APPLIED PROGRAMMING TECHNIQUES IN C

APPLIED PROGRAMMING TECHNIQUES IN C

Terry A. Ward

Programmer Analyst

Academic Computing Services
University of Northern Iowa

Scott, Foresman and Company
Glenview, Illinois • London

The author and publisher would like to thank the following sources for use of their material:

The program lpr.c: The Line Printer Utility on p. 39–45 is reprinted from Zolman, Leor. *BD Software C Compiler* version 1.5. (BD Software: Brighton, MA 1982) by permission of Leor Zolman.

The program othello.c: Game Program to Play Othello on p. 276–288 is reprinted from Zolman, Leor. *BD Software C Compiler* version 1.5 (BD Software: Brighton, MA 1982) by permission of Leor Zolman.

The program cmp.c: File Comparison Program on p. 52–57 is reprinted from Zolman, Leor. *BD Software C Compiler* version 1.5. (BD Software: Brighton, MA 1982) by permission of Leor Zolman.

The program teledit.c: Telecommunications Program on p. 226–274 is reprinted from Zolman, Leor. *BD Software C Compiler* version 1.5. (BD Software: Brighton, MA 1982) by permission of Leor Zolman.

The program ed2: A Full Screen Editor on p. 101–196 is reprinted from Ream, Edward. *ED2 Editor—BDS C Version* (Ed Ream: Madison, WI 1982) by permission of Edward Ream.

Library of Congress Cataloging in Publication Data

Ward, Terry A.
    Applied programming techniques in C.

    Bibliography: p.
    Includes index.
    1. C (Computer program language)   2. Microcomputers—
Programming. I. Title.
QA76.73.C15W37   1985   001.64'24   84-14119
ISBN 0-673-18050-6

To my parents
Mary Lee and Vince Ward
and to my wife
Shelly Danner Ward

Trademark List

UNIX is a trademark of Bell Laboratories.

OTHELLO is a trademark of CBS Toys.

muMATH is a trademark of Software House.

Ada is a trademark of the U. S. Department of Defense.

MS-DOS is a trademark of Microsoft Corporation.

PCDOS, IBM PC, IBM are trademarks of International Business Machines, Inc.

Apple II, Lisa, Macintosh are trademarks of Apple Computer, Inc.

CP/M, CP/M-80, CBASIC, CBASIC-2, Pascal/MT+ are trademarks of Digital Research Inc.

Z-80, Z-80A is a trademark of Zilog, Inc.

Turbo Pascal is a trademark of Borland Software.

Pascal/Z is a trademark of Ithaca Intersystems.

UCSD Pascal is a trademark of Softech Microsystems.

PET is a trademark of Commodore International.

MINCE, SCRIBBLE are trademarks of Mark of the Unicorn.

Valdocs, GRAFTRAX, MX-80, QX-10 are trademarks of Epson America.

WordStar is a trademark of Micropro, Inc.

Preface

This is a text on applied programming techniques and software tools in the C programming language. It can be used by readers familiar with computer programming. A brief synopsis of the C programming language is presented for readers unfamiliar with this popular programming language.

The C language was developed at Bell Laboratories and was originally designed to be run under the UNIX operating system (UNIX is a trademark of Bell Laboratories.) Increasingly, C is run under other operating systems and is rapidly becoming the language of choice for microcomputer programming applications. Its conciseness and power, coupled with its speed of execution, have made C a formidable contender for the standard microcomputer programming language of the next decade. This book was written to follow the C standards as specified by Brian W. Kernighan and Dennis M. Ritchie in their book *The C Programming Language* (Englewood Cliffs, NJ: Prentice-Hall, 1978) as implemented in the excellent microcomputer C compiler by B D Software (BDS C). This compiler environment provides excellent facilities for program development and implementation. Details are provided for transporting the programs included in this text to other implementations of the C programming language.

The text begins with an analysis of the factors involved in the selection of a programming language and support environment for implementing software. Next a capsule summary is presented of the C programming language that provides sufficient details of the language to make the text understandable.

The bulk of the text is devoted to the presentation of actual, working programs written in C. In addition to presenting software, each chapter includes references to additional material on the topic of interest as well as tutorial introductions to the specific tools presented.

File tools are the topic of the first tool chapter, which includes software to concatenate files, compare files, and eliminate leading records from a file. In addition, three programs are included for printer output formatting. Finally, a tool for writers, a word counting utility, is included.

A second tool chapter includes two tools for compressing text files. One replaces strings of spaces with tabs, and the other tool reverses this text compression process.

A major portion of the book is devoted to the theory and practice of text editing.

Specifically, a full-screen text editor is presented complete with source code. This editor provides such facilities as full-screen operation, splitting and joining of lines, and other advanced features desired in text-editing software.

In conjunction with the text editor, the text presents a text formatter that can be used to produce final printed copy from the text editor. Presented in a modular fashion (like the text editor), this formatter can be expanded at will by the reader to include any features that might be desired to produce a sophisticated text processing system.

The field of microcomputer communications is represented by a chapter that details a telecommunications program that converts a microcomputer to a time-sharing terminal complete with error-correcting file transfer capabilities.

A collection of sorting routines and programs is presented in the chapter on sorting. These programs include an internal text sort and an external, unlimited capacity sorting program.

Finally, a chapter is included that provides a program to play the game of Othello.

A directory of C compilers, books, periodicals, and articles is included in an appendix to the text. This directory to other C resources includes approximately 500 entries. A directory of public domain software available in the C programming language is also included. This is the most complete directory available to the approximately 15 megabytes of C software available for little or minimal cost.

Finally, notes on converting the programs in the text to other C compilers and programming environments are presented.

ACKNOWLEDGMENTS

The author would like to thank the following people for providing the indicated programs or tools used in the text:

Leor Zolman   lpr.c, othello.c, cmp.c, and teledit
Ed Read   ed2.c

Thanks are due also to James E. White, Regional Manager, and the Harris Corporation for providing a copy of their excellent C compiler used during the preparation of this text.

Thanks are due also to the University of Northern Iowa and their Academic Computing Services which supplied computer facilities and services for the preparation of the text.

Finally, much loving and heartfelt thanks are due my wife Shelly who provided me with constant encouragement throughout this project.

Contents

APPLIED PROGRAMMING TECHNIQUES IN C

1

Selecting a Programming Language

In the beginning, life was simpler. Computers were large, expensive, and equipped with one high-level language—FORTRAN. The early history of data processing is essentially the story of the successful implementation of FORTRAN compilers on virtually all the computer systems existing then. Today, we are blessed with a situation of virtual "compiler-babble." The languages available to us range from the sublime (e.g., Ada) to the ridiculous (e.g., tiny-BASIC) and include all manner of specialized languages for robotics or control applications (FORTH), artificial intelligence (LISP or PROLOG), symbolic mathematics (muMATH, MACSYMA), and countless other computing tasks.

The process of selecting an implementation language for our software tools can be divided into the tasks of (1) establishing criteria for language selection and (2) determining which language or languages best embody the desired traits.

As should be obvious by the title of this book, the language chosen for our purposes is the C programming language. The reasons and criteria for selecting this particular programming language and the particular compiler (B D Software, also known as BDS C) are discussed in this chapter.

The criteria presented in this chapter for language selection are applicable to the determination of any suitable programming language and compiler support environment. Had our task been artificial intelligence programming or robotic control, the language chosen would perhaps have been either LISP or FORTH, respectively.

The task before us then is the selection of a programming language and environment for the implementation of an extensive set of software tools. Before beginning, we should be clear that we are interested not simply in selecting a language in the abstract but also in selecting a tool for constructing our software. This insistence upon the "real" nature of computer language use requires that we select both a language and a programming environment. The most ideal, theoretical language is of little (if any) value if it takes hours to compile programs with it. The task of program development requires both a programming language (C, FORTH, FORTRAN, etc.) and a programming environment (compiler, library manager, linker/loader, etc.) that allows one to use the language in the most productive manner possible.

The initial requirements for choosing a programming language are first the selection of a suitable language and then the determination that there exists a sufficiently powerful realization of this language for the desired computer environment. Our first task then is to specify the expected target machine for our software tool programs and in so doing to set the limits for our programming language selection.

The world of microcomputers can be subdivided on the basis of operating system, and this division will provide the basis for our discussion of the target machine. There are essentially three unique operating systems currently predominating in the marketplace. On the one hand there is the proprietary system on the Apple II computers. On the other hand, there is MS-DOS or PCDOS as implemented on the IBM PC computer. Finally there is the more portable CP/M system on a wide variety of microcomputer CPUs (e.g., CP/M has been implemented on everything from the 8080 8-bit microcomputer chip to the 32-bit giant 68000). Because of the wide variety of CP/M-based systems, our target machine will be using this operating system as its base. (The fact that I personally own a CP/M system probably played no small part in this selection process of a target machine.) While this choice might seem to run counter to the current compatibility craze, we will see that with our choice of programming language the problem of portability is quite minimal. In fact, Appendix C contains information on the transportability of the software tools in this book to any other computing environment.

To keep the target machine requirements as generic as possible, a few other caveats might be useful. To begin, a relatively small (in terms of disk storage) programming environment would be desirable. While mass storage is becoming less expensive, it would be ideal if the compiler, linker, and so forth could fit on a single-sided, single-density diskette (i.e., be approximately 125k or smaller in total size). Second, the target machine should also provide for the maximum 64k of CP/M memory that is available. With memory prices as low as they are, this requirement is virtually always met. Finally, the compiler must be available in a format that is usable by the target machine. Again, with the great commercial successes of microcomputers, most compilers are available for most machines in one form or another.

Our target machine is thus seen to require a CP/M based operating system. This makes no assumption about the underlying microcomputer CPU chip. CP/M currently operates on the following microcomputer CPUs:

8 bit:	8080 series:	Intel 8080, 8085
	Z80 series:	Zilog Z80
16/8 bit:	8086 series:	Intel 8086, 8088
32/16 bit:	68000 series:	Motorola 68000

Having decided on a target-machine (CP/M-based), the actual process of language selection can begin.

At one time, the language selection process for microcomputers was much simplified. Any language was suitable, as long as it was BASIC. The only language available on microcomputers for many years was BASIC and varieties of extended-BASIC. Happily today the situation is much more multilingual. Professional languages available for microcomputers include APL, BASIC, C, Pascal, and PL/I. Our task is the selection of an appropriate language and of the specific compiler and environment for our applications development.

In data processing evaluations of machines and languages, a remnant of our primitive past still haunts us—the benchmark. A benchmark is a measure of speed (e.g., compilation or execution) of a "typical" program. As we will see in our analysis of the language selection process, the benchmark, per se, is a relatively minor consideration. I simply mention it at this point so that you will know what to expect when someone expounds on the speed of a particular language. Speed alone does not a programming environment make!

LANGUAGE SELECTION CRITERIA

We can divide the criteria for language selection into three major categories. First, we have the category of management criteria. The preeminence given these criteria reflects the current state of the art of programming and program development. The costs of program design and development reside principally in the "people" costs (programmer time, ease of program interaction) rather than in purely technical factors. As we will see, there are several components associated with management criteria.

A second category of language selection parameters is the more technical criteria such as data representation facilities and control structures. This is accorded second place because all the major microcomputer languages (those mentioned above are likely candidates) have adequate language features. In general, any language could probably have the facilities to accomplish our tool constructing task. The selection here will revolve around programmer preferences and minor features of the respective languages vis-à-vis each other.

The final and least important criterion for language selection is that of benchmark performance. I have intentionally relegated the most quantitative measure of program performance to this last position. In general (excluding the obviously slow group), most microcomputer languages perform adequately fast for our purposes. Also, the benchmark is notoriously sensitive to algorithm selection. As we shall see below, a clever programmer can reduce the benchmark speed by more than half. So, benchmarks are nice and quantitative but should be used with extreme caution in arguments about language selection.

Management Criteria

A major proportion of the criteria for language selection fall under the general rubric of management/personnel considerations. We will focus on three broad general areas of interest in our discussion of management criteria.*

We can distinguish three phases of costs in any programming project. The first phase is the initial development time cost. The second is the system operational phase costs (also known as the system effectiveness) and the third is life-cycle maintenance. It might seem unusual to categorize a microcomputer programming project in this way, but I think a strong case can be made that all programs go through these three phases until they reach a point where they are either discarded, replaced, or made a permanent part of the program library.

The idea of costs seems obvious in a commercial application such as payroll, but what of a microcomputer program to play an outer-space type game. Costs? Surely the author jests.

No, I am quite serious; all programs have associated costs. In the case of a commercial endeavor the costs are obvious—computer time, programmer time, and so on. In the case of a home or personal computer, the costs are just as real, if not quite as obvious. Your time developing a program is worth something. If a properly selected language can reduce the time spent developing a program, you can then write more programs or do other noncomputing activities (if you have any other such activities!). A language that encourages good programming practices will provide you with a more

---

*For the discussion that follows, I am indebted to the article "Selecting a Programming Language, Compiler, and Support Environment: Method and Example" by Gordon E. Anderson and Kenneth C. Shumate (*IEEE Computer*, vol. 8, August 1982, pp. 29–36).

thoroughly tested and reliable program. Reliability in program execution is always desirable whether the application is a payroll program or a chess-playing program. Finally, system maintenance, like the poor of the Gospel story, will always be with us. Whether we are fixing bugs or simply improving our program (payroll or game), the choice of language can either hinder or enhance the system life-cycle maintenance process.

The first management-related criterion to be considered is that of development time and cost. In general, this is a relatively small, fixed proportion of the entire programming cost. Typically, the costs and elements involved at this juncture are compiler cost, compiler machine requirements (e.g., additional disk storage requirements), ease and speed of initial compilations, debugging and trace facilities, and some imponderables such as programmer satisfaction, availability of outside help, such as support and training materials, and aesthetic criteria (i.e., is the language fun to use).

At this point, it might be useful to consider the various factors that will influence our final selection in terms of actual languages. We will consider the following languages as likely candidates for a microcomputer programming project: BASIC, CBASIC, APL, FORTRAN, C, Pascal, and PL/I.

Development Time and Start-Up Costs

In terms of development times and costs, we can summarize the language possibilities as follows.

BASIC   BASIC will in general have very small or no start-up costs. Almost without exception, some version of BASIC is available on every microcomputer in existence at little or no additional cost. The machine requirements are generally minimal, and so no additional equipment is required and BASIC is very easy (recall that it is an acronym: **B**eginner's **A**ll-Purpose **S**ymbolic **I**nstruction **C**ode) to learn and use. As we will see, these positive features are quite overshadowed by the technical deficiencies of the language, and this criticism applies to all BASIC dialects. CBASIC provides more structured facilities, but it is still essentially BASIC. In addition, CBASIC generally requires the purchase of an additional pseudocompiler and the use of a screen editor at a cost of approximately $125.

In terms of our imponderables, BASIC has a limited amount of material available for outside help. For example, there are numerous books of programs available in a generic form of BASIC for use. Quite frequently these programs are so trivial as to be of little value. Also, BASIC is relatively unpopular in the professional programming community. All is not lost however. BASIC does provide excellent facilities for program development. The integrated interpreter/editor environment of BASIC is perhaps unequaled for speed and ease of program development. The price of this ease however is the tendency to program "on the fly" without prior analysis of the problem. This will have its consequences in the final life-cycle maintenance phase of management selection criteria.

APL   APL (**A P**rogramming **L**anguage) is a relative newcomer to the stable of microcomputer programming languages. In terms of initial start-up costs, it is perhaps the most expensive language under consideration. At present the only professional APL interpreters available are for the IBM Personal Computer. This initial equipment outlay is further increased by the cost of the APL interpreter (currently between $500 and $750). Obviously, without compelling reasons to use APL, the initial start-up costs are likely to be prohibitive. The user support community for APL, however, tends to be quite vocal and insistent with their thesis that APL is *the* computer language par excellence. Personally, I have my doubts as to the viability of APL as a tool-making language for the average microcomputer user or programmer. The labyrinthine structure of the language and its limited availability render it even less usable than BASIC for microcomputer users. In one case, however, its status is assured. In conjunction with a mainframe environment that uses APL extensively, program testing and development on microcomputers would be a viable option.

In addition there is a lack of extensive materials for the new APL programmer. While it is used somewhat in computer science education, it falls far behind the more commonly taught languages (BASIC, FORTRAN, Pascal and COBOL) in terms of trained programmers.

FORTRAN   FORTRAN (**FOR**mula **TRAN**slation) is the grand old man of programming languages. Anyone with any amount of data processing experience has probably programmed in FORTRAN. Typically, until quite recently, FORTRAN was the initial programming language taught at the university level. (It has now been supplanted by Pascal.) However, like many things, older is not necessarily better. With an initial cost of approximately $500, FORTRAN suffers from the same problem of high start-up costs as APL or PL/I. Coupled with this is the limited selection of FORTRAN compilers available.

FORTRAN is also a "dead" language. It is rapidly becoming the Latin language of the computer industry. As a high school student, I often wondered at the value of studying the Latin language (a dead language in terms of usefulness for everyday communication). FORTRAN is in a very similar situation. Few new applications are being written in FORTRAN, and its continued existence is in large part due to the difficulty of translating programs from FORTRAN to anything else. A second factor in

FORTRAN's survival is the number of older scientists and engineers who are familiar only with FORTRAN.

There are several advantages to FORTRAN that should be mentioned. The original software tools of Brian Kernighan and P. J. Plauger are written in RATFOR (a **RAT**ionalized dialect of **FOR**TRAN) and there is an active users group for the RATFOR software tools. Also, the availability of a FORTRAN compiler on virtually all larger mini- or mainframe computers makes FORTRAN a possible candidate for software tool construction language.

Pascal   Pascal is a relative newcomer on the programming scene, and this is reflected in its excellent structured programming features. Like our previous candidates (excluding BASIC), with one exception noted below, Pascal suffers from the problem of high initial start-up cost for the compiler. Again, the cost will be between $500 and $750 for a professional quality compiler.* In addition, some Pascal compilers are quite large in terms of disk storage, and this may involve unwanted expense in terms of system expansion or an undesirable number of mechanical operations (e.g., switching diskettes among editor, compiler, and linker). Finally, many Pascal implementations (such as UCSD Pascal) require a run-time interpreter to execute the intermediate code produced by the compiler.

However, there are numerous positive features of Pascal that would make it a very likely candidate for tool status. The initial RATFOR tools of Kernighan and Plauger have been reissued in a Pascal implementation. In addition, there is a fairly wide selection of public-domain or quite inexpensive diskettes containing Pascal code for many common tool applications. (However, as we will see below, C has the greatest diversity and variety of software available in the public domain for ready access and use.)

There are many textbooks and materials available to learn and use Pascal, and its use as the introductory language in computer programming curricula is now quite established. Finally, the number of Pascal implementations is very large, ranging across the entire microcomputer spectrum from Apple to Zenith.

In general, Pascal is quite suited for the software tools programming environment. Its major drawbacks are a high initial start-up cost (although Turbo Pascal seems to have solved this problem) and the need for hardware extensions (particularly disk storage capacity) for easy use.

---

*As this book was in its final stages of preparation, the microcomputer community was blessed with a professional quality Pascal for the ridiculously low price of $50. This Pascal, called Turbo Pascal, seems to be an excellent product and may do more than anything else to make Pascal an increasingly popular language for microcomputers.

PL/I   PL/I (Programming Language I) was at one time considered the programming language for all time. Designed in an IBM mainframe environment, it included all the features (and then some) needed for real programming. Unfortunately, it has never really caught on in the microcomputer world. There is no gainsaying its technical features. It can do anything. However, from the standpoint of development time and cost it suffers from some serious problems.

To begin, the only microcomputer PL/I compiler available (from Digital Research) costs approximately $500. This, coupled with very large disk storage requirements, makes the initial start-up cost quite high.

In addition, there is relatively little material available in either printed or machine-readable form for the neophyte PL/I programmer. Further, the limited availability of PL/I in the mainframe environment means that few university or college computer science departments teach the language.

In general, the conclusion regarding PL/I is quite similar to that for APL. If you are working in an environment where the language (APL or PL/I) will be ported to larger mainframe machines, the microcomputer version may represent a reasonable alternative to the other languages presented here. If not, perhaps Pascal or C would be a better choice.

C   Like the other non-BASIC languages considered above, C requires the purchase of the compiler. Unlike those for the other languages considered previously, C compilers are available for virtually all microcomputer environments and at very reasonable costs. The lowest priced C compilers for CP/M (e.g., small-C or C/80 from Software Toolworks) are available for less than $50. (A full guide to the wide variety of C compilers is presented in Appendix A. While inexpensive, these are still professional quality compilers and quite well suited to tool construction work. The B D Software C compiler is available for approximately $125 and includes a complete programming environment: C compiler, linker, debugger, and program trace facility, a telecommunications program, and several game programs as examples of C programming. In addition BDS C provides the source code for the complete library of over 150 functions. It has probably the best price/performance ratio of any microcomputer software product on the market today. Unfortunately, BDS C is available for CP/M-80 systems only. Users of other microcomputers might consider C/80 (Software Toolworks $50) or Aztec C II (all microcomputers $150).

The amount of resource material available for the aspiring C programmer is staggering in its variety. Over 15 megabytes of public domain software is available from users groups (see Appendix B). In addition, a large amount of commercial software is customizable by anyone with access to a C compiler (e.g., Mark of the Unicorn's excellent text processing and editing software is so customizable).

C also is supported by a wide variety of books and materials (e.g., *Dr. Dobb's Journal*) that can teach one a great deal about the language. C, as a relatively modern language, also possesses all the features of structured programming and structured design concepts that we have come to expect in a useful programming language.

In conclusion then, the choice of language (in terms of development time and cost) is between three languages, FORTRAN, Pascal, and C. FORTRAN has the advantage of availability on mainframe machines and the RATFOR software tools environment. Pascal likewise has these advantages. Both Pascal (with the exception of Turbo Pascal) and FORTRAN are quite a bit more expensive in terms of initial cost and machine requirements than C. C, then seems to possess all the desirable traits for the start-up and development phase of a software tools project.

At this point, we have effectively excluded APL and PL/I from consideration and so will focus on the remaining candidate languages, BASIC, FORTRAN, Pascal and C. We can now consider the second of our three management criteria, namely system effectiveness.

System Effectiveness

BASIC   For all of its myriad failings and faults reflecting its humble origins as a "beginner's" language, BASIC is still a very effective language in terms of its programming environment. The integration of interpreter and editor within one environment is a stroke of design genius. By allowing the programmer to make changes and to see the effects of those changes virtually instantaneously, BASIC makes a great language for "quick and dirty" programs. Unfortunately this "ad hoc–ness" of BASIC is also a problem. By allowing, and even encouraging, such program design, BASIC permits the development of unmanageable programs that can be quite difficult to modify or generalize. Also, as we will see, interpreted BASIC is relatively slow in terms of execution speed. Finally, in terms of system effectiveness, there are some technical deficiencies that make it difficult to manage large programming projects in BASIC. These deficiencies include the lack of local variables, the lack of modular programming facilities (procedures or functions), and the tendency to encourage very short (and hence difficult to remember) variable names.

These deficiencies are corrected in CBASIC-2 to a certain extent, and so in terms of system effectiveness, CBASIC-2 remains a marginally viable software tools programming language. The more common BASICs (interpreted BASIC) fail at this point, however. The deficiencies of BASIC are not remedied in their compiled versions. Compiler BASICs remain BASIC in their program structures, and the compilation generally provides only speedier execution times.

These deficiencies of the language are now currently being addressed by the original creators of BASIC, who are now working on what will be called TRUE BASIC. This new language is designed to remedy many of the deficiencies of the current microcomputer BASIC dialects available.

Pascal   There are currently four Pascal compilers (or pseudocompilers) available to the microcomputer tool builder: Pascal/Z from Ithaca Intersystems, Pascal/MT+ from Digital Research, UCSD Pascal from Softech Microsystems, and Turbo Pascal from Borland International. The other major Pascal, Pascal/M from Sorcim has recently been discontinued. While not the abundant harvest presented by C compilers (see Appendix A), the available Pascal compilers are all excellent products. In terms of system effectiveness, Pascal/MT+ with its Speed Programming Package (SPP), UCSD Pascal, and Turbo Pascal are perhaps the most tailored to production and development of computer software. Any of these compiler environments presents a useful option for tool construction.

Despite the fact that their power is somewhat offset in the case of Pascal/MT+ and UCSD Pascal by the initial high cost of acquiring the software and the rather extensive machine requirements in terms of disk storage, Pascal (at least in these three implementations) is still very much in the competition for software tool language.

C   With a ratio of approximately 50 between the least expensive C compiler (small-C) to the most expensive (Whitesmith's), the range of compiler environments available to the interested C programmer is diverse. In general, the available C compilers can be categorized as follows. On the one hand, there are the offshoots of small-C, which often contain numerous enhancements to the original small-C and are not to be overlooked for production programming. The best example of a small-C type C compiler is the C/80 compiler from Software Toolworks. While this software costs only $50, it includes an assembler, linker, and virtually all the C language features needed for programming in the "large." As an example, much of the other software from Software Toolworks is written in C/80. This other software includes everything from editors to LISP interpreters. Surely this product variety is a testimony to the power of this inexpensive C compiler. A wide selection of C/80 compatible software is also available in the public domain. Finally, for those specialized applications that might require it, Software Toolworks has available a MATHPACK enhancement to C/80 to provide the commonly needed mathematical functions for floating point manipulations.

At the other end of the scale are those compilers that attempt to emulate the standard UNIX/C environment as closely as possible. One example is Whitesmith's C that is a massive (and massively priced) product. In all truthfulness, Whitesmith's C is simply not worth the exceptional expense vis-à-vis its less expensive competitors for microcomputers.

However, there are other large C compilers that approach the UNIX/C standard of which Digital Research's C is a prime example. It provides virtually all the features of UNIX/C and even includes a facility similar to LINT for syntax checking of C programs. The cleverly named LINT is designed to check C programs for common errors such as array boundary problems and improper function calls.

If the developed software tools are likely to be ported to UNIX or other C compilers, one of the following standard C compilers would be an appropriate choice: Digital Research, Aztec, or Lattice. These are all excellent compilers and are well suited for the task at hand. They have only two drawbacks. First, the amount of available public domain software specifically written for them is relatively limited. This is principally due to the newness of the compilers, and is certainly no reflection on their quality. In fact, more and more software in C is being written in a generic fashion for porting to this growing, UNIX-compatible compiler family. A second problem with this class of compilers is their rather extensive disk storage requirements.

A third and virtually independent category of C compilers is represented by BD Software's C. This product is unusual in its construction and presentation. BDS C is designed to enhance the programmer-machine interface as much as possible. BDS C includes over 150 intrinsic functions for doing everything from allocating memory to doing a quicksort of an array in memory. This wealth of library facilities is one reason for the success of BDS C. It is generally never necessary to code anything in assembler if one is using BDS C.

Second, BDS C comes with its own linker and library manager so that no additional assembler is necessary (as opposed to the other C compilers considered). Finally, BDS C is incredibly compact. On a miniscule 90k diskette, I have the BDS C compiler, linker, loader, library files, two printer utilities, and a program text editor. Eliminating the need to ever swap out the compiler disk speeds the process of program development considerably.

BDS C does, I must admit, have several drawbacks. First, it is not totally UNIX/C compatible at some points. While this is not an insurmountable problem, it does represent a problem to people hoping to port BDS C to UNIX/C environments. Second, BDS C does not include the means to handle floating point numbers in its standard repertoire. However, to be honest, floating point, long, and BCD (for business applications) extensions are available for the compiler through additional library facilities as enhancements. Some of these facilities are even available from the public domain for little or no cost.

This last point also reflects something of great value in terms of BDS C. The vast majority of public domain software written in C is written in BDS C. At last count this includes approximately 15 megabytes of source code for everything from virtual editors to text formatters to C compilers themselves!

Finally, BDS C is quite inexpensive. This amazing software product is available for only $125.

At this point in our investigation of managerial criteria for language selection, we have reduced our list of candidates to the following:

Product	Price
Turbo Pascal (Borland International)	$49.95
Pascal+/SPP (Digital Research)	$750.00
UCSD Pascal (Softech Microsystems)	$750.00
Lattice C (Lifeboat Associates)	$300.00
C (Digital Research)	$300.00
Aztec II C (Manx Software)	$150.00
CBASIC (Digital Research)	$125.00
C (B D Software)	$125.00
C/80 (Software Toolworks)	$50.00

At this point we need to consider the final managerial factor that goes into our language selection process. This is perhaps the easiest of the criteria to evaluate.

Life-Cycle Maintenance

The major cost (and I might say aggravation) of any programming project is in the area of system maintenance and modification. Any language destined for tool construction should provide modular programming facilities as well as allowing separate compilation of modules and such nice things as debugging or trace facilities. I am happy to report that all our candidate languages listed above meet these criteria handily.

I would, in fact, argue that any language that fails this life-cycle requirement should probably be eliminated from consideration as a professional programming language. In real programming, the current, working version of a program is always one version removed from the desired end product!

Technical Criteria

One might question why the technical criteria have been postponed until this moment. As you will soon see, all our remaining candidate compilers have the requisite technical richness to accomplish our tasks. The question will eventually be decided upon nontechnical grounds. However, for the sake of completeness, I would like to present the technical factors that should be considered in the selection of a programming language. We can distinguish six major categories of technical criteria. They are shown below:

1. Portability
2. Modularity
3. Reliability
4. Human factors
5. Technical richness
6. Speed (benchmarks)

For the sake of brevity, we will consider each of these six factors in turn.

Portability

Portability may be defined as the ease with which a program can be moved from one environment to another. In terms of our candidate languages we can group the compilers as follows:

> **microcomputer portability: all**
> **micro-mainframe portability: Pascal and the C compilers (except BDS C)**

All of our candidate languages are available on a wide variety of microcomputers and so present few difficulties in this portability. In terms of micro to mainframe portability, CBASIC-2 and BDS C fail the test. CBASIC-2 does not have a counterpart in the mainframe world. BDS C presents the problem of a nonstandard C. It should be noted however that BDS C can in general be converted to standard C with little difficulty. It is, however, a step that is considerably lessened with the more standard C compilers. The basic problem is the richness of the BDS C library functions (recall the function for doing an in-memory quicksort). These functions are included to make BDS C a complete programming environment and in so doing make it unusual.

Modularity

Modularity is the ability to break a problem down into smaller component parts and attack each of these programming tasks in turn. All of our languages provide this facility. This greatly simplifies something like tool construction where we generally build components into larger units until we have constructed an often very large tool.

Our candidate languages all provide some means of achieving modularity of program design and construction. CBASIC-2, for example, allows real subroutines and allows them to be called by name. This is a vast improvement over the normal BASIC procedure of calling GOSUBs by number only.

Pascal allows the separation of a program into smaller units that can be compiled individually. C likewise allows the separate compilation of functions to be included later into the overall, larger program.

Reliability

Reliability refers to the characteristics of a language that enforce good, safe programming practice. Here, Pascal excels. Designed as a pedagogical language, Pascal virtually forces the programmer to write structured program code without much chance for deviation. Feuer and Gehani in their comparison of C and Pascal (FEUE82) conclude that this is one of the major areas of difference between C and Pascal.

C, on the other hand, is a much more flexible (and hence less reliable) language. Designed for the real, and often nasty, world of computing, C has features which can lead to unreliable programs. This is the price the designers have paid for the power of such things as the extensive pointer and address operations available in C. C has been designed with virtually no internal limitations for the programmer.

Human Factors

The human factors of a language include those important, but inherently qualitative, measures such as documentation quality, simplicity of implementation, and speed of compilation (increasing productivity). While admittedly a subjective measure, these factors are nonetheless important in the selection of a language. If the documentation is so dense as to be virtually unusable, the language is not likely to be a productive programming tool.

In terms of program documentation, BD Software C ranks at the very pinnacle. The current compiler release (version 1.50) includes approximately 500k of program files (compiler, telecommunications program, library files, example programs, assembler utilities, etc.) and close to 200 pages of typeset documentation. The remaining programs all include excellent documentation, but in terms of sheer volume, complete-ness, and quality BDS C stands alone.

A second factor in the computer-human interface is the ease of program use. Here UCSD Pascal, Turbo Pascal, and BDS C rank at the top. Turbo Pascal and UCSD Pascal both provide an integrated programming environment of compiler and editor. This provides a rapid means of program design and development. While BDS C does not provide an integrated editor, it nonetheless is compact enough to allow the editor, compiler, linker, and entire set of library files to reside on a single-density diskette (approximately 90k). This means that the user of a two-drive system need never swap diskettes to load an assembler or an editor. This combined with the speed of the BDS C compiler makes for very rapid program development. Nothing is more aggravating than to load an editor disk, change a program, load a compiler disk, compile a program, load an assembler disk, and then (after this disk-intensive process) discover a small error that restarts the long, tiresome process. Turbo Pascal, UCSD Pascal, and BDS C all prevent this "disk-o" madness.

Technical Factors

Finally, we come to what many consider to be the only criterion worth evaluating: technical factors. Yet, as the experience of PL/I shows, technical facilities alone do not insure a language's popularity. In the case of our present candidate languages, Pascal and C have the most variety in terms of technical richness. Pascal provides all the major structured features desirable in a language as well as access to lists, records, sets, and other desirable features for complex programming applications. Perhaps the only area where Pascal falters is in the machine-level interface. Here, Pascal betrays its academic roots. In general, Pascal's access to specific machine features is somewhat complex. C, on the other hand, provides ready access to machine-specific features and in general presents an environment where little if any assembly language programming is required. In terms of technical qualities of the language, C provides all the structured facilities of Pascal with the added versatility of extensibility so that such things as coroutines, classes, and generators can be added (see Appendix A for articles on C's extensibility).

Benchmarks

Finally, we come to the last, and I would say least important, criterion for evaluating a language—sheer, raw speed. I place this in last position, for in general, time is not particularly crucial in most applications and all the languages considered are adequately fast. However, there are a few distinctions that can be made. A complete discussion of benchmark results for a wide variety of computer languages (ranging from tiny-BASIC to IBM assembler) and computer types (from a PET to a Cray!) can be found in the excellent series of articles by the Gilbreath's (GILB81, GILB83).

Our candidate languages can be classified as follows:

Slowest (pseudocompilers)	CBASIC
	UCSD Pascal
Slower (interpreters)	BASIC
Mid-range (compilers)	Pascal/MT+ and SPP
Fastest (compilers)	C/80
	BDS C
	Turbo Pascal

Any of our candidate languages would be suitable for all but those few tasks requiring great speed (e.g., real-time control, data acquisition, animation).

CONCLUSION

We have now come to the end of our tale of language selection and the reader may be forgiven for wondering if perhaps data processing is less scientific and quantitative than previously thought. We have talked of things like simplicity, ease of use, and modularity and very little of such things as speed or instructions-per-second execution time.

Well, sad to say, programming is still more art than science and the criteria for selecting a language are often more prosaic than "high-tech." Our criteria have lead us to conclude that the language of choice for software tool development is C. Specifically, we will use the implementation of C by B D Software for the remainder of this text.

In a manner analogous to college football team standings, the final rankings are subject to dispute, but a choice has to be made. Tools are written in real languages on real machines. Our conclusion is that the trade-offs among speed, performance, capability, and price favor BDS C, followed by C/80, as the languages of choice for our application. If we were interested in a Pascal implementation, Turbo Pascal would be the clear choice.

The next chapter will explore the nature of C and BDS C in more detail, and then we will jump immediately into the exciting world of software tools and their development.

2

C and BD Software C

Interested Bystander: "What language are you writing about?"
Author: "C."
Confused Bystander: "How do you spell that?"

The dialogue above is a reproduction of countless conversations that I have had with people when they learn that I have been writing a book. C is at present a relatively little known language, but people are discovering that C is a powerful and sophisticated language particularly well suited to microcomputer applications. Perhaps when you finish with this book, you too can tell all your friends how to spell "C."

This chapter introduces the C language in a very brief schematic manner. It is impossible to teach an entire programming language in a few pages; this chapter will just review C and present a synopsis of the language features. A more detailed introduction to the C programming language can be found in the books listed in Appendix D.

Second, this chapter will also discuss the nature and peculiarities (i.e., strengths, weaknesses, and differences) of C (as defined in Kernighan and Ritchie, *The C Programming Language*) and B D Software C. With this information, it is possible to transport the programs within this book to virtually any C compiler environment.

Over the years in working with various computer languages (from assembler to the old FORTRAN II to Pascal to C), I have developed a theory of language development that I think you might find interesting.

Basically, I have concluded that you can tell a great deal about a computer language simply from its name. Hear me out before you decide this is a crazy theory. . . .

We all know that names can make or break a person (the country-western song "A Boy Named Sue" springs to mind). It seems to me that something similar can be discerned in the very nature of programming languages themselves.

Think of BASIC, a nice beginner's language with basic features, or LISP with its *Lots* of *Irritating Single Parentheses*. Pascal, named for the French philosopher and mathematician, is more suited to the academy than the marketplace. Finally, C. The name is terse to the point of being missed in conversation. The name couldn't be simpler or less prepossesing (think of all the commonplace words that use the letter "c"). As a language it is powerful but concise, important but straightforward.

As we will see in the technical part of this chapter on C, the language may be described as a higher low-level language. In many applications, its higher level features, such as control structures and data types, rival those of any other language. On the other hand, its lower level capabilities (e.g., speed, machine independencies, I/O control, pointer manipulations, and addressing capabilities) allow it to be used instead of assembly language in many applications.

In many respects, C provides us with the best of both worlds. It is concise and powerful enough for "real" programming on microcomputers, and with its access to machine features, it is also suitable for traditional assembly applications.

SIMPLIFIED GUIDE TO THE SYNTAX OF C

C has a simple and relatively straightforward syntax that reflects the latest concepts in structured programming and structured design techniques. It provides the standard capabilities of do-while loops, for-loops, switch statements (i.e., a "case" statement), and even the much maligned "goto" statement.

The inclusion of the latter might seem to be a language bug rather than a language feature. The advocates of structured programming have rightly criticized the goto statement as the bane of many a programmer's existence. To be honest, the problem with goto's is not the "goto" but the "come from." Anyone who has attempted to trace program "logic" through a maze of jumping goto statements might wonder at the logic of its inclusion within a highly structured language like C. Yet this reflects the nature of C. Unlike a purely pedagogical language (such as Pascal), C reflects the real world. Occasionally, a goto is the most efficient and straightforward means of solving a programming problem. Rather than exclude it for essentially philosophical reasons, C includes the goto but provides enough features so that there is no reason for excessive use of it.

C traces its origins to the justly famous Bell Laboratories. The language was developed in 1972 by one man, Dennis Ritchie, and this sole authorship is reflected in the structure and style of the language. Unlike PL/I, which shows the influence of committee input and committee politics, C has enough features to do virtually anything without "extensions" that simply confuse compilers and compiler designers. Lest one doubt the power of C (even after reading the programs in this book), I might point out that the entire operating system of the Digital Equipment Corporation PDP-11 and VAX computers was written in C. According to a reliable source (the introduction to *The C Programming Language* by Brian W. Kernighan and Dennis M. Ritchie), one of the authors doesn't even know PDP-11 assembler language!

The essential unit of C programming is the function. A function may or may not return a value to the calling program or function. Functions may be either intrinsic to the language (for such things as input/output) or defined by the user (as will be seen below in our software tools).

A trivial, but complete, C program is shown below. Even if you are completely unacquainted with C, you should be able to discover that this small program prints the message "This is a trivial C program."

```
/* This program prints a message for */
/* readers of this book.              */
main()
{
printf("This is a trivial C program.\n");
}
```

That's all there is to it. The first two lines are obviously comments. In C, comments are delimited from the body of the program by "/*" and "*/" pairs. The next statement is required in all C programs and is a function called "main." It marks the beginning point for the program. The next line (containing the "{") marks the beginning of a compound statement. Anything within the paired "{" and "}" will be treated as a complete unit. The braces perform much the same function in C as the "begin" and "end" of Pascal.

The lengthy, next statement provides the meat of the program. This statement calls a built-in C function called "printf" that takes as arguments a set of parameters within parentheses. In this particular case, the first portion of the argument is the phrase, "This is a trivial C program." The second portion of the argument is the odd-looking "\n" (backslash n). The first portion of the argument (i.e., the phrase) supplies the text to be printed. The odd-looking "\n" is C's technique of telling the printing device to perform the line-feed to the next line. The C function, printf, takes these arguments and prints the specified text on the system printer or console.

Suppose we wanted to print our simple text message a number of times. We could simply repeat the "printf" statement a given number of times with the "{", "}" pair. While this would obviously work, it seems a fairly foolish programming technique.

This need for repetitive processing brings us to the second feature of C, namely, control structures. This fancy phrase from the realm of computer science refers to those commands in a language that allow the execution sequence of a program to be changed. Some typical control structures include the jump or goto types and the looping types (such as the DO-loop in FORTRAN). In BASIC, for example, we could write a program for repetition using a counter variable and a FOR . . . NEXT loop to produce our multiple message program.

The process in C is quite similar. We could use a control structure (the while statement) to print our message as shown below:

```
main( )
/* A trivial C program that prints a message three (3) times */
int i;
i = 1;
{
while (i++ <= 3)
    {
    printf("This is a trivial C program in triplicate.\n");
    }
}
```

Our initial program has been modified to include a while loop control structure. The while loop specifies the terminating condition for our loop (when i is greater than 3) and the means of incrementing and testing this counter. In this example, the counter will be incremented after the test. The indented braces above and below the printf statement delimit a compound statement for the while loop. Anything and everything between these two braces will be executed once during each loop operation.

The unusual syntax of the "i++" shows us one of the problem areas with C programming syntax. The elegance and power of C is often obtained at the expense of legibility or readability. In many languages, loop behavior is always constant; i.e., we always change the counter and test the condition before or after executing the statements within the loop. C provides for either possibility. The ++i (prefixed i) syntax is tested before the loop is performed, while the postfixed form (i++), which is used above, is tested after the loop is performed. Obviously the power of this capability can also lead to very obscure program bugs.

Like any higher level language, C features an adequate selection of data types. All versions of C include both character and integer types; in fact, most programming in C is done using only these two types. However, in more complete C implementations, the range of data types extends from these simple character and integer types to the long integers, to floating point, and even up to double precision data types. In B D Software C, the long and floating point data types are handled through extensions to C through the use of library functions. While this is somewhat less convenient than intrinsic data facilities, their absence is rarely missed. As an example of the power of floating point—less computing, I might mention that the very powerful MINCE text editor is written entirely in BDS C.

A final data type present in C is the special escape sequences that we have already encountered under the guise of the "\n." These special escape sequences are represented by a "\" (backslash) followed by a character to represent the appropriate special characters such as tab or newline. For example, "\n" is newline (i.e., linefeed—carriage return), and "\t" is the tab character.

Another area where the power of C is evident is in the scoping of variable types allowed. Unlike BASIC, C provides for local and global variables. This means that in a C program, a variable can be used in a function without affecting anything outside that function. This facility is used extensively in the ED2 editor where the various modules are designed to interact in known and predictable ways with their other program compatriots. Logically, a "local" variable is one whose influence is limited to the locality of the function only. A simple example of local and global variables is shown below:

Global Variable   (The program below will print out the global variable value of 100):

```
int x;
x=100;                  /* global variable */
main()
{
```

```
printf("%d\n",x);       /* %d\n is the format for */
                        /* printing integers      */
}
```

Local Variable   (The program below will print out the local variable and the value of 999):

```
int x;
x=100;                  /* global variable */
main()
{
int x;
x = 999;                /* local variable */
printf("%d\n",x);
}
```

This second program shows the insulating power of local variables. In BASIC, all variables are global. Therefore, any reference to a variable can have catastrophic side effects if it has been used previously. This is particularly a problem in large BASIC programs where it can be difficult to keep track of all the variable names that have been used previously. In C, a locally declared variable will have no such untoward side effects.

OPERATORS

C is a concise language in virtually all respects save one. The power of C is evident in a dizzying variety of operators. We have already been given a hint as to the complexity involved with our brief mention of pre-versus post-fixed operators. In a language like BASIC, the usual mathematical operators are present: plus (+), minus (–), multiplication (*), division (/), and exponentiation (** or ^). The other operators in BASIC include the logical operators (such as NOT, EQV, AND). Finally, BASIC has a group of relation operators such as equal (=) or not equal (<>).

C has all of these and many, many more. In fact the number of operators is so great that I will simply present a brief synopsis of those available. In general, any of the textbooks on the C programming language (see C Language Reference for BDS C, p. 29) will include discussions of C's operators and their uses.

UNARY OPERATORS (operators with one argument)

*p	Pointer to p
	The value is the value of the object currently pointed to by p.
&x	Address of x
	Returns a pointer to x
+x	States that x is positive
	Returns the same value of x
-x	Negative of x
	Returns the negative of x
++x	Increment x (prefixed)
	Increase the value of x by one and use this new value.
--x	Decrement x (prefixed)
	Decrease the value of x by one and use this new value.
x++	Increment x (postfixed)
	Use the value of x and then increase x by one.
x--	Decrement x (postfixed)
	Use the value of x and then decrease x by one.
~x	Returns the ones complement of x. [tilde x]
!x	Not x
	The result is 1 if x is 0, otherwise 0.
(type-name) x	Convert x to the type "type-name."
	Returns the value obtained by converting the value of x to the specified data type
sizeof (type)	The result is an integer equal to the size in bytes of an object of type "type."

BINARY OPERATORS (operators with two arguments)

$p*q$	Multiply
	The result is the product of p and q.
p/q	Divide
	The result is the quotient of p divided by q.
$p\%q$	Remainder
	The result is the remainder of p/q.
$p+q$	Add
	The result is the sum of p and q.
$p-q$	Subtract
	The result is the difference of q from p.
$p<<q$	Shift left
	The result is p shifted left q bits.
$p>>q$	Shift right
	The result is p shifted right q bits.
$p<q$	Less than comparison
	The result is 1 if p is less than q, else the result is 0.
$p>q$	Greater than comparison
	The result is 1 if p is greater than q, else the result is 0.
$p<=q$	Less than or equal comparison
	The result is 1 if p is less than or equal to q, else the result is 0.
$p>=q$	Greater than or equal comparison
	The result is 1 if p is greater than or equal to q, else the result is 0.
$p==q$	Equal comparison
	The result is 1 if p is equal to q, else the result is 0.
$p!=q$	Not equal comparison
	The result is 1 if p is not equal to q, else the result is 0.
$p\&q$	AND
	The result is the bit-wise AND of p and q.

p^y   Exclusive OR
The result is the bit-wise EXCLUSIVE OR of p and q. (Note that this is the same symbol for exponentiation in BASIC.)

p|q   Inclusive OR
The result is the bit-wise INCLUSIVE OR of p and q.

p&&q   Logical connective AND
The result is 0 if p is zero. Evaluates strictly left-to-right so that if p is 0, q is not evaluated. Otherwise the result is 1 only if both p and q are nonzero. Typically used in logical expressions such as:

```
    if(p==q && q==r)p=r;
```

which stops evaluation as soon as the expression becomes false.

p||q   Logical connective OR
The result is 1 if either p or q is nonzero. Used in a similar manner to the logical connective AND (cf. above).

c?t:f   Conditional expression
This compact statement acts like the following C program code:

```
    if (c) /* condition to be tested */
        {
        t; /* true condition */
        }
    else
        {
        f; /* false condition */
        }
```

The conditional expression returns the result of the evaluation. Our program for word counting (wc) uses a conditional expression to provide a convenient facility for rounding of integer values correctly.

p=q   Assignment
The result (which is p) is the value of q.

p*=q	Equivalent to p = p*q
p/=q	Equivalent to p = p/q
p%=q	Equivalent to p = p%q
p+=q	Equivalent to p = p+q
p-=q	Equivalent to p = p-q
p<<=q	Equivalent to p = p<<q
p>>=q	Equivalent to p = p>>q
p&=q	Equivalent to p = p&q
p^=q	Equivalent to p = p^q
p|=q	Equivalent to p = p|q
p,q	Comma operator. Used in for statements to separate multiple expressions.

This whole area of operators in C is obviously quite complex and powerful. In general, most C programming can be done without many of the more obscure features. As noted above, any of the textbooks covering the C language can provide a detailed discussion of operators and their uses.

CONTROL STRUCTURES

C has benefited from the recent ideas concerning the nature of desirable control structures. It has all the modern types such as the if, while, and do loops. In addition, it also includes the goto statement for the few cases where it is really needed. To anyone familiar with Pascal, the control structures of C are quite straightforward. As an example, the if statement is shown below:

```
if (the condition here is true)
   {
   execute this group of
   statements within the
   braces
   }
else
   {
   execute these things
   }
```

A second, and quite familiar control structure in C is the for statement. Its format is shown below:

```
for (initial condition; conditional test; re-evaluate condition)
    {
    this line will be executed
    and so will this one
    }
```

The syntax of the control structures for C are shown below in the tabular presentation of the syntax for C.

FUNCTIONS

Now we have come to the very heart of C. In BASIC, programs are designed either with straightline code (i.e., do this, then this, then this) or around subroutine (GOSUB) calls. C operates on the basis of functions. This is the key to C's power and versatility.

A function in C is a self-contained segment of program code that performs a specific task. We have already seen an example of a function in our trivial example—the printf function. As you recall, printf is an intrinsic function that accepts as arguments text and formats to be printed on the standard output device.

In general, any C program is simply a series of functions united together with the appropriate control structures to produce a desired outcome or result.

To see a function in action, we might take a look at a simple program to calculate factorials. The program shown below will produce factorials for the numbers 6, 5, 4, 3, 2, 1:

```
main()
/* initial C declarations */
{
int i;
i=0;
while (++i < 6)   /* Loop to produce the numbers that we will */
                  /* use to calculate factorials.            */
```

```
printf("%d! is %d\n", i, factorial(i));
                        /* The printf function has embedded within */
                        /* it the factorial function call. This    */
                        /* is a general feature of functions; they  */
                        /* may be used wherever a simple variable   */
                        /* may appear.                              */
}                       /* This bracket ends the main program.      */
/* Here is the factorial function. */
/* Input is the number i;        */
/* return value is i! in the     */
/* variable n.                   */
/* As a practical matter, a      */
/* function could be compiled at */
/* a different time than the main */
/* program and then linked       */
/* together when needed          */
factorial(n)
int(n);
   {
   if (n == 1)
      return (1);      /* Check for the odd case of 1.   */
else
                        /* Note that C is also recursive. */
                        /* The factorial function calls   */
                        /* itself:                        */
   return (n * factorial(n-1));
}
```

This concludes our cursory examination of the C programming language. Obviously much more can be learned of the language. The syntax of C (with particular reference to BDS C) is presented in the following section.

An excellent approach to learning C would be to use one of the C textbooks listed in Appendix D and then implement the programs presented in this book. By actually implementing the programs, one will learn all there is to C!

SYNOPSIS OF BDS C SYNTAX AND FORMATS

A complete description of the particulars of BD Software's implementation of C is available in the documentation that accompanies the compiler package. Incidentally, the documentation for BDS C is perhaps the finest in the microcomputer industry. The current compiler version (version 1.50) includes close to 200 pages of professional documentation.

The official definition of the C programming language is contained in Appendix A of Brian W. Kernighan and Dennis M. Ritchie, *The C Programming Language* (Prentice-Hall, 1978).

C LANGUAGE REFERENCE FOR BDS C

Preprocessor Directives

#define identifier string	Substitute string for identifier: #define AUTHOR "Terry A. Ward"
#define identifier macro	Substitute expanded macro for identifier: #define max(A,B) ((A) > (B) ? (A) : (B))
#undef identifier	Cause previously #defined identifier to be "forgotten": #undef AUTHOR
#include <sysfile>	Replace this line with contents of system file sysfile: #include <bdscio.h>
#include "localfile"	Replace this line with contents of local file localfile: #include "B:HARDWARE.H"
#if constant expression	Compile if constant expression is true: #if MODE == 2
#ifdef identifier	Compile if identifier is defined: #ifdef CPM
#ifndef identifier	Compile if identifier is not defined: #ifndef IBM_PC
#else	Compile if previous if condition false;

#endif	#endif terminates conditional compile:

```
#if MODE == 2
    Compile this if MODE == 2
#else
    these lines will be compiled
#endif
```

Constants

Type	*Example format*
decimal number	675
hexadecimal number	0x2e3f
octal number	0127
character	'c'

Special Characters

backspace	'\b'
backslash	'\\'
carriage return (CR)	'\r'
double quote	'\"'
form feed (FF)	'\f'
newline (CR-FF)	'\n'
octal constant	'\ddd' (backslash and three octal digits)
single quote	'\''
tab	'\t'

Variable Declarations

char	Character unsigned (8-bit unsigned within range 0–255). Note: Char variables in BDS C can never have a negative value!
int	Signed integer
long	Available in supplementary long integer package only (cf. BDS C compiler documentation for details)
float	Available in supplementary float integer package only (cf. BDS C compiler documentation for details)

char *ptr	Variable ptr points to data of type character
char board[ ]	Definition of an array named "board" of characters
struct book	Definition of complex data type, book with members
{	
char author[40];	book.author,
char title[60];	book.title,
char publisher[40];	and publisher (all arrays of characters)
} biblio;	Declaration of variable biblio of type struct name
union mishmash	Definition of overlay of different data types
{	
char c;	The member over.c shares its storage area
int i;	with the integer over.i
} over;	Declaration of a variable over

C Statement Formats

comments	Comments in C are enclosed by slash-asterisk, asterisk-slash pairs:
	/* This is a comment. */
simple statements	Simple statements in C are terminated with a semicolon:
	x = 1;
	or may simply include a null body:
	;
compound statements	Compound statements are enclosed within curly braces and may be used wherever a simple statement is allowed:
	{
	temp = a;
	a = b;
	b = temp;
	}

label	A label followed by a colon marks a statement for use with the goto statement: 　　error: printf("Bad input\n");
if (condition) 　statement1	If the condition is true (i.e., x less than 0 below), then perform this statement. Note: the else clause is optional: 　　if (x < 0) 　　　x = -x

if (condition)
　statement1;
else
　statement2;
	If the condition is true, then
	perform statement1
	otherwise
	perform statement2:
	　　if (x < 0)
	　　　x = -x;
	　　else
	　　　printf("positive\n");

do
statement;
while (condition);
	Do
	this statement or compound statement
	until the condition is false.
	Note: The do . . . while is often used when it is desired to execute a loop at least once:
	　　do
	　　　{
	　　　c = getchar();
	　　　}
	　　　　while (c == ' ');

for(init,cond,reeval)
statement
	Perform initialization (i.e., init statement) once. Evaluate the condition (i.e., cond). If the condition value is nonzero then the statement is executed and the expression is reevaluated (i.e., reeval) and the process continues as long as cond is nonzero. Note: If the condition is FALSE initially, the statement will not be executed.
	/* initialize array to zero: */
	for(i=1; i < 10; i++)
	　array[i] = 0;

while (condition)
statement;

While the condition is nonzero (i.e., TRUE), then execute this statement. Note: Since the condition is evaluated before the execution of the statement, it is possible that the statement will never be executed.
while (i < ARRAY.SIZE)
    array[i++] = 0;

switch (condition)
{
case c1: stat1;
case c2: stat2; break;

●
●

default: statements;
}

Evaluate the condition and goto appropriate case statement [i.e., the matching constant (e.g., c1)] and fall through unless a break exits you from the switch.

The default is used to handle the situation where no case constant matches the condition (generally recommended for good programming practice):
switch (option)
    {
    case 'E': edit(); break;
    case 'X': exit(); break;
    case 'I': insert(); break;
    default: printf("error\n");
    }

break

The break statement terminates the while, do, for, or switch statements.

continue

The continue statement goto the bottom of while, do, or for loop construction.

goto label;

Unconditional jump to statement preceded by label. goto badloop;

Formatted Output (printf)

printf(fmt,arg1,arg2,.)

Formatted print function. Output goes to the standard output. Conversion characters supported by BDS C:
d   decimal integer format
u   unsigned integer format

c   single character
s   string (null-terminated)
o   octal format
x   hexadecimal format

Note: Long and floating print functions
       are available in their respective
       library packages. Each conversion
       is of the form:

% [–] [[0] w] [.n] <conversion char>
where
–(optional) specifies left justification. If
  omitted field will be right justified.
w specifies the width of the field. Default 1.
n (optional) specifies the maximum
  number of characters to be printed out
  of a string conversion.

3
File Tools

If you ask someone what a computer is, they will typically respond with an arithmetic, computational analogy. Such responses might be things like a computer is a super brain, or a computer is a giant calculator. While these responses are true, they are somewhat misleading.

Computers do excel at the mathematical tasks given them, but they are more at home, and used more frequently, for nonmathematical tasks. The analogy for a computer is no longer the adding machine or the pocket calculator; rather, the symbol of modern data processing is the file cabinet and the file folder.

The model, or paradigm, for the vast majority of computing done today is that of office supplies and equipment. The typewriter has been replaced by the word processor, the file cabinet has given way to the diskette, and the old, dependable manila file folder has given way to the disk file. If you think this analogy of mine is far-fetched, we might look at a state-of-the-art computer system like the Apple Macintosh or Lisa. Here, we see the use of *icons* as commands. These icons, or pictures, represent such things as file deletion (a garbage can icon) or file storage (a file folder picture). The fundamental unit of computing is no longer the floating-point number, but rather the character of text.

As an aside, you might recall that the standard BDS C compiler does not even include floating point numbers as valid data types in the standard library of functions supplied with the language. They are included (along with long integer numbers) in an extension to the language. In general, this is not a major handicap.

This radical shift in perspective in computing practice from numerical to textual has not been matched by a corresponding shift in personal and professional attitudes.

Most computing courses are still taught from the perspective of mathematics/computer science. It is unclear to me why computer literacy requires any knowledge of hexadecimal arithmetic. This math orientation is probably one of the major causes of the much noted "computer phobia" of my generation. If you've never been good with numbers and computers are simply mathematical machines, of course it follows that you should fear these silicon-based beasts.

The time has come when we (in the computer field) can, and probably should, admit that much of what we do is related to textual information and not specifically numbers. Our computers act as very sophisticated typewriters or produce very detailed financial reports, but in the final analysis, it is often the text and its presentation, not the numbers, that matter.

This shift in emphasis is represented in the selection of software tools for inclusion in this book. Missing are tools to do square roots or factorial calculations. Honestly, when was the last time you needed to calculate a hyperbolic cosine?

This emphasis upon character or text manipulation also represents the aspect of computing problems that software tools are designed to address. In any program, the computational aspects are relatively straightforward. A matrix inversion, once programmed, is likely to be transportable to most any other computing environment. The computational statements are the most portable parts of any programming language.

The case of text or character manipulations is quite the opposite. In general, the major problems in large programs lie with the text manipulations and not the numerical calculations. As examples, we might consider the problem (or challenge) of text formatting with the wide variety of printer brands available (all with varying command sets for such things as "top of page"). The classic problem of character sets (ASCII versus EBCDIC) would fall in this textual problem area.

Finally, I might mention that this textual rather than numerical orientation shows C at its best. For mere calculations, any language is probably adequate—a square root is a square root! For text manipulation, C and perhaps BASIC stand alone. FORTRAN will handle text and characters only reluctantly, if at all. COBOL is superb for text writ large (reports, inventory lists, etc.), but the **C**ommon **B**usiness **O**riented **L**anguage seems a bit large and unwieldy for constructing tools for character and text file manipulations.

Here, C, as a higher low-level language is most at home in its element. Sophisticated enough to handle any computing task, it is also concise and fast enough to be used for text-intensive tool crafting.

The initial set of tools that we will present will be file manipulation tools and filters. At the simplest level, a filter is a program or tool that is designed to facilitate the transmission of data (possibly with changes in the process) from one location to another. At the most primitive level, we are dealing with a filter any time we interact with a computer.

Internally, the computer operates upon bits of information encoded as electrical impulses and represented as a string of zeros (0) and ones (1). To the computer, the following is a perfectly adequate statement:

10010110 10010010

In fact, the above sequence of bits represents the phrase *ok* in binary form. Obviously, when we need to communicate with the computer, we would rather deal with *o*'s and *k*'s rather than their internal binary representations.

Here is the first level filter that we encounter. The hardware of our computer terminal and computer make the encoding and decoding of character data transparent to us, the users.

The group of tools in this chapter may be subdivided into the four categories shown below:

1. file → printer directing tools
2. file → report tabulator tools
3. file → file filtering tools
4. file ↔ file comparison tools

The set of tools represented by the first group, the file to printer utilities, are relatively simple programs that make the printer a more useful component in the entire data processing chain. In the CP/M operating system environment, for example, the following command will send a copy of the contents of the file MYFILE.TXT (on disk drive B:) to the printer:

A>PIP
*LST:=B:MYFILE.TXT

Even with the many options available to the user via the PIP program, there are still additional features that would be nice to have in a printer utility. Some of these enhanced features will be the subject of tool construction later in this chapter.

A typical need, particularly if one is dealing with multiple copies of files (such as will occur in the process of developing programs), is the need for a time/date stamp on the printer listing, as well as the ability to title each page of printed output with the specific file name. These two relatively simple requests will make the task of keeping track of program contents vis-à-vis program name much simpler.

Our program lpr that follows does just this titling operation. In addition, as you will see, we have included notes on how to automate the time/date stamping of program listings.

The second tool, related to this one, is a simple tool to get numbered program listings. It is frequently necessary to have a numbered listing of a program. Our tool, pnum, gives us this feature.

The final tool in this category of file-to-printer utilities that we will present is a header file for use with an Epson printer to allow rapid and convenient setting of printer parameters.

A very common and popular type of microcomputer printer available today is the dot-matrix printer. These printers use a matrix of print elements (generally seven by nine elements) to form the characters to be printed. In many of these printers, the printing font is programmable. With this type of printer and an appropriate program, one can print pica, elite, italic, bold face, and any number of other specialized type fonts without changing the printer physically in any way. In fact, the reference section for the mxprint.h tool gives the address of a very fine commercial software product that gives a dot-matrix printer the capability of producing everything from Greek/scientific to Gothic to Russian character sets! Incidentally, plain old English is also available.

Our program for the printer is simply a header file that permits rapid setting of the printer codes for an Epson MX-80 printer equipped with Graftrax printer ROMs.

Our second class of file tools in this chapter is represented by a utility (wc) that will count the number of characters, words, and lines in a text file. As a writer, I find this particular tool very helpful. This tool also provides an approximate measure of average word length. In addition, references are provided so that the program can be expanded to include more sophisticated calculations of readability and FOG (comprehensibility) indices.

The final two categories of tools in this chapter comprise file to file transfer programs and file to file comparison programs.

The file to file transfer tool is represented by two programs. The first, chop, takes a file and "chops" off a given number of records from the beginning of a file. The second tool, concat, takes advantage of the sophisticated BDS C features of directed input-output and wildcard expansion to provide a file concatenation facility.

Finally, a software tool cmp is presented that takes two files and compares them on a byte-by-byte basis and provides information concerning their differences. This is a particularly useful utility during program development when several versions of the same program are likely to reside on a diskette at any given time.

The following tools will be presented in the remaining portion of this chapter:

1. lpr   Line printer formatter for producing titled and numbered file listings on a conventional printer.

2. pnum   Line printer formatter for producing numbered file listings on a conventional printer.

3. mxprint Header file to facilitate the use of special printer features in C programs. Specifically designed for Epson MX-80 printers, the tool is modifiable for any printer with special features and print codes.

4. wc   Word counting utility to produce a statistical report on the number of characters, lines, and words in a given text file. Also provides an approximate measure of average word length.

5. chop   Remove or "chop" a specified number of lines from the beginning of a text file.

6. concat   Concatenate a specified set of files together into a larger output file.

7. cmp   Compare two files on a byte-by-byte basis and report the differences.

Utility/Tool

lpr.c   Format text file for line printer output with time/date stamp.

Usage

lpr <fn,fn. . . fn>   Format all files given on the command line and then ask for more until null line is typed.

lpr <return>   Format given files until null line is typed.

control–Q   Aborts current printing operation and begins next file.

Function

lpr copies the given file to the line printer with a heading of filename and date. Each file printed begins upon the same phase of fan-fold paper.

Example

To print some of the files in this chapter on the line printer:

lpr lpr.c mxprint.h wc.c

To print only two files in response to queries by lpr:

lpr
lpr.c
wc.c
<cr>   {null line}

Theory of Operation

The line printer utility lpr.c can be outlined in pseudocode (an English-like description of program operation) as shown below:

```
initialize
while there are still filenames
if filename arguments use these names
else query for filename until null response
check filename for validity abort on error
check page phasing, if OK
    print header
    print filename until done or until ^Q (control-Q aborts)
else if page phase not OK
    page break
    print filename until done or until ^Q (control-Q aborts)
```

C Function	Purpose/Function
linepr(string)	Print a line of text on the CP/M LST: device (normally the printer) and return TRUE if formfeed encountered in the text.
putlpr(c)	If page phase OK then send character to LST: device.
formfeed()	If formfeed character encountered then put formfeed to LST: device, otherwise while there are lines left on the page, put line feeds until no lines left. Reset lines left to page length.

IMPLEMENTATION NOTES

1. The version listed below uses a simple interactive query to obtain the date stamp. A more sophisticated program could make use of any hardware time/date facilities available (such as a chronoboard) to obtain the data automatically. An example of BDS C software for this type of time-stamping is available in Bolton's article (BOLT81) listed in Appendix D.

2. The program could be modified to allow the insertion of options such as variable number of lines per page, alternating page number headings, or automatic lower-case to uppercase conversion.

3. The use of bios (5,c) in the putlpr function shows one of the strengths of C and CP/M. The exact location in terms of hexadecimal address of the bios (basic input output system) is irrelevant. By definition, the fifth bios jump-table function is the sending of a character to the standard list output (LST:).

POSSIBLE PROBLEM AREAS

1. This filter is quite limited. It will simply transmit from the file to the printer whatever it finds. A possible enhancement would be to confirm that we are printing text rather than executable files (.COM in the CP/M environment).

/* lpr.c—Line Printer Utility */

```
/* Line printer formatter */
/* Supplied courtesy of Leor Zolman and B D Software. */
/* First prints all files named on the command line, and then */
/* asks for names of more files until a null line is typed. */
/* Control-Q aborts current printing and goes to next file. */
/* Paper should be positioned ready to print on the first page; */
/* each file is always printed in an even number of pages so that */
/* new files always start on the same phase of fan-fold paper. */
/* Tabs are expanded into spaces. */
#include     "BDSCIO.H"
#define     FF      0x0c      /* formfeed character, */
                             /* or zero if not supported */


#define     PGLEN   54       /* lines per lineprinter page */
#define     ON      1
#define     OFF     0
int pgflag;
int pg;
int count;
int colno, linesleft;
main(argc,argv)
char **argv;
{
   int i, pgno, fd;
   char date[30], linebuf[135];   /* date and line buffers */
   char fnbuf[30], *fname;        /* filename buffer & ptr */
char ibuf[BUFSIZ];          /* buffered input buffer */
char *gets();
char *pgstr;
char pgnmbuf[10];
pg = count = 0;
pgflag= ON;
pgno = colno = 0;
linesleft = PGLEN;
```

```
printf("What is today's date? ");   /* With the appropriate hardware */
   gets(date);                      /* capabilities, the acquisition */
                                    /* of the date could be made an */
                                    /* automatic operation. */
while (1)
{
   if (argc-1)
      {
         fname = *++argv;
         argc--;
      }
   else
      {
         printf("\nEnter file to print, or CR if done: ");
         if(!*(fname=gets(fnbuf))) break;
         printf("\nEnter page to print, CR for all: ");
         if (*(pgstr=gets(pgnmbuf))) {
            pg=atoi(pgstr);
            }
         else pg=0;
      }
   if ((fd = fopen(fname,ibuf)) == ERROR)
      {
         printf("Can't open %s\n",fname);
         continue;
      }
   else printf("\nPrinting %-13s",fname);
/* force formfeed */
   for (pgno = 1; ; pgno++)
      {
         if (pg) {
            if (pg==pgno) {
               pgflag=ON;
               }
            else pgflag=OFF;
            }
         else pgflag=ON;
         putchar('*');
```

```
        sprintf(linebuf,"\n%28s%-13s%5s%-3d%20s\n\n",
            "file: ",fname,"page ",pgno,date);
        linepr(linebuf);
  loop: if (!fgets(linebuf,ibuf)) break;
        if (kbhit() && getchar() == 0x11) break;
        if (linepr(linebuf)) continue;
        if (linesleft > 2) goto loop;
        formfeed();
        }
    formfeed();
    if (pgno % 2) formfeed();
    fabort(fd);
    }
}
/* Print a line of text out on the list device, and */
/* return true if a formfeed was encountered in the */
/* text.          */
linepr(string)
char *string;
{
    char c, ffflag;
    ffflag = 0;
    while (c = *string++)
      switch (c) {
      case '{':
      count+=1;
      putlpr(c);
      break;
      case '}':
      count-=1;
      if (count==0) ffflag=1;
      putlpr(c);
      break;
      case FF:
      ffflag = 1;
      break;
      case '\n':
      putlpr('\r');
```

```
        putlpr('\n');
        colno = 0;
        linesleft--;
        break;
          case '\t':
        do {
          putlpr(' ');
          colno++;
        } while (colno % 8);
        break;
          default:
        putlpr(c);
        colno++;
      }
    if (ffflag) formfeed();
    return ffflag;
}
putlpr(c)
char c;
{
    if (pgflag) bios(5,c);
}
formfeed()
{
    if (FF) putlpr(FF);
    else while (linesleft--) putlpr ('\n');
    linesleft = PGLEN;
}
```

Utility/Tool

<table>
<tr><td>pnum</td><td>Format text file for line printer output with line numbers.</td></tr>
</table>

Usage

<table>
<tr><td>pnum <fn></td><td>Format the file given by fn to the printer.</td></tr>
</table>

Function

pnum takes the given file and prints the file contents on the standard list device with line numbers.

Example

To print a copy of itself to the line printer with line numbers:

```
pnum pnum.c
```

Theory of Operation

The line printer utility pnum.c can be outlined in pseudocode (an English-like description of program operation) as shown below:

```
get arguments
if not OK print usage error message
else
open file (abort on error)
print file to LST: device with line numbers
```

IMPLEMENTATION NOTES

1. A bit of C bragaddocio: the entire printing operation takes place in one (short) statement.

/* pnum.c—Program File Numbering Utility */

```
main(argc,argv)
char **argv;
{
```

```
    int fd, lnum;
    char ibuf[134], linebuf[132];
    if (argc != 2) {
      printf("Usage: pnum filename\n");
      exit();
    }
    if ((fd = fopen(argv[1], ibuf)) == -1) {
      printf("cannot open: %s\n",argv[1]);
      exit();
    }
    lnum = 1;
    while (fgets(linebuf, ibuf))
      printf("%3d: %s",lnum++,linebuf); /* powerful C printf statement */
}
```

Utility/Tool

chop   Remove the leading records from a file and output the shortened file into a specified output file.

Usage

chop fn1 fn2 nn   Chop the leading nn records from fn1 and place the resulting shorter file into the file named fn2.

Function

chop removes the specified number of leading records from a file and produces a shortened output file.

Example

To remove the first 20 lines from file "LONGFILE.FIL" and place the shorter output into "OUT.FIL":

chop LONGFILE.FIL OUT.FIL 20

Theory of Operation

The file utility chop.c can be outlined in pseudocode (an English-like description of program operation) as shown below:

```
initialize
syntax check (abort on error)
if OK open files
count records to skip
print remaining records onto output file
```

IMPLEMENTATION NOTES

1. An interesting enhancement would be to modify chop so that it would accept a parameter to specify chopping from the rear of a file rather than from the front.

/* chop—Eliminates Leading Records of a File */

```
int nskip, recnum;
int infd, outfd;
char buf[128];
main(argc,argv)
int argc; char *argv[];
{
puts("File Chopper, V1.0\n");
if (argc != 4)
    { puts("Bad command line\n"); exit (); }
    if ((nskip = atoi(argv[3])) == 0)
    { puts("No records to skip\n"); exit(); }
    /* open files */
    if ((infd = open(argv[1],0)) == -1)
    { printf("%s","File not found: ", argv[1]); exit(); }
```

```
   if ((outfd = creat(argv[2])) == -1)
     { printf("%s","Cannot creat: ",argv[2]); exit (); }
   printf("Skipping %u records\n", nskip);
   for (recnum = 0; recnum < nskip; recnum++)
     { if (read(infd,buf,1) <= 0)
       { printf("%u","File read error at record",recnum); exit (); }
     }
   while (read(infd,buf,1) > 0)
     { if (write(outfd,buf,1) == -1)
       { printf("Output file error at record %u",recnum); exit (); }
     }
   puts("All Done!");
close(outfd);
}
```

Utility/Tool

concat   Concatenate text files onto output file.

Usage

concat file1 file2 file3 >file4   Takes file1, file2 and file 3 and concatenates
                                    them together to produce file4.

Function

concat takes as input a group of files and concatenates them onto an output file.

Example

To concatenate "INTRO.TXT" onto "BODY.TXT" to produce CHAPTER. TXT, the following command would be used:

concat INTRO.TXT BODY.TXT >CHAPTER.TXT

Theory of Operation

The file utility concat.c can be outlined in pseudocode (an English-like description of program operation) as shown below:

```
initialize wildcard expansion module
initialize directed input/output routines
while there are files
    putchar to output
    when done get next file
close files with dio flush
```

The operation of concatenation is simplified considerably with the inclusion of wildcard and directed input/output facilities with the BDS C compiler. This is another example of the quality of this software product.

This is also a good example of the modularity of the C programming language. We need not be concerned with the internals of the wildcard or directed I/O facilities. We simply need be concerned with the calling protocols. The use of such "black boxes" of tested code is a strength of the modular languages (such as C, Pascal, or Modula-2).

C Function	Purpose/Function
wildexp(&argc,&argv)	BDS C utility function to allow ambiguous file names to appear on the command line. Automatically expands the parameter list to contain all files that fit the ambiguous specifications given. These filenames are specified with the following wildcard characters: ! NOT (logical NOT) * any file name ?c match the given character c
dioinit(&argc,argv)	Initialize directed input-output package for BDS C. Redirection allows input/output from keyboard or disk file. The following redirection characters are available:

> file	output to file
+ file	output to file and console
< file	getchar from file not keyboard
command:prog	send the standard output of command to the standard input of the program.
dioflush( )	Flush directed output file, if open, and close all directed I/O files.
getchar( )	Directed I/O version gets a character from the device or from a directed file if specified.
putchar( )	Directed I/O version puts a character to the device or to a directed file if specified.

IMPLEMENTATION NOTES

1. This utility/tool requires the use of the BDS C directed input-output (DIO) library. This library facility should be included in the linking (clink) operation.

/* concat.c—File Concatenation Program */

```
#include "bdscio.h"
#include "dio.h"
#define STDERR 4
main(argc, argv)
char **argv;
{
  int c;
  int i;
  char ibuf[BUFSIZ];
  wildexp(&argc, &argv);
  dioinit(&argc, &argv);
```

```
if (argc == 1)
  while ((c = getchar()) != EOF) putchar c;
else
  for (i=1; i < argc; i++)
  {
    if (fopen(argv[i],ibuf) == ERROR)
      {
      fprintf(STDERR,"\nCan't open %s\n", argv[i]);
      continue;
      }
  while ((c = getc(ibuf)) != EOF && c != CPMEOF)
    putchar(c);
  }
dioflush();
}
```

Utility/Tool

cmp.c   Compare (byte for byte) two files and print
                          differences.

Usage

cmp <file1> <file2> {-a -b<hex number>}

The optional arguments are as follows:

-a   ASCII files (terminate on 1AH)
-b <hex-number>   begin at <hex-number> address

Function

cmp compares two files on a byte-by-byte basis and prints their differences on the
console.

Theory of Operation

The file comparison utility cmp.c can be outlined in pseudocode (an English-like description of program operation) as shown below:

```
initialize
check syntax
compare files
    if unequal text print text strings and end.
    else if checkfile EOF
        print checkfile shorter and end.
    else if masterfile EOF
        print masterfile shorter and end.
    else
    files equal.
```

C Function	Purpose/Function
fcompare(mfile,cfile,adrs,ascii)	Compare input master file (mfile) with check file (cfile) beginning at address (adrs). Print message of file differences. Give address and mismatched text.
err_exit(msg)	Generic error exit function
hextoi(string)	Convert hex string to integer.
i_error()	Error function for invocation errors
xl(c,xlate)	Translate ASCII control characters to their printable representations.

/* cmp.c—File Comparison Program */

```c
#define EOFF -1      /* end of file marker returned by getc( ) */
#define EOF 0x1A     /* ascii end of file mark */
#define NOFILE -1    /* no such file indication given by fopen( ) */
#define FALSE 0
#define TRUE 1
```

```
main( argc,argv )
  int argc;
  char *argv[ ];
  {
  int fdin,fdout,ascii;
  unsigned start_adrs,hextoi( );
  char *ptr;
  char mstbuf[134],chkbuf[134];
  ascii = FALSE; /* assign the defaults */
  start_adrs = 0;
  if( argc < 3 || argc > 5 )
    i_error( );
  else if( (fdin = fopen(argv[1],mstbuf)) == NOFILE )
    printf("No such file %s\n",argv[1]);
  else if( (fdout = fopen(argv[2],chkbuf)) == NOFILE)
    printf("No such file %s\n",argv[2]);
  else {
    while( argc > 3 ) {
      ptr = argv[--argc];
      if( *ptr++ != '-' )
        i_error( );
      switch ( tolower(*ptr++) ) {
        case 'a':ascii = TRUE;
        break;
        case 'b':start_adrs = hextoi(ptr);
        break;
        default: puts("Unrecognized option. Aborted\n\n");
        i_error( );
        } /* end switch */
      } /* end while */
    fcompare( mstbuf,chkbuf,start_adrs,ascii);
    }/* end else */
  exit( );
  }
fcompare( mfile,cfile,adrs,ascii)
char mfile[];   /* the input file buffer */
char cfile[];   /* the output file buffer */
unsigned adrs;   /* the address of begin of file */
```

```
int ascii;   /* flag of whether these are ascii files */
{
int mc,cc;   /* 1 char buffers */
char erflg;   /* flag that an error has occurred */
translate control chars */
char str1[6],str2[6];   /* temporaries for strings */
char xlate[10];   /* string used in ascii control char translation */
erflg = 0;
while( ! ( (mc = getc(mfile)) == EOFF || (ascii && mc == EOF)) ) {
   if( (cc =getc(cfile)) == EOFF || ( ascii && cc == EOF )) {
   puts("Checkfile shorter than Master file\n");
   return;
   }
else if( mc != cc ) {
   if( ! erflg ) {
erflg = 1;
puts("\nRelative Master Check");
puts("\nAddress File File Mismatch");
puts("\n------- ---- ---- --------\n");
      } /* end if */
   if( ascii ){
strcpy(str1,xl(mc,xlate)); /* Fudge because parameters are */
strcpy(str2,xl(cc,xlate)); /* evaluated before being passed. */
printf("%4x  %-4s %-4s %8b\n",adrs,str1,str2,mc^cc);
      }
   else
printf("%4x  %2x  %2x  %8b\n",adrs,mc,cc,mc ^ cc);
   } /* end else if */
   else
      ;
   adrs++;
   } /* end while */
if(! ( (cc = getc(cfile)) == EOFF || (ascii && cc == EOF) ) )
puts("Masterfile shorter than checkfile\n");
return;
   } /* end fcompare() */
err_exit(msg)
   char *msg;
```

```
    {
    exit( puts( msg ) );
    }
unsigned hextoi( string )
    char *string;
    {
    unsigned number;
    char c;
    number = 0;
    c = tolower( *string++ );
    while( isalpha(c) || isdigit(c) ) {
      if( c > 'f' )
        return number;
      number *= 16;
      if( isdigit(c) )
        number += c -'0';
      else
        number += c - 'a' + 10;
      c = tolower( *string++ );
      }
    return number;
    }
i_error( )
{
puts("Correct invocation form is:\n");
puts(" CMP <file1> <file2> {-a -b<hex-num>}\n\n");
puts("Where optional arguments are:\n\n");
puts("-a              => these are ascii files (terminate on 1AH )\n");
puts("-b<hex-num> => begin of file is address <hex-num> ");
puts("default is 0\n");
exit( );
}
char *xl( c,xlate )
    int c;
    char *xlate;
    {
    if( c > 0x7f || c < 0 )
      strcpy( xlate,"????" );
```

```
    else if( c == Ox7f )
      strcpy(xlate,"del ");
    else if( c > Oxlf ) {/* Then it is printable. */
      xlate[O] = c;
      strcpy(xlate+1,"      ");
      }
    else
      switch (c) {
        case Ox7: strcpy(xlate,"bel");
          break;
        case Ox8: strcpy(xlate,"bs");
          break;
        case Ox9: strcpy(xlate,"tab");
          break;
        case Oxa: strcpy(xlate,"lf");
          break;
        case Oxc: strcpy(xlate,"ff");
          break;
        case Oxd: strcpy(xlate,"cr");
          break;
        case Oxlb: strcpy(xlate,"esc");
          break;
        default:xlate[O] = '^'; /* show control chars as */
          xlate[1] = c + Ox40; /* ^ <char> e.g. ^A is */
          xlate[2] = '\O'; /* control A */
break;
      }
return xlate;
}
```

Utility/Tool

wc.c   Count characters, lines, and words in a text
                             file.

Usage

wc <filename>   Count the characters, lines, and words in the given file and output information to console.

Function

wc counts the characters, alpha characters, lines, and words and calculates average word length.

Example

wc wc.c   Analyzes this portion of the present chapter.

Theory of Operation

The file utility wc.c can be outlined in pseudocode (an English-like description of program operation) as shown below:

```
initialize
check syntax (abort on error)
while not EOF
   getchar(c)
   increment character counter
   if c == EOL
      increment line counter
   if alpha character
      increment alpha character counter
   if first letter of word
      increment word counter
calculate average word length
end
```

IMPLEMENTATION NOTES

1. A word is defined as a sequence of characters that begins with an alpha character.
2. Enhancements can be made to the word counting utility to include features such as FOG index or reader level calculations. In general, these more sophisticated

measures of written complexity use algorithms to measure such things as sentence length, number of syllables, and clause lengths. The two articles by Parry (PARR81) and Roberts (ROBE82) listed in Appendix D detail two approaches to this more complex task of measuring reading level. Both include programming details that could be included in an enhanced version of wc.

POSSIBLE PROBLEM AREAS

1. The program uses integer division, the modulus operator and a conditional expression to calculate average word length. The expression on our last printf is evaluated as follows: If the remainder of the division of na (number of alpha characters) by the number of words (nw) is greater than half the number of words (nw/2), then the first expression [i.e., ((na/nw)+1)] of the conditional expression is returned. This is the case where we need to round up the average to the next larger integer. If no rounding is required, the false conditional is returned (i.e., no rounding is performed). The reason for this obscure code is that the use of floating point numbers in BDS C is somewhat clumsy. For the purposes of simple text analysis, the approximation given here is adequate. If floating point numbers are available, the final printf statement would simply print the floating point value for average word length and print it with the %f specification.

/* wc.c—Word Counting Utility */

```
#include "BDSCIO.H"
main(argc, argv)
   int argc;
   char *argv[];
{
   int c, nl,nw,nc,na,inword;
   char iobuf [BUFSIZ];
   nl = nw = nc =na =0;
   inword = NO;
   if (argc < 2)
     {
```

```
        printf ("\nUsage: wc filename\n");
        exit( );
        }
    if (fopen(*++argv, iobuf) == ERROR)
        {
        printf("\nFile I/O error, check filename for spelling\n");
        exit( );
        }
    while ((c = getc(iobuf)) !=EOF && c != CPMEOF)
        {
            ++ nc;
        if (c == EOL)
            ++ nl;
        if (isalpha(c))
            ++ na;
        if (isspace(c))
        inword = NO;
        else if (inword == NO)
            {
        inword = YES;
        if (isalpha(c)) ++nw;
            }
        }
    printf("\n");   /* Begin on new line. */
    printf("File %s\n",argv[0]);
    printf("The number of lines is: %d\n",nl);
    printf("The number of words is: %d\n", nw);
    printf("The total number of characters is: %d\n",nc);
    printf("The number of alpha characters is %d\n",na);
/* The following printf prints the rounded number of */
/* characters per word. The conditional expression */
/* is used so that rounding of the integer division */
/* will occur rather than simply truncation. In a C */
/* compiler with floating point numbers, this would */
/* be replaced with a floating point number and %f */
/* specification in the printf. */
    printf("Approximate average word length: %d\n",
```

```
((na%nw) > (nw/2)) ? ((na/nw)+1) : (na/nw));
fclose(iobuf);
}
```

Utility/Tool

mxprint.h   Header file for Epson MX-80/Graftrax
                             printer.

Usage

#include mxprint.h   Include these constants and functions in any
                             program (such as an enhanced text format-
                             ter) that needs to take advantage of the
                             sophisticated printing capabilities of the
                             Epson MX-80 printer.

Function

mxprint.h provides a convenient method of isolating the printer-specific features for use in other C programs. Unlike the other tools in this book, mxprint.h is provided as a starting point for inclusion in your programs. It also provides an example of the use of C header files and can be modified to fit any printer available.

Theory of Operation

The line printer utility mxprint.h can be outlined in pseudocode (an English-like description of program operation) as shown below:

This tool is mainly a lengthy series of #define's that establish the characteristics of the Epson MX-80 printer for use in C programs. The functions included in the listing are presented simply as examples to be expanded into the appropriate program by the reader.

C Function	Purpose/Function
printout(c)	Sample function to send one character to the CP/M LST: device.

escprint(c)   Sample function to send one escape charac-
                   ter sequence to the standard CP/M LST:
                   device.

italicon(c)   Sample function demonstrating how the pre-
                   vious #define's can be used to simplify set-
                   ting the printer modes. In this case, the print-
                   er's italic mode is initialized.

IMPLEMENTATION NOTES

1. This tool is not directly usable as presented here. It is designed to be included in any printer utility that would like to use the printing capabilities of the Epson MX-80 printer. Some of the features of this printer include underlining, super- and subscript-ing, italic mode, and limited graphics capabilities.

2. The header file is obviously machine-specific to the Epson MX-80 printer equipped with the Graftrax ROM-set. Isolating such machine-specific code in a header file is a good C programming practice. The modularity of our text formatter (see Chapter 7) makes the inclusion of such machine-specific features relatively easy. Readers with other machines may want to take this file and modify it to take advantage of its unique printer characteristics.

/* mxprint.h—Printer Header File */

```
/* mxprint.h Header file for Epson MX-80 printer constants */
/* #include at the beginning of any program that needs to use */
/* the printing capabilities of the Epson MX-80 printer with */
/* the Graftrax ROM set. */
#define NUL     0       /* terminator for TABS */
#define BEL     0x07    /* sounds buzzer for 1/3 second */
#define BS      0x08    /* Backspace. Empty the printer buffer. */
                        /* Backspace print head one space. */
#define HT      0x09    /* Horizontal tabulation. Advance print */
                        /* head to next tab stop */
```

```
#define LF      0x0A    /* Line feed. Printer empties buffer and */
                        /* does line feed at current position. */
#define VT      0x0B    /* Vertical tab. Single line feed. */
#define FF      0x0C    /* Formfeed. Advance paper to next */
                        /* logical top of form. */
#define CR      0x0D    /* Carriage return. Print buffer contents */
                        /* and reset buffer character count to zero. */
#define SO      0x0E    /* Shift out. Turn on double width mode to */
                        /* end of line unless cancelled by DC4. */
#define SI      0x0F    /* Shift in. Turns on compressed character */
                        /* mode. Does not work with emphasized */
                        /* mode. Stays on until cancelled by DC2. */
#define DC2     0x12    /* Turns off compressed characters and */
                        /* empties print buffer. */
#define DC4     0x14    /* Turns off double width mode (SO only). */
#define ESC     0x1B    /* ASCII code for ESCAPE. Generally used */
                        /* to prepare printer to receive special */
                        /* control codes. */
#define ESC#    0x23    /* Accept eighth bit "as is" from the */
                        /* computer. */
#define ESC-    0x2D    /* Underline mode. N = 0 → underline OFF. */
                        /* N>0 → underline ON. Format of call: */
                        /* <ESC> - N */
#define ESC0    0x30    /* set line spacing to 1/8" */
#define ESC1    0x31    /* set line spacing to 7/72" */
#define ESC2    0x32    /* set line spacing to 1/6" */
#define ESC3    0x33    /* set line spacing to n/216". Format: */
                        /* <ESC> <ESC3> <n> */
#define ESC4    0x34    /* italics ON */
#define ESC5    0x35    /* italics OFF */
#define ESC8    0x38    /* ignore paper out sensor */
#define ESC9    0x39    /* enable "paper out" sensor */
#define ESC_C   0x3C    /* unidirectional print on */
#define ESC_D   0x3D    /* clear eighth bit (i.e., set to zero) */
#define ESC_E   0x3E    /* set eighth bit to 1 */
#define ESC40   0x40    /* reset all modes to power up state */
#define ESCA    0x41    /* set spacing of line feed to n/72". */
                        /* Format: <ESC> <ESCA> <N> */
```

```
#define ESCC    0x43    /* Set form length to N lines. Format: */
                        /* <ESC> <ESCC> <N> or */
                        /* set form length to N inches. Format: */
                        /* <ESC> <ESCC> <NUL> <N> */
#define ESCD    0x44    /* reset current tabs and set up to 28 */
                        /* horizontal tabs. Format: */
                        /* <ESC> <ESCD> <N1> <N2> ... <NUL> */
                        /* terminate sequence of tabs with NUL */
#define ESCE    0x45    /* turn ON emphasized mode */
#define ESCF    0x46    /* turn OFF emphasized mode */
#define ESCG    0x47    /* turn ON double strike mode */
#define ESCH    0x48    /* turn OFF double strike, superscript */
                        /* and subscript modes */
#define ESCJ    0x4A    /* set line spacing to N/216" and empty */
                        /* printer buffer. Format: */
                        /* <ESC> <ESCJ> <N> */
#define ESCK    0x4B    /* set low resolution dot graphics mode ON */
#define ESCL    0x4C    /* set high resolution graphics mode ON */
#define ESCN    0x4E    /* set skip over perforation to N lines */
                        /* Format: <ESC> <ESCN> <N> */
#define ESCO    0x4F    /* resets skip over perforation to 0 */
#define ESCQ    0x5B    /* set column width. Format: */
                        /* <ESC> <ESCQ> <N> */
#define ESCS    0x5D    /* set super or subscript mode. Format: */
                        /* <ESC> <ESCS> N; N = 0 → superscript */
                        /* N > 0 → subscript */
#define ESCT    0x5E    /* reset subscript or superscript */
#define ESCU    0x5F    /* unidirectional printing */
#define ESCW    0x61    /* double width print ON */
/* The following are rudimentary printer control functions that */
/* use the previously defined constants to control an Epson MX-80 */
/* printer with the Graftrax ROM set. These functions could be */
/* included in any sophisticated printer control program. */
/* printer output */
printout (c)
char c;
{
```

```
    bios(5,c) /* send output to line printer 1st: device */
    return;
}
/* escape sequence print */
escprint (c)
char c;
{
    printout (ESC);
    printout (c);
    return;
}
/* set italics character set ON */
italicon (c)
char c;
{
    escprint (ESC4);
    return;
}
/*      Note: this last function would be repeated for the */
/* various printer capabilities desired. By changing the name */
/* of the function, we would isolate the printer control definitions */
/* into one header file and make the software more portable from */
/* printer to printer. */
```

4

Text Compression

You can never be too rich, too thin, or have too much disk
storage.

Ancient American proverb, ca. 1980

The facetious quotation above encapsulates the basic problem faced by microcomputer
users. Namely, our computers generally are lacking in sufficient disk space. Typically,
we use machines with a storage capacity between 100k and 256k characters. While
this is adequate for most of our purposes, it is often necessary to pack more information
onto a diskette. (To those fortunate few readers with hard disks of 20 megabytes
capacity, this chapter is not for you.) For the rest of us, we can read on and learn more
about the whole problem of text compression and expansion.

    This chapter presents two relatively simple programs for text compression and
expansion that implant or remove tab characters within a file to conserve disk space. In
addition, material is presented directing the interested reader to a much more sophisticated text compression facility available in the public domain.

    The need for text compression can arise in one of two ways. For the isolated
microcomputer user, the problem of text compression arises out of the need to store
more and more information on the relatively small 5-inch diskettes used by most
microcomputers. For the communicating microcomputer user who is accessing the
nationwide databases of public domain files, the problem arises with the cost of
telephone connections. If a file can be transmitted in a compressed form, the telephone

connection and transmission charges can be minimized. The SQUEEZE/ UNSQUEEZE programs from the CP/M Users Group fall into this latter category.

The basic process of text compression can be represented as shown below:

original file → encoding → compressed file

The reverse process involves the task of decoding the compressed file to restore it to its original configuration:

compressed file → decoding → restored file

Text compression or data compression depends upon the ability to predict redundancy within a data file and then to encode this information with an algorithm that permits the redundancy to be removed without losing any information from the file. As an example, suppose we know that in our file every sixth character is a blank space. Obviously this regularity can be encoded into a much smaller file using the rule that when we decode the file, we print five characters from the file and then produce a blank space. While this example is artificial and contrived, all text compression programs operate on this same basis. Namely, first we discover redundancies. Second, we encode these redundancies to save space. Third, in decoding the file, we use the encoding algorithm to restore the original content of the file. A technical definition of data compression is that it is the process of predicting redundancy and then encoding data to eliminate the redundancy.

We can distinguish five basic schemes for text compression. At the simplest level (which is the level of the programs presented in this chapter), we are dealing with what is known as run-length encoding and decoding. In this simple procedure, we locate runs or sequences of characters within a file and then replace them with a marker of the character in the run and a special representation of the number of recurrences. Consequently, we can reduce the amount of file disk space used. As an example, suppose the file contains the line:

"AB . . . . CD"

(For clarity, each blank space is shown by a period mark.) Our example line thus contains the letters A and B followed by seven spaces and then the letters C and D. The task of run-length encoding involves encoding each run as a single representative character and a count of the number of occurrences. For example, we might decide that the "\" character is to be used to represent a run of blanks. In a real program, the representational character should be one that does not occur in the file normally. Our sample line would become:

AB\7CD

We have reduced the size of the file from 11 bytes (seven blanks and four characters) to 6 bytes. Obviously the most efficient use of run length encoding is possible in files that are known to contain long runs of redundant characters. (A good candidate for such run-length encoding is program listings with extensive indentations and hence redundant blank spaces.)

A second and simple process for compressing program text is presented by Gustafson (GUST82) in his article "Compress It." This article takes advantage of a specialized form of redundancy: Computer programs are written in computer languages that typically contain a very few reserved words. For example, BASIC contains such reserved words as READ or INPUT, while C contains such things as if . . . then . . . else or #include. Using this information, we can write a program to replace these keywords with shorter tokens to conserve space. This technique of compression is known as keyword replacement. Gustafson (GUST82) presents a program for keyword replacement in NorthStar BASIC programs.

A third and similar technique involves the more general process of substituting shorter abbreviations for recurring segments of text within a file. This technique is often used in the construction of dictionary files for spelling checker programs. The basic process here involves taking a file and producing an output file with the following format:

dictionary portion	abbreviation 1	expanded form 1
of file	abbreviation 2	expanded form 2
text portion of file	abbreviation1-ing second and fourth word of the file	

The compressed file contains a glossary of abbreviations used and their expanded forms. The text portion of the file then contains the text with the abbreviated forms used whenever possible. Obviously this technique is applicable on only the largest text files and only those with some measure of regularity (such as very large word or name files). An example of this abbreviation technique is presented by Tropper in an article on constructing dictionary files with what is called "binary-coded text" (TROP82). In that article he notes that the sequence *the* represents approximately 7% of the sample text examined and that 104 words comprise approximately 47% of the written language examined. On the basis of these evidences of redundancy, the author presents a technique known as binary coding of text to reduce the storage requirements for normal text files.

A fourth and even more sophisticated method of text encoding makes use of the discovery that not all character sequences are created equal. Basically, this method of text compression, known as frequency distribution characteristic encoding involves three steps. First, we must measure the differences between the most common and least common letter sequences. Because of programming complexities and the structure of noncomputing languages (such as English), the unit of comparison is generally the digraph (i.e., the two letter pair). The second step of the encoding process involves replacing the most common letter sequences with a shorter representational code. An excellent example of frequency distribution characteristic encoding is the International Morse Code. In this telegraphic code, the letter e, which occurs with a 13% frequency in English, is represented by the very compact single dot "." The much rarer character j, with an occurrence of only 0.13%, is represented by the longer ". –––" (dot-dash-dash-dash) sequence. An example of digraph encoding for text compression is presented by Cortesi (CORT82; CORT83) in his book on CP/M-80 utilities and in a related *Byte* magazine article.

The final technique of text compression in common usage is Huffman encoding. A detailed introduction to Huffman encoding is available in Tanenbaum and Augenstein's text on Pascal (TANE81). The actual process of Huffman encoding is beyond the scope of this book. This powerful text compressing technique is available in the public domain software programs SQUEEZE/UNSQUEEZE.

Huffman encoding operates on the basis of recoding the underlying character code representation itself. The normal ASCII code which uses 7 bits can obviously be stored more efficiently in an 8-bit microcomputer word. In the normal ASCII scheme of things we are ignoring one eighth of the possible storage space in a file. Suppose we have a simple file that contains only four letters A, B, C, D, and they are encoded in a simple coding scheme as follows:

A 00
B 01
C 10
D 11

Let's further assume that A occurs 50% of the time, B occurs 25% of the time, and C and D occur only 12.5% of the time. Note that with the fixed-length encoding shown above, we are wasting a great deal of space. If we could replace the fixed length (two digits) encoding scheme above with a variable length code as shown below, we could save some storage space:

A 0
B 10
C 110
D 111

This technique is not without its costs however. Because it involves bit manipulations it is quite complex to program and can be slow in terms of execution speed. Also, it is very vulnerable to transmission errors unless special precautions are taken. As a consequence, the best prospect for implementing a text compression facility using this technique is the publicly available SQUEEZE/UNSQUEEZE program from the CP/M Users Group. Specifically, the programs are contained on volume 85 of the CP/M Users' Group diskette series. These programs are also available from the C Users Group. (See Appendix B for information on sources of public domain software.) Need I even mention that these programs are written in BDS C!

This chapter presents two programs, TAB and DETAB, that are simple but effective text compression and expansion filters. As their names suggest, they restore or remove (as the case may be) tabs and blank spaces in text files. Their greatest utility is with program listings (typically containing extensive amounts of white space surrounding indented portions of a program). They are least useful with simple textual material, such as this paragraph, which generally has little if any redundant blank spaces.

Utility/Tool

tab.c   Convert sequences of spaces into tabs when-
                     ever possible, thus conserving storage space.

Usage

tab oldfile newfile Take the "oldfile" and replace space with
                     tabs producing the "newfile."

Function

Tab replaces spaces in a file with the tab character whenever possible to reduce the amount of extraneous "whitespace" within a file.

Example

tab a:big a:small   Takes a file called "big" on disk drive a and replaces spaces with tabs to produce a file named "small" also on disk a.

Theory of Operation

The text compression utility tab.c can be outlined in pseudocode (an English-like description of program operation) as shown below:

```
initialize
check syntax (abort on error)
getchar from file
if EOF quit
else switch(c):
    CR:         Putchar CR reset column count.
    LF:         Putchar LF reset space count.
    blank:      Collect blanks in 8-blank units (CP/M default for tabs).
                Output tab character.
                Output remaining blanks.
    tab:        Output tab to appropriate tab column assuming tabs set
                every eight columns (CP/M default).
    ":          Do not compress blanks (assumes quotes will enclose
                text strings that must remain exact such as program
                constants, etc.). Fail if double quote unmatched.
    default:    Putchar (c).
```

IMPLEMENTATION NOTES

1. There shouldn't be any control characters within the file, except for carriage returns and linefeeds, or the program will fail.

2. Also, there shouldn't be any double quotes (") within the file except as string delimiters; i.e., tabify shouldn't be used on itself because of the quote in this sentence and the double quotes enclosed within single quotes further down in the file.

3. The input file isn't altered; the result is a new file named by the second argument. A common use of this program is to tabify text files which you've loaded in over the phone from a computer system (like UNIX) that tends to turn all tabs into spaces for 300 baud DECwriters.

/* tab.c—Tab Insertion Filter */

```
main(argc,argv)
char **argv;
{
  int scount, column, ifd, ofd, i;
  int c;
  char ibuf[134], obuf[134];
  if (argc != 3) {
    printf("usage: tab oldfile newfile\n");
    exit();
  }
  ifd = fopen(argv[1],ibuf);
  ofd = fcreat(argv[2],obuf);
  if (ifd == -1 || ofd == -1) {
    printf("Can't open file(s)\n");
    exit();
  }
  scount = column = 0;
  do {
    c = getc(ibuf);
    if (c == -1) {
      putc(0x1a,obuf);
      break;
    }
  switch(c) {
      case 0x0d: putc1(c,obuf);
        scount = column = 0;
        break;
      case 0x0a: putc1(c,obuf);
```

```
        scount = 0;
        break;
case ' ':column++;
    scount++;
    if (!(column%8)) {
        if (scount > 1)
        putc1('\t',obuf);
        else
        putc1(' ',obuf);
        scount = 0;
    }
    break;
case '\t': scount = 0;
    column += (8-column%8);
        putc1(c,obuf);
    break;
case '"': for (i=0; i<scount; i++)
        putc1(' ',obuf);
    putc1('"',obuf);
    do {
        c = getc(ibuf);
        if (c == -1) {
            printf("Quote error.\n");
            exit();
        }
        putc1(c,obuf);
    } while (c != '"');
    do {
        c = getc(ibuf);
        putc1(c,obuf);
    } while (c != 0x0a);
    column = scount = 0;
    break;
case 0x1a: putc(0x1a,obuf);
    break;
default: for (i=0, i<scount; i++)
        putc1(' ',obuf);
    scount = 0;
```

```
            column++;
            putcl (c,obuf);
        }
    } while (c != 0x1a);
    fflush(obuf);
    close(obuf);
    close(ibuf);
}
putcl(c,buf)
char c;
{
    putchar(c);
    if (putc(c,buf) < 0) {
    printf("\n\ntabify: disk write error.");
    exit();
    }
}
}
```

Utility/Tool

detab.c   Convert tab characters into sequences of
                        spaces.

Usage

detab oldfile newfile   Take the "oldfile" and replace tab characters
                        with spaces producing the "newfile."

Function

detab is the converse program for the preceding utility tool tab. It replaces the tab character in a file with the appropriate number of spaces.

Example

detab a:small a:big   Takes a file called "small" on disk drive a
                        and replaces tabs with spaces to produce a
                        file named "big" also on disk a.

Theory of Operation

The text compression utility detab.c can be outlined in pseudocode (an English-like description of program operation) as shown below:

```
initialize
check syntax (abort on error)
while not EOF
   getchar(c)
   switch (c):
      CR:        reset column counter
      LF:        output LF
      tab:       output spaces and increment column counter until
                 column counter equal to 8 space CP/M tab default
      default:   output character and increment column counter
```

IMPLEMENTATION NOTES

1. The detab program operates on a default of 8 spaces per tab character (i.e., the CP/M default). An interesting enhancement to the program would be to modify it to allow the user to specify the modulus for tab to space conversion.

2. The input file isn't altered; the result is a new file named by the second argument.

/* detab.c—Detabify Filter */

```
/* Prog to take a text file full of tabs */
/* and turn them into the right number of spaces: */
#define CR 0x0d
#define LF 0x0a
#define BS 0x08
#define EOF 255
#define CPMEOF 0x1a
#define ERRORCODE -1
#define TAB 0x09
```

```
char ibuf[134], obuf[134];
main(argc,argv)
char **argv;
{
  int fd1, fd2, col;
  char c;
  int i;
  fd1 = fopen(argv[1],ibuf);
  fd2 = fcreat(argv[2],obuf);
  if (fd1 == ERRORCODE || fd2 == ERRORCODE) {
    printf("Open error.\n");
    exit();
  }
  col = 0;
  while ((c=getc(ibuf)) != EOF) {
    switch(c) {
        case CR: col = 0;
        case LF: putc2(c,obuf);
          continue;
        case TAB: do {
          putc2(' ',obuf);
          col++;
          } while (col%8); /* CP/M default of eight spaces per tab */
          continue;
        default: col++;
      }
      putc2(c,obuf);
    }
  fflush(obuf);
  close(fd1);
  close(fd2);
}
putc2(c,obuf)
char c;
{
  putchar(c);
  putc(c,obuf);
}
```

5

Text Editing I: General Overview and User Guide

INTRODUCTION

This chapter, and the chapter following, comprise the longest topic in the book; namely, text editing. In case you might doubt that editing is the prototypical computer activity, we will recount a little history of data processing.

In the beginning, computers were essentially vast, cumbersome mathematical calculators and were the sole province of mathematicians and their ilk. Computers quickly infiltrated the less purely mathematical realm of business and accounting, and today they have even found their way into elementary schools and the home.

With this transition of computing's locus of operation has come a fundamental shift in emphasis. The initial mathematical orientation has given way almost totally to a symbol and text manipulation emphasis. The largest selling microcomputer programs are the word processors. These range all the way from "WordStar" to "Bank Street Writer." The former is an absolutely professional product that can do virtually anything and is somewhat complex and complicated to master. The latter editor/word processor is routinely used in elementary schools to teach writing skills. Even programmers, who do little if any writing in the traditional literary sense, constantly use editors in the preparation of their programs.

In a very real sense then, editing has become the paradigmatic or typical computing activity. This explains the length and prominence given this and the succeeding chapter.

Text editing is somewhat like spicy, ethnic food in that "There's no accounting for tastes." Just as we all have our favorite ethnic dish (mine is spicy Chinese), everyone has his or her own favorite text editing program. The very abundance of commercial text editing programs reassures us that there is no one perfect editor.

The editor presented in this chapter is not claimed to be the perfect, end-all editor. It does, however, have certain very nice features. Most importantly, it includes a complete listing of the program code for itself. Thus, if you don't like it, you can (unlike the weather) do something about it—you can change it to suit your fancy.

GENERAL THEORY OF EDITORS

Before presenting the editor itself, it might be useful to discuss the theory and practice of text editors as well as provide a brief guide to the vast literature available on this most interesting aspect of text processing.

The initial software tool editor ("edit") presented by Kernighan and Plauger in their classic *Software Tools* (KERN76) operates in what is known as a line-oriented mode. Commands operate on the basis of lines, and there is no type of full-screen display orientation. This batch- or line-editor was for many years the only type of editing facility available on any computer. The CP/M editor ED is a remnant of this class of text editors. The editor available within the popular versions of Microsoft BASIC is also a line-oriented editor. As anyone who has ever used ED knows, this editor class is far from ideal. While often quite powerful, the lack of ability to view multiple lines or files is often a hindrance in complicated editing sessions.

Today, virtually all editors are what is known as full-screen or video editors. The availability of more sophisticated computer and terminal hardware has facilitated this development. Quality microcomputer software has also fueled the creation of excellent full-screen editors. WordStar is a classic example of a full-screen editor. Basically, a full-screen editor provides a "window" into a text file where we can see the text that we are manipulating, and through this window we can make changes in the text file.

Technically, an interactive editor is a tool that allows a user to create and revise a target document. The content of this document may range from the fictional prose of an author to the technical details of a computer program.

All text editing involves a basic four-stage process. Initially, we select what part of the document is to be viewed and manipulated. In general, the length of a text far exceeds the display capacity of our computer system. A typical video screen of 24 lines by 80 characters allows only 1920 characters to be displayed at a time. Obviously, this first task of text editing involves the use of text buffers and display routines to allow us to efficiently manipulate the much larger text files that we are interested in.

The second task of any text editor is to format the internal representation of the text into the displayed text that we will view on our video screen. Some examples of this formatting are the use of the display to reflect the physical character set used (e.g., italics, boldface, etc.). Editors for the Apple Macintosh machine and the Epson QX-10 VALDOCS system allow direct representation of multiple character sets on their display screens.

Our text editor in this chapter is much more modest. We simply want the editor to display the text so that words are not arbitrarily split between lines and perform other more mundane tasks.

The third step in any text editing system is the specification and execution of a requested operation. In text editing parlance, an operation can include anything from deleting or inserting characters to splitting and rejoining separate lines of text. In our editor, this stage of operation takes place in either the command or the edit mode. The insertion of characters takes place in the third mode, the insert mode.

The final step of any text editing program is the updating of the display screen to reflect the changes made in the document file in step three above.

This initial description of text editing is obviously woefully incomplete. The amount of material available on text editing is incredible in its diversity and breadth. Listed in Appendix D are some recent articles on editing and editors.

C TEXT EDITORS

In addition to ed2 presented in this and the succeeding chapter, there are several other editors available that include source code or include details concerning custom user modification using the C programming language. Presented below is a list of the major editors available to users of the C language that are modifiable by the purchaser.

MINCE

Mark of the Unicorn
222 Third Street
Cambridge, MA 02142
(617) 576-2760

C Screen Editor

Northwest Microsystem Design
P.O. Box 10853
Eugene, OR 97401, or
Programmer's Shop
128-D Rockland Street
Hanover, MA 02339

ed2
(initial editor of this chapter in small-C)

C User's Group
415 E. Euclid
McPherson, KS 67460, or
Algorithmic Technology
P.O. Box 278
Exton, PA 19341-0278

RED

Ed Ream
150 Summit Avenue
Madison, WI 53705

edit

J. E. Hendrix
Route 1, Box 585
Oxford, MS 38655

ed2: GENERAL OVERVIEW OF PROGRAM OPERATION

One of the major strengths of the C programming language is its modularity. Large programs (such as ed2) can be designed in smaller, more manageable units that can be combined to form the final, integrated software package. This section of the chapter will present a brief overview of the entire ed2 program. This presentation will be at the level of modules and functions. Comments concerning individual lines of code or segments of the C program are included with the source code presented in the next chapter.

The text editor is divided into thirteen separate files or modules. Four of these files include only definitions and macros used by the other program modules.

A quick glance at the table of modules reveals that modifying the editor should be relatively straightforward. As an example, the addition of more commands could be accomplished by modifying two modules. Specifically, we would need to modify the main module (ed2.bds) to permit the selection of our additional commands. Further, the new commands would need to be included into the command mode commands module (ed3.bds). By separating the functions of the editor in this manner, the task of expanding or modifying the program is simplified considerably.

A complete list and brief description of the modules is presented below:

ed2 MODULES

Module Name	Function	Description
bdscio.h	standard header file	Defines I/O constants, general purpose symbolic constants, port numbers, modem numbers, etc. The bds C equivalent of the UNIX stdio.h header file. Generally included in most bds C programs.
ed2.h	nonuser defined globals	Global definitions for text lines, and miscellaneous constants.
ed1.ccc	special key definitions	File containing the #define statements for keyboard definitions (e.g., up arrow, insert char key, etc.). Must be modified for specific user hardware before compilation.
edext.cc	static definitions	Definitions for static C variables. Includes such items as tabs, buffer indices, buffer flags, etc.
ed2.bds	main command program	Main program. Interprets commands and dispatches execution sequence appropriately.
ed3.bds	command mode commands	Module for command mode commands.
ed4.bds	window module	Module for display formatting and windowing of buffer text.
ed5.bds	output format module	Output routines for display and list devices.
ed6.ccc	terminal output module	Terminal specific output

		functions. This file must be customized by the user before compilation of the editor.
ed7.bds	prompt line module	Module handles messages and prompt line input/output.
ed8.bds	operating system module	Module for lower level system interfaces (e.g., file input/output, console input/output, etc.). This module would need to be changed if the editor is to be used on a non-CP/M operating system.
ed9.bds	general utilities	Catch-all module for miscellaneous utility functions, such as character-integer conversions and error handling functions.
ed10.bds	buffer module	Module to handle buffering of text for use by the editor. Functions include clearing and keeping track of the status of the buffer. All inserting and deleting of lines, for example, takes place here.

The operation of the editor can also be described relatively easily due to its modular structure. The pseudocode shown below presents an overview of the editor's operation. The modular nature of command execution is particularly evident there.

PSEUDOCODE LISTING FOR THE ed2 TEXT EDITOR

```
initialize and enter command mode
while not done
    check for mode (edit/command/insert/exit)
    execute chosen mode
```

command mode

save current line
while not done
  format screen and get command
  if edit/insert
    check for line changes
      if no changes
        get current line and redraw screen
      else
        update line and screen
    if edit
      return (editmode)
    else
      return (insertmode)
  else check for command letters
  command letter execution

case:g	$\rightarrow$	goto	{edgo function}
append	$\rightarrow$	append	{append function}
change	$\rightarrow$	change	{change function}
clear	$\rightarrow$	clear	{clear function}
delete	$\rightarrow$	delete	{delete function}
dos	$\rightarrow$	exit	return (exitmode)
find	$\rightarrow$	find	{find, edgo functions, return (editmode)
else if find fails			return (commandmode)}
list	$\rightarrow$	list	{list function}
load	$\rightarrow$	load	{load function}
name	$\rightarrow$	name	{name function}
resave	$\rightarrow$	resave	{resave function}
save	$\rightarrow$	save	{save function}
search	$\rightarrow$	search	{search function}
tabs	$\rightarrow$	set tabs	{tabs function}
else error	$\rightarrow$	invalid command	

edit mode

initialize prompt line
get edit command
  if commandmode $\rightarrow$ enter command mode

```
        if insertmode      → enter insert mode
      else continue in editmode
    check for edit command
      " "      →    right      {edright function}
      b        →    begin      {edbegin function}
      d        →    down       {check bottom and scroll if OK}
      e        →    end        {edend function}
      g        →    goto       {save x,y and edgo function}
      k        →    kill       {edkill function}
      s        →    search     {edsearch function}
      u        →    up         check buffer and scroll if OK
```

insert mode

```
  initialize prompt line
  get command
    if commandmode → enter command mode
    if editmode      → enter edit mode
    else stay in insertmode
    check for special characters
    if special characters execute appropriate insert command
      split          →    {edsplit function}
      abort          →    {edabort function}
      delete char    →    {eddel function}
      delete line    →    {edzap function}
      move up        →    {edup function}
      insert up      →    {ednewup function}
      move down      →    {eddn function}
      insert down    →    {ednewdn function}
      left           →    {edleft function}
      right          →    {edright function}
```

exit mode

```
  exit from editor.
```

ed2 SCREEN EDITOR: USER GUIDE

Basic Terms

The terms mode, command, special character, prompt line, cursor, the current line, and the buffer are used extensively in this documentation. You will learn about the screen editor more easily if you become familiar with these terms. Let's look at each in turn.

The screen editor is comprised of several *modes*. You can switch between modes, but the editor cannot be in two modes at the same time. The editor behaves differently in each mode, so you use each mode to do a particular type of editing.

There are three modes: *edit* mode, *command* mode and *insert* mode. You use edit mode for making small changes in many different lines. Command mode is used for making larger (and hence potentially more dangerous) changes to the whole file you are editing. You must be in command mode to do anything that will change files on the disk. You use insert mode for making a series of insertions into the text. First drafts are generally entered in this mode.

You use *commands* to make things happen in each mode. Which commands you can use depends on what mode you are in. Do not confuse the terms *commands* and *command mode*. Every mode has a set of commands that you can use in that mode. Command mode has its own set of commands.

Special characters are one-letter commands. Special characters must be control keys, so that you can use these commands in places where the editor might not otherwise expect a command.

The *prompt line* is the top line of the screen. It tells you things like what line you are editing and what mode you are in. If you get confused about what mode you are in, you can always glance at the prompt line.

Several edit-mode commands consist of two or more letters. These edit-mode commands are called *extended commands*. After you type the first letter of such a command, but before you type the last letter, the prompt line will indicate that you must type one more letter to finish the extended command. For example, after you type an "s" to enter the edit-mode search command, the prompt line's mode field will contain "edit: search."

The *cursor* is a distinctive character on the screen. On most video terminals this marker is a character shown with reverse video. In command mode you always type commands on the bottom line so the cursor is always on the bottom line. In edit mode and insert mode the cursor is always on the current line.

The *current line* is the only line you can edit. In command mode the current line may not show on the screen, but in edit and insert modes the current line is shown and it contains the cursor. If you want to make a change to a line you must first move the cursor to that line.

The *buffer* is a part of the computer's storage that holds the file you are editing. In order to edit a disk file, you must first read the disk file into the buffer using the load command. As you edit the file, the changes you make are made only to the buffer, not to your disk file. Before you end your editing session you must copy the buffer back to a disk file using the save or resave commands. The editor keeps track of whether you have done this; it won't let you forget to save your work.

The *window* is a part of the screen that shows a portion of the buffer. In edit and insert modes the window fills all of the screen except the prompt line. You can think of the file as a scroll of parchment that unwinds under the window as you move the cursor. The window is not shown in command mode.

Now let's look more closely at the editor's commands. We'll start with special characters, which are commands that may be used in either insert or edit modes. Then we will look at other commands that are unique to a particular mode.

Special Characters

Special characters act the same in all modes. Special characters must be control characters so that the editor may always distinguish special characters from regular text.

There are 14 special characters; all 14 may be used in either edit mode or insert mode. Only a few may be used in command mode.

You can use the configuration program to choose which keys on your keyboard to use for each special character. Thus, we won't be able to be specific about what key on your keyboard you will actually hit in order to type, for instance, the down key. I'll often refer to special characters as special keys; for example, I'll call the down special character the down key.

The *left and right keys* just move the cursor. They do not cause changes to lines. These keys are always "anchored" to the current line; you can't move off the current line by using these keys. If you hit the right key while the cursor is at the right margin, nothing will happen. Similarly, nothing will happen if you hit the left key while the cursor is at the left margin.

The *up and down keys* move the cursor up and down on the screen. You can't move the cursor above line 1 of the file, nor can you move the cursor below the last line of the file. Both these keys also switch the editor to edit mode.

The *insert up key* inserts a blank line above the current line while the *insert down key* inserts a blank line below the current line. Both these keys also switch the editor to insert mode.

The *delete character key* deletes the character to the left of the cursor. This key is anchored to the current line; nothing is deleted if the cursor is at the left margin. The *delete line key* deletes the entire line on which the cursor rests.

The *undo key* always undoes whatever editing you have done on the current line since the last time the cursor came to the current line.

The *insert key* switches the editor to the insert mode. Similarly, the *command key* switches the editor to command mode and the *edit key* switches the editor to edit mode.

The *split key* splits the current line into two pieces. Everything to the left of the cursor stays right where it is. All other characters are moved from the current line to a new line which is created below the original line.

The *join key* is the opposite of the split key; it combines two lines into one line. The join key appends the current line to the line above it, then deletes the lower line.

Edit Mode

Edit-mode commands are normal letters; you don't need to use special keys. This speeds typing. You can, however, use the special keys in edit mode if you want to.

In addition to the special characters, you can use the following one-letter edit-mode commands: space, b, c, d, e, g, i, k, s, u, and x. These letters stand for **b**egin, **c**ommand, **d**own, **e**nd, **g**o, **i**nsert, **k**ill, **s**earch, **u**p, and e**x**change. Note that all these commands may be typed either in uppercase or in lowercase. Letters that are neither edit-mode commands nor special keys are simply ignored. The following paragraphs explain what these commands do in greater detail.

The *space bar* moves the cursor right one column. Nothing happens if the cursor is already on the rightmost column of the screen.

The *b command* puts the cursor at the beginning (left hand margin) of the line.

The *c command* switches the editor to command mode.

The *d command* causes the cursor to move down rapidly. The cursor keeps moving until it reaches the last line of the file or until you type any key.

The *e command* moves the cursor to the right end of the line.

The *i command* switches the editor to insert mode.

The *g command* moves the cursor to another line. The g command is an extended command; after you type the g the cursor will move to the prompt line. The prompt line will show "edit: goto." Now type a line number followed by a carriage return. The cursor will move to the line whose number you typed. If you do not type a valid number the g command does nothing. Leading blanks or minus signs are not allowed. The cursor will move to the last line of the buffer if the number you type is larger than the number of lines in the buffer.

The *k command* is a two-letter command. The second letter you type (the first character after the k) is a search character. The k command deletes from the cursor up to, but not including, the next occurrence of the search character to the right of the cursor. Everything from the cursor to the end of the line is deleted if the search character does not appear to the right of the cursor on the current line. After you hit the k and before you hit the search character the prompt line will show "edit: kill." If you wish to cancel the k command you can hit any control character. The k command will be stopped and no deletion will be made.

The *s command* is another two-letter command. The second character you type (the first character after the s) is a search character. The s command moves the cursor to the next occurrence of the search character which appears to the right of the cursor. The cursor moves to the end of the current line if the search character does not occur to the right of the cursor. After you hit the s and before you hit the search character the prompt line will show "edit: search."

The *u command* moves the cursor up rapidly. The cursor keeps moving until it reaches the first line of the file or until you hit any key.

The *x command* is another two-letter command. The second character you type replaces the character under the cursor. The prompt line will show "edit: eXchange" until you hit the second character. If you hit a control character no change is made and the x command is cancelled.

Insert Mode

Use insert mode to insert many lines of text at once. In insert mode anything you type (except special keys) will be inserted into the text to the left of the cursor. You may use special keys in insert mode exactly as in edit mode.

Command Mode

You use command mode to do potentially dangerous things, such as making multiple changes to the buffer or updating your files. For this reason, all command-mode commands require you to type several characters with a carriage return at the end.

The editor starts off in command mode after you invoke it from your operating system.

You may use either the edit key or the insert key to exit from command mode. You can also use the g command-mode command or the find command-mode command to leave command mode. When the editor leaves command mode the screen is redrawn to show the current line.

The cursor is on the bottom line of the screen whenever the editor is in command mode. This line is called the command line. As you type commands, what you type will be shown on this line. Use either the delete character key or the right key to delete the last character you typed. Use the undo key to delete the entire command line.

Several command-mode commands take arguments. There are three types of arguments: range arguments, file names, and line numbers. In the description below, range arguments will be denoted by <line range>, file name arguments will be denoted by <filename> and the line numbers will be denoted by <n>.

Range arguments denote the range of lines in the buffer for which a command will take effect. For example,

list 25 50

means list all lines from line 25 to line 50 inclusive,

list

means list all the lines of the buffer, and

list 300

means list line 300 and all following lines. Range arguments, if present, must be non-negative integers. If two numbers are entered, the first must be no larger than the second. 0 is equivalent to 1. A number larger than the largest line number is equivalent to the largest line number.

Filename arguments are the name of a file to be used in a command. For example:

load myfile.doc

causes the file myfile.doc to replace whatever is in the buffer. Note that no quotation marks are used around filename arguments. Filename arguments optionally may be preceded by disk drive names. For example:

load b:myfile.doc

loads the buffer from the file myfile.doc which must be found on drive b.

The editor protects you from destroying the buffer unintentionally. If a command would cause the buffer to be erased and you have not already saved the buffer on a disk file the editor will ask:

buffer not saved. proceed ?

If you type y or Y the command will be done and the buffer will be erased. If you type anything else, no change will be made to the buffer and the message "cancelled" will be printed on the screen. Note however, that the delete command does *not* protect you in this way. Use the delete command with caution.

You may interrupt or cancel the change, find, list, and search commands. If you type any character *except* a blank, the command will be cancelled immediately. If you type a blank the command will be temporarily suspended. Type another blank to continue or any other character to cancel the command.

The following paragraphs discuss all the command-mode commands.

append <filename>

The append command inserts the named file into the buffer after the current line. In other words, the position of the cursor affects where the file will be inserted. This command adds to the buffer; it does not delete what is already there.

change <line range>

The change command searches all lines in <line range> for an instance of a search mask. If the search mask is found it is replaced by the change mask. After you type change <line range> the command will ask:

search mask ?

At this point, type the pattern you are searching for, followed by a carriage return. Then you will be asked:

change mask ?

Now you type the pattern you want the search mask to be replaced by. For example:

**change 100 300
search mask ? abc
change mask ? xyz**

will change abc to xyz in all lines from 100 to 300. Thus, the line:

know your abc's.

would be changed into:

know your xyz's.

Only the first instance of abc on each line would be changed. The line:

know your abc's. The abc's are very important.

would be changed to:

know your xyz's. The abc's are very important.

Question marks may be used in both the search mask and the change mask. A question mark in the search mask matches any character at all. The search mask:

12?34

will match any string of five characters that starts with 12 and ends with 34. A question mark in the change mask matches the letter that matched the corresponding question mark in the search mask. For example:

change 99 109
search mask ? trailing?
change mask ? ?leading

would change the line:

trailingA

into the line:

Aleading

The question mark in the search mask matched the A, so the question mark in the change mask became an A. You can use as many question marks as you like, but there must be at least as many question marks in the search mask as there are in the change mask. As another example:

**change
search mask ? wh??e
change mask ? fath??**

would change the line:

where is here.

to the line:

father is here.

If the first character of the search mask is an up arrow (ˆ), the search mask is anchored to the start of the line. In other words, the search mask will only match patterns that start at column 0. For example, the search mask

ˆabc

will only match lines that contain abc in columns 0, 1 and 2. Anchoring the search mask dramatically increases the speed of the change command.

An up arrow which is not the first character of the search mask is treated as a regular up arrow. An up arrow in the change mask never has any special significance.

clear

The clear command erases the entire buffer. If you have not saved the buffer you will be asked whether you want to proceed.

delete <line range>

The delete command erases all lines in the line range. This command must be used cautiously because no check is made to see whether the buffer has been saved.

dos

The dos command exits the editor and returns to the operating system. If the buffer has not been saved, this command makes sure that you really wanted to exit without saving the buffer.

find

The find command searches for the next occurrence of a search mask. If the search mask is found, the editor switches to edit mode and the cursor is set to the start of the pattern. If the search mask is not found the editor remains in command mode. You specify the search mask exactly as in the change command.

g <n>

The g command exits the edit mode. Line <n> is drawn on the top line of the window and becomes the current line. Typing g without the <n> is the same as typing the edit key.

list <line range>

The list command lists all lines in the line range to the current list device, i.e., the printer. Lines are formatted just as they are on the screen, but the length of the print line, not the width of the screen, determines where lines will be truncated if they are too long. Listing may be stopped at any time by typing any key.

load <filename>

The load command replaces whatever is in the buffer by the contents of the named file. If the buffer has not been saved on disk when the load command is given, the editor makes sure you really wanted to erase the previous contents of the buffer. If the named file exists, then <filename> becomes "the current file" and <filename> is shown on the prompt line. This file becomes the file used in the save and resave commands. The current file name does not change if the named file does not exist.

After the file has been completely read from the disk into the buffer, the screen is redrawn to show the first several lines of file.

name <filename>

The name command sets the name of the file that will be used in the save and resave commands. This command is not often used because the load command is the usual way to set this file's name. The name command does not cause any action immediately; it simply affects which file the save and resave commands will use.

resave

The resave command saves the entire buffer in the current file. The current file is set by either the load or the name commands and always appears on the prompt line. Note that this command does *not* take any arguments. All arguments to this command are ignored.

The resave command requires that the current file already exists; if the file does not exist, a warning is printed and nothing happens.

save

The save command works just like the resave command except that the file must *not* exist for the command to work. If the file does exist, a warning is printed and nothing happens. This protection insures that files cannot be overwritten inadvertently.

search <line range>

The search command prints on the screen all lines in <line range> that contain an instance of the search mask. As soon as the search command is typed the editor will ask:

search mask ?

Now type the search mask. Just as in the change command, a question mark matches any character and a leading up arrow anchors the search mask to the start of the line.

tabs <n>

The tabs command controls how lines are listed on the screen and on the printer. Specifically, the tabs command sets tab stops every <n> columns. <n> must be an integer. tabs 0 is equivalent to tabs 1.

ed2: SCREEN EDITOR: COMMAND SUMMARY

Special Characters

All special characters may be used in edit and insert modes, but only the command, edit, insert, undo, and delete character keys may be used in command mode. The function of each special character is given below:

up key	(default is line feed) Move the cursor up one line unless the cursor is already at the top line of the file. Enter edit mode.
down key	(default is carriage return) Move the cursor down one line unless the cursor is already at the bottom line of the file. Enter edit mode.
right key	(default is control-r) Move the cursor right one character.
left key	(default is back space) Move the cursor left one character.
insert up key	(default is control-u) Insert a new line above the current line and enter insert mode.
insert down key	(default is control-d) Insert a new line below the current line and enter insert mode.
delete character key	(default is del) Delete the character to the left of the cursor.
delete line key	(default is control-z) Delete the line on which the cursor rests.
insert key	(default is control-n) Enter insert mode.
command key	(default is escape) Enter command mode.
edit key	(default is control-e) Enter edit mode.
undo key	(default is control-x) Undo any editing done since the cursor last came to the current line.
split key	(default is control-s) Split the current line into two lines.
join key	(default is control-p) Append the current line to the line above it. Then delete the lower line.

Edit Mode

The following are the edit mode commands:

<space>	Move the cursor right one character.
b (beginning)	Move the cursor to the beginning of the current line.
c (command)	Enter command mode.

d (scroll down)	Scroll the cursor down rapidly. Hit any key to stop scrolling.
e (end)	Move the cursor to the end of the line.
g <line #> (go to)	Move the cursor to the start of the indicated line.
i (insert)	Enter insert mode.
k <char>	(kill up to <char>) Delete from the cursor up to, but not including, <char>. Delete to the end of the line if <char> does not appear to the right of the cursor. Do not delete anything if <char> is a special character.
s <char>	(search for <char>) Move cursor to the next occurrence of <char> to the right of the cursor. Move cursor to the end of the current line if <char> does not appear to the right of the cursor.
u (scroll up)	Scroll the cursor up rapidly. Hit any key to stop.
x <char>	(exchange one character) If <char> is not a special character then <char> replaces the character under the cursor.
anything else	(ignored) If <char> is neither a special character nor an edit-mode command it is completely ignored.

Insert Mode

Use insert mode to enter multiple lines of text into the buffer. All characters that are not special characters are simply inserted into the buffer.

Command Mode

Use command mode to load or save files or to do things that might cause drastic changes to the edit buffer. Here is a list of the command mode commands and what they do:

append <filename>	Append the file <filename> to the main buffer at the current cursor position.

change <line range>	Change the first instance of <search mask> on each line in the line range to <change mask>. Question marks match any character in <search mask>. Question marks in <change mask> match the character that the corresponding question mark matched in <search mask>. A leading up arrow (^) anchors the search mask to the start of the line.
clear	Erase the entire buffer.
delete <line range>	Delete all lines with numbers in <line range>.
dos	Return to the operating system (exit from the editor).
find	Search for the next occurrence of <search mask>. Enter edit mode if <search mask> is found. Otherwise, stay in command mode. The '?' and '^' characters are treated just as in the change command.
g <n>	Enter edit mode and set the cursor on line <n>. If you do not type <n>, the current line is used for <n>.
list <line range>	List all lines with numbers in <line range> on the list device (printer).
load <filename>	Erase the buffer, then load it with the file named by <filename>. <filename> becomes the current file name, which is used by the save and resave commands.
name <filename>	Make <filename> the current file name for use by the save and resave commands.
resave	Save the buffer in the file named in the load or name commands. The file must already exist.
save	Save the buffer in the file named in the load or name commands. The file must *not* already exist.
search <line range>	Print all lines on the display that contain an instance of <search mask>. The '?' and '^'

characters are treated just as in the change command.

tabs <number>   Cause tabs to be printed as <number> blanks on the screen and on the list device.

Presented below is a summary of the commands used in the various modes of the ed2 editor of this chapter.

SPECIAL CHARACTER COMMANDS

Special Character	Function
up key	Move cursor up one row and enter edit mode.
down key	Move cursor down one row and enter edit mode.
* left key	Move cursor left one character.
right key	Move cursor right one character.
insert up key	Insert line above current line and enter edit mode.
insert down key	Insert line below current line and enter edit mode.
* delete char key	Delete character to left of cursor.
* delete line key	Delete the current line.
* undo key	Undo all changes to the current line.
* insert key	Enter insert mode.
* edit key	Enter edit mode.
command key	Enter command mode.
split key	Split the current line into two lines.
join key	Combine two lines into one line.

Note: All the special characters are valid in edit mode and insert mode. A few special characters are also operable in the insert mode and these are noted above with an asterisk, "*".

EDIT MODE COMMANDS

Command	Mnemonic	Function
space	(over)	Move cursor right one character.
b	(begin)	Move cursor to start of line.
c	(command)	Enter command mode.
d	(down)	Scroll screen down.
e	(end)	Move cursor to end of line.
g <n>	(goto)	Go to line number <n>.
i	(insert)	Enter insert mode.
k <char>	(kill)	Delete from cursor up to <character>.
s <char>	(search)	Move cursor right to <character>.
u	(up)	Scroll screen up.
x <char>	(exchange)	Replace cursor with <character>.

COMMAND MODE COMMANDS

Command	Arguments	Function
append	<filename>	Insert file into buffer at cursor.
change	<line range>	Make changes to lines in <line range>.
clear		Erase the buffer.
delete	<line range>	Delete the lines in <line range>.
dos		Exit from editor to operating system.
find		Search for pattern; enter edit mode.

g	\<n\>	Enter edit mode and goto line \<n\>.
list	\<line range\>	Print lines in \<line range\> on line printer.
load	\<filename\>	Replace buffer with file.
name	\<filename\>	Set name of current file.
resave		Save buffer to an existing file.
save		Save buffer to a new file.
search	\<line range\>	Print all lines that match a pattern.
tabs	\<n\>	Set tab stops at every \<n\> columns.

6

Text Editing II:
Installation, Configuration, and Programming

<hr>

Due to the complexity of the text editing program, the material on text editing has been divided into two parts. Chapter 5 presented a general overview of editors and a user's guide to the ed2 editor. This chapter presents the actual program code and installation instructions for the editor.

Utility/Tool

ed2   Full-screen text editor

Usage

ed2   ed2 invokes the ed2 editor, clears the
           screen, and places you in the command
           mode awaiting further commands.

Function

ed2 provides a complete full-screen text editor for use by anyone with access to a C compiler. The editor is customizable to specific hardware configurations and includes notes to configure the editor for the specific terminal and screen codes used with a particular microcomputer.

IMPLEMENTATION NOTES

1. Due to the wide variety of terminal types available, ed2 uses two files, ed1.ext and ed6.ccc, to tailor the editor to your specific keyboard and video display hardware, respectively. If you are entering the editor source code directly from this chapter, you will need to modify these two files to use the appropriate values for your microcomputer equipment. The two files include comments detailing the default values for the specified codes. If you have obtained a copy of the ed2 editor from a public domain software diskette (such as the C Users Group), the program config can be used to automatically generate the files ed1.ext and ed6.ccc.

2. The powerful editor contains all necessary features for full-screen editing. The users guide and command summary are presented below.

3. Due to the complexity of the software presented in this chapter, a users guide to the editor is included and is presented before the implementation details.

POSSIBLE PROBLEM AREAS

1. The major limitation of this editor is the requirement that the entire text file be present in memory during operation. A vastly improved version of the ed2 editor called RED overcomes this limitation. It has vastly improved capabilities in addition to this virtual file operation. RED is available directly from Ed Ream (see Appendix B); a description is given in the July and August 1983 issues of *Dr. Dobb's Journal*.

2. The editor presented in this chapter is designed for operation under CP/M, version 2 or later. The source code available from the public domain diskettes includes material in the module ed8.bds for operation under earlier versions of CP/M (specifically version 1.4).

ed2 Notes

The initial ed2 editor was written by Edward K. Ream in small-C and appeared in the January 1982 issue of *Dr. Dobb's Journal* ("A Portable Screen-Oriented Editor," pp. 18–61). Errata to this article appeared in a letter to the editor in the May, 1982, issue (pp. 4–7). Finally, Alan Howard has written a lengthy article detailing enhancements to the ed2 editor and conversion to Software Toolwork's C/80 syntax as well as customization for the Heath/Zenith series of microcomputers Alan Howard, "Enhancing the C Screen Editor," *Dr. Dobb's Journal*, (May, 1983, pp. 38–63).

This editor is in the public domain, and diskettes containing the complete source code are available from the following sources:

C Users Group	Small-C and BDS C versions (numerous disk formats available)
Algorithmic Technology	Enhanced Howard C/80 version (numerous disk formats available)
Ed Ream	8-in. CP/M small-C or BDS C only

Finally, as mentioned, a vastly improved version of ed2 called RED has been written by Ed Ream and is presented in the July and August 1983 issues of *Dr. Dobb's Journal*. RED is also available directly from Ed Ream in standard 8-in. CP/M format.

ed2 SCREEN EDITOR: CONFIGURATION AND INSTALLATION GUIDE

This section tells you how to get the screen editor up and running on your system. To do this you need the following:

1. A CP/M version 2.2 operation system that runs on an 8080, Z-80 or 8085 based computer.
2. At least 48K of central memory.
3. A video display that has a goto, x,y cursor positioning function.

To get the screen editor up and running on your system all you need to do is follow these five steps.

Step 1   Back up the diskette. Make a backup copy of your diskette. Do it now!

Step 2   Modify the files ed1.ext and ed6.ccc for your specific video and keyboard hardware. If the public domain diskettes are available, run the configuration program. Start the configuration program by typing "config" from CP/M.

The configuration program tailors the screen editor for your particular keyboard and display screen. The configuration program asks you three sets of questions. After you finish answering all the questions, it creates two files that describe your keyboard and video display. These two files are included into the screen editor during step 3.

Note that the values you enter should either be less than 32 or be equal to 127. Avoid values greater than 127 or less than 0.

After you answer all these questions, you will be asked if all the answers are correct. If you say no, then you will be asked the same questions over again.

Step 3   Next, compile the editor using the BDS C compiler. Versions 1.43 and later will work. You will need to compile ed2.bds through ed10.bds, including ed6.ccc. The submit file edcomp.sub (which is generally included on public domain software diskettes) will do it all at once.

If you get an error, you may have made a mistake when you typed in the sequences of bytes for the configuration program. Such an error will show up when the compiler is compiling the file ed6.ccc. If there is an error on file ed6.ccc you must restart the installation process at step 2.

Something is wrong with the files on your disk if you get any other error. No error you can make using the configuration program should cause an error that shows up in any file except ed6.ccc. Get a fresh copy of the disk from your backup diskette and start over again from step 2.

Step 4   Link the editor, using the BDS C clink program to create ed2.com. The file edlink.sub shows how to call the linker. You should set the linker "r" switch as follows: clink ed2 -r1000 ed3 ed4 ed5 ed6 ed7 ed8 ed9 ed10.

Step 5   You are now ready to test and use the editor. Invoke the editor by typing "ed2" from CP/M. It should clear the screen, draw the prompt line at the top of the screen, and tell you what version you are using.

If that doesn't happen, you probably modified the files ed1.ext and ed6.ccc incorrectly. The most likely problem area is the goto x,y cursor function. Remember, when you specify the goto xy function : x means the COLUMN number, y means the ROW number. Make sure you have specified the row and column numbers in the order your terminal expects. Take a deep breath and repeat steps 2 through 6.

If the screen looks reasonable, try out all the commands from the users guide. Be sure to check whether the hardware screen scrolling is working properly.

Note that the program cannot handle keyboard keys that produce more than one character. If you want to use such keys, you will have to modify the file ed2.bds. Then, of course, you will have to recompile and link the new editor. I recommend that you get the editor working before you attempt to modify it.

NOVICE'S GUIDE TO COMPILING AND LINKING

1. Copy the editor source files and the submit files to an empty disk (PIP A:=B:ED*.* will do it). Add a copy of the standard BDS C header file BDSCIO.H, the compiler (CC?.COM), linker (CLINK.COM), runtime package (C.CCC), library (DEFF?.CRL) and finally SUBMIT.COM.

2. Boot the system with this disk in drive A and type submit edcomp.

3. Get a cup of coffee (the process will take a few minutes).

4. If all is well, type submit edlink and finish your coffee.

5. The resulting editor will be called ed2.com. Good luck!

ed2.h—Nonuser Defined Globals

```
/* ed2: Screen editor: nonuser defined globals */
/* Module name: ed2.h */
/* Define global constants. */
/* Define constants describing a text line. */
#define MAXLEN      133     /* max chars per line */
#define MAXLEN1     134     /* MAXLEN + 1 */
/* Define operating system constants. */
#define SYSFNMAX    15      /* CP/M file name length + 1 */
/* Define misc. constants */
#define EOS         0       /* Code sometimes assumes \0 */
#define ERR         -1      /* must be same as ERROR. */
#define YES         1       /* must be nonzero */
#define NO          0
#define CR          13      /* carriage return */
#define LF          10      /* line feed */
#define TAB         9       /* tab character */
#define HUGE        32000   /* practical infinity */
```

ed1.ccc—Special Key Definitions

```
/* ed2: Screen editor: special key definitions */
/* This file was created by the configuration program. */
/* Module name: ed1.ccc */
/* Define which keys are used for special edit functions. */
#define UP1          10      /* line feed */
#define DOWN1        13      /* carriage return */
#define UP2          21      /* control u */
#define DOWN2         4      /* control d */
#define LEFT1         8      /* backspace */
#define RIGHT1       18      /* control r */
#define INS1         14      /* control n */
#define EDIT1         5      /* control e */
#define ESC1         27      /* escape (esc) */
#define DEL1        127      /* delete (del) */
#define ZAP1         26      /* control z */
#define ABT1         24      /* control x */
#define SPLT1        19      /* control s */
#define JOIN1        16      /* control p */
/* Define length and width of screen and printer. */
#define SCRNW        64      /* screen width (columns) */
#define SCRNW1       63      /*screen width - 1 */
#define SCRNL        16      /* screen length (rows) */
#define SCRNL1       15      /* screen length - 1 */
#define SCRNL2       14      /* screen length - 2 */
#define LISTW        80      /* printer width (columns) */
```

edext.cc—External Definitions

```
/* Screen editor: external definitions */
/* Module name: edext.cc */
/* Define statics for the command module—ed3.bds. */
```

```
char filename[SYSFNMAX];          /* file name for (re)save */
/* Define statics for the window module—ed4.bds. */
char editbuf[MAXLEN];             /* the edit buffer */
int editp;                        /* cursor: buffer index */
int editpmax;                     /* length of buffer */
int edcflag;                      /* buffer change flag */
/* define statics for the format module—ed5.bds */
int fmttab;                       /* max length of tab character */
int fmtdev;                       /* device—YES/NO = LIST/CONSOLE */
int fmtwidth;                     /* device width. LISTW/SCRNW1 */
/* fmtcol[i] is the first column at which buf[i] is printed. */
/* fmtsub() and fmtlen() assume fmtcol[] is valid on entry. */
int fmtcol[MAXLEN1];
/* define statics for the terminal module—ed6.ccc. */
int outx, outy;                   /* coordinates of the cursor */
/* define statics for the prompt line module—ed7.bds. */
char pmtln[MAXLEN];        /* mode */
char pmtfn[SYSFNMAX];      /* file name */
/* define statics for the operating system module—ed8.bds. */
/* constants defined in bdscio.h— */
/*      #define NSECTS 8 */
/*      #define SECSIZ 128 */
/*      #define BUFSIZ(NSECTS * SECSIZ + 6) */
int iormode;                      /* YES if file is read mode */
char iobufl[BUFSIZ];              /* file buffer */
/* Define statics for the buffer module—ed10.bds. */
/* Buffer [] must be the last external variable and it */
/* must have a nonzero dimension. */
int bufcflag;                     /* main buffer changed flag */
char *bufp;                       /* start of current line */
char *bufpmax;                    /* end of last line */
char *bufend;                     /* last byte of buffer */
int bufline;                      /* current line number */
int bufmaxln;                     /* number of lines in buffer */
char buffer[1];                   /* start of buffer */
```

MODULE NAME: ed2.bds

Function: Main Command Program

C Function	Purpose/Function
edit ()	Edit mode. Handle edit mode. Execute proper routine based upon one-character commands.
insert ()	Insert mode.
control(c)	Check for control character. Return YES if character is a control character.
special(c)	Handle the default action for all special keys. Return YES if a special key.
command()	Command mode. Execute command routines while in command mode.
lookup(line,command)	Check for command. Return YES if line starts with a command.
getcmnd(args,offset)	Get command into argument buffer.

ed2.bds—Main Program

```
/* Screen editor: main program—BDS C version */
/* Module name: ed2.bds */
/* Transliteration of small-C version of September 5, 1981. */
/* Define globals. */
#include   ed2.h
#include   bdscio.h
#include   ed1.ccc
#include   edext.cc
/* Define signon message. */
#define   SIGNON   "BDS C editor, version 2: December 20, 1981."
/* The main program dispatches the routines that */
/* handle the various modes. */
#define CMNDMODE 1        /* Enter command mode flag. */
```

```
#define INSMODE   2    /* Enter insert mode flag. */
#define EDITMODE  3    /* Enter edit mode flag. */
#define EXITMODE  4    /* Exit editor flag. */
main()
{
int mode;
  /* Fmt output by default goes to screen. */
  fmtassn(NO);
  /* Set tabs, clear the screen, and sign on. */
  fmtset(8);
  outclr();
  outxy(0,SCRNL1);
  message(SIGNON);
  outxy(0,1);
/* Clear filename [] for save (), resave (). */
name ("");
/* Clear the main buffer. */
bufnew();
/* Start off in command mode. */
mode=CMNDMODE;
/* Get null line 1 for edit(). */
edgetln();
while(1){
  if (mode == EXITMODE) {
    break;
  }
  else if (mode == CMNDMODE) {
    mode=command();
  }
  else if (mode == EDITMODE) {
    mode=edit();
  }
  else if (mode == INSMODE) {
    mode=insert();
  }
  else {
    syserr("main: no mode");
```

```
        mode=EDITMODE;
    }
  }
}
/* Handle edit mode. */
/* Dispatch the proper routine based on one-character commands. */
edit()
{
char buffer [SCRNW1];
int v;
int x,y;
char c;
/* We can't do edgetln() or edgo() here because */
/* those calls reset the cursor. */
  pmtedit();
  while(1){
    /* Get command. */
    c=tolower(syscin());
    if (c == ESC1 || c=='c') {
      /* Enter command mode. */
      return(CMNDMODE);
    }
    else if (c == INS1 || c=='i') {
      /* Enter insert mode. */
      return(INSMODE);
    }
    else if (special(c) == YES) {
      if (c == UP1 || c == DOWN1) {
        return(INSMODE);
      }
      else {
        continue;
      }
    }
    else if (control(c) == YES) {
      continue;
    }
    else if (c == ' ') {
```

```
        edright();
        pmtcol();
      }
    else if (c == 'b') {
        edbegin();
        pmtcol();
      }
    else if (c == 'd') {
        /* Scroll down. */
        pmtmode("edit: scroll");
        while (bufnrbot() == NO) {
          if (chkkey() == YES) {
            break;
          }
          if (eddn() == ERR) {
            break;
          }
        }
        pmtedit();
}
      else if (c == 'e') {
        edend();
        pmtcol();
      }
      else if (c == 'g') {
        /* Save x,y in case don't get number. */
        x=outgetx();
        y=outgety();
        pmtcmnd("edit: goto: ",buffer);
        if(number(buffer,&v)) {
          edgo(v,0);
        }
        else {
          outxy(x,y);
        }
        pmtedit();
      }
      else if (c == 'k') {
```

```c
            pmtmode("edit: kill");
            c=syscin();
            if (special(c) == NO &&
              control (c) == NO) {
              edkill(c);
            }
            pmtedit();
        }
        else if (c == 's') {
        pmtmode("edit: search");
        c=syscin();
        if (special(c) == NO &&
          control(c) == NO) {
          edsrch(c);
        }
        pmtedit();
    }
    else if (c == 'u') {
        /* Scroll up. */
        pmtmode("edit: scroll");
        while (bufattop() == NO) {
          if (chkkey() == YES) {
            break;
          }
          if (edup() == ERR) {
            break;
          }
        }
        pmtedit();
    }
    else if (c == 'x') {
        pmtmode("edit: eXchange");
        c=syscin();
        if (special(c) == NO &&
          control(c) == NO) {
          edchng(c);
        }
```

```
      pmtedit( );
    }
    /* Do nothing if command not found. */
  }
}
/* insert mode. */
/* In this mode the UP1, UP2 keys reverse their roles, */
/* as do the DOWN1, and DOWN2 keys. */
insert( )
{
char c;
  pmtmode("insert");
  while ( 1 ) {
    /* Get command. */
    c=syscin( );
    if ( c == ESC1 ) {
      /* Enter command mode. */
      return( CMNDMODE );
    }
    else if ( c == EDIT1 ) {
      /* Enter edit mode. */
      return( EDITMODE );
    }
    else if ( c == INS1 ) {
      /* Do nothing. */
      ;
    }
    else if ( special(c) == YES ) {
      if ( c == UP2 || c == DOWN2 ) {
        return( EDITMODE );
      }
      else {
        continue;
      }
    }
    else if ( control(c) == YES ) {
      /* Ignore nonspecial control chars. */
```

```
            continue;
        }
        else {
          /* Insert one char in line. */
          edins(c);
          pmtcol();
        }
      }
}
/* Return YES if c is a control char. */
control(c) char c;
{
    if (c == TAB) {
      return(NO); /* Tab is regular. */
    }
    else if (c>=127) {
      return(YES); /* del or high bit on */
    }
    else if (c< 32) {
      return (YES); /* control char */
    }
    else {
      return(NO); /* normal */
    }
}
/* Handle the default actions of all special keys. */
/* Return YES if c is one of the keys. */
special(c) char c;
{
int k;
    if (c == JOIN1) {
      edjoin();
      pmtline();
      return(YES);
    }
    if (c == SPLT1) {
      edsplit();
      pmtline();
```

```
    return(YES);
}
if (c == ABT1) {
  edabt();
  pmtcol();
  return(YES);
}
else if (c == DEL1) {
  eddel();
  pmtcol();
  return(YES);
}
else if (c == ZAP1) {
  edzap();
  pmtline();
  return(YES);
}
else if (c == UP2) {
  /* Move up. */
  edup();
  pmtline();
  return(YES);
}
else if (c == UP1) {
  /* Insert up. */
  ednewup();
  pmtline();
  return(YES);
}
else if (c == DOWN2) {
  /* Move down. */
  eddn();
  pmtline();
  return(YES);
}
else if (c == DOWN1) {
  /* Insert down. */
  ednewdn();
```

```
        pmtline();
        return(YES);
    }
    else if (c == LEFT1) {
        edleft();
        pmtcol();
        return(YES);
    }
    else if (c == RIGHT1) {
        edright();
        pmtcol();
        return(YES);
    }
    else {
        return(NO);
    }
}
/* Command() dispatches command routines while in command mode. */
command()
{
int v;
char c;
char args [SCRNW1];
char *argp;
int topline;
int ypos;
int oldline;
int k;
/* Command mode commands may move the current line. */
/* Command mode must save the current line on entry */
/* and restore it on exit. */
    edrepl();
    /* Remember how the screen was drawn on entry? */
    oldline=bufln();
    ypos=outgety();
    topline=oldline-ypos+1;
    while(1) {
        outxy(0,SCRNL1);
```

```
fmtcrlf();
pmtmode("command:");
getcmnd(args,0);
fmtcrlf();
pmtline();
c=args [0];
if (c == EDIT1 || c==INS1) {
  /* Redraw screen. */
  if (oldline == bufln()) {
    /* Get current line. */
    edgetln();
    /* Redraw old screen. */
    bufout(topline,1,SCRNL1);
    outxy(0,ypos);
  }
  else {
    /* Update line and screen. */
    edgo(bufln(),0);
  }
  if (c == EDIT1) {
    return (EDITMODE);
  }
  else {
    return (INSMODE);
  }
}
else if (tolower(args [0]) == 'g'){
  argp=skipbl(args+1);
  if (argp [0] == EOS) {
    edgo(oldline,0);
    return(EDITMODE);
  }
  else if (number(argp,&v) == YES) {
    edgo(v,0);
    return(EDITMODE);
  }
  else {
    message("bad line number");
```

```
      }
    }
    else if (lookup(args,"append")) {
      append(args);
    }
    else if (lookup(args,"change")) {
      change(args);
    }
    else if (lookup(args,"clear")) {
      clear();
    }
    else if (lookup(args,"delete")) {
      delete(args);
    }
    else if (lookup(args,"dos")) {
      if (chkbuf() == YES) {
        return (EXITMODE);
      }
    }
    else if (lookup(args,"find")) {
      if ((k = find()) >= 0) {
        edgo(bufln(),k);
        return(EDITMODE);
      }
      else {
        /* Get current line. */
        bufgo(oldline);
        edgetln();
        /* Stay in command mode. */
        message("pattern not found");
      }
    }
    else if (lookup(args,"list")) {
      list(args);
    }
    else if (lookup(args,"load")) {
      load(args);
    }
```

```
    else if (lookup(args,"name")) {
      name(args);
    }
    else if (lookup(args,"resave")) {
      resave();
    }
    else if (lookup(args,"save")) {
      save();
    }
    else if (lookup(args,"search")) {
      search(args);
    }
    else if (lookup(args,"tabs")) {
      tabs(args);
    }
    else {
      message("command not found");
    }
  }
}
/* Return YES if line starts with command. */
lookup(line,command) char *line, *command;
{
  while(*command) {
    if (tolower(*line++) != *command++) {
      return(NO);
    }
  }
  if(*line == EOS || *line == ' ' || *line == TAB) {
    return(YES);
  }
  else {
    return(NO);
  }
}
/* Get next command into argument buffer. */
getcmnd(args,offset) char *args; int offset;
{
int j,k;
char c;
```

```
    outxy(offset,outgety());
    outdeol();
    k=0;
    while ((c=syscin()) != CR) {
      if (c == EDIT1 || c == INS1) {
        args [0]=c;
        return;
      }
      if (c == DEL1 || c == LEFT1) {
        if (k>0) {
          outxy(offset,outgety());
          outdeol();
          k--;
          j=0;
          while (j < k) {
            outchar(args [j++]);
          }
        }
      }
      else if (c == ABT1) {
        outxy(offset,outgety());
        outdeol();
        k=0;
      }
      else if (c != TAB && (c < 32 || c == 127)) {
        /* Do nothing. */
        continue;
      }
      else {
        if (k+offset < SCRNW1) {
          args [k++]=c;
          outchar(c);
        }
      }
    }
  args [k]=EOS;
}
```

MODULE NAME: ed3.bds

Function: Command Mode Commands Module

C Function	Purpose/Function
append (args)	Load file into main buffer at current location. The current file name is NOT changed.
change (args)	Global change command.
clear()	Clear main buffer and file name.
delete(args)	Multiple line delete command.
find()	Find. Search all lines below the current line for a given pattern. Return −1 if not found, otherwise return column number of pattern.
list (args)	List lines to output device.
load (args)	Load file into buffer.
name (args)	Change current file name (uses function name1).
name1(args, filename)	Check command syntax, copy to filename, return OK if name is valid.
resave()	Save the buffer in an already existing file.
save()	Save the buffer in a new file.
search (args)	Global search command (uses function search1).
search1(from,to,flag)	Search lines in given range for a pattern. If flag == YES; stop at the first match. Return −1 if no match found. Otherwise return column number of pattern match.
tabs(args)	Set tab stops for fmt (formatting) functions.
chkbuf()	Function to check if buffer has changed. Returns YES if buffer has been changed. This function is used to prevent accidental exit from the editor without saving the work done.
message(s)	Generalized message function to print a message from a command.
get2args(args, val1,val2)	Get two arguments. No arguments implies HUGE. One argument implies both arguments the same.

skiparg (args)	Skip over all except EOS and blanks.
skipbl (args)	Skip over all blanks.
chkkey ()	Check if user has pressed any key. Return YES if key pressed.
amatch(lin, pat, col)	Anchored search for text pattern (pat) in text line (lin) at column (col). Returns YES if pattern starts at column col.
replace(oldline,newline,oldpat,newpat,col)	Replace old text pattern (oldpat) in old line (oldline) by new pattern (newpat) starting at column number col. Result is placed in newline. Returns number of characters in newline.

ed3.bds—Command Mode Commands

```
/* Screen editor: command mode commands—enhanced */
/* Module name: ed3.bds */
/* Transliteration of small-C version of September 5, 1981. */
/* Define globals. */
#include ed2.h
#include bdscio.h
#include ed1.ccc
#include edext.cc
/* data global to these routines */
/* comment out ----- */
/* char filename [SYSFNMAX]; */
/* ----- end comment out */
/* Append command. */
/* Load a file into main buffer at current location. */
/* This command does NOT change the current file name. */
append(args) char *args;
{
char buffer [MAXLEN]; /* disk line buffer */
int file;
int n;
```

```
int topline;
char locfn [SYSFNMAX]; /* local file name */
  /* Get file name that follows command. */
  if (namel(args,locfn) == ERR) {
    return;
  }
  if (locfn [0] == EOS) {
    message("no file argument");
    return;
  }
  /* Open the new file. */
  if ((file=sysopen(locfn,"r")) == ERR) {
    message("file not found");
    return;
  }
  /* Read the file into the buffer. */
  while ((n=readline(file,buffer,MAXLEN)) >= 0) {
    if (n > MAXLEN) {
      message("line truncated");
      n=MAXLEN;
    }
    if (bufins(buffer,n) == ERR) {
      break;
    }
    if (bufdn() == ERR) {
      break;
    }
  }
  /* Close the file. */
  sysclose(file);
  /* Redraw the screen so topline will be at top */
  /* of the screen after command() does a CR/LF. */
  topline=max(1,bufln()-SCRNL2);
  bufout(topline,2,SCRNL2);
  bufgo(topline);
}
/* global change command */
change (args) char *args;
```

```c
{
char oldline [MAXLEN1]; /* Reserve space for EOS. */
char newline [MAXLEN1];
char oldpat [MAXLEN1];
char newpat [MAXLEN1];
int from, to, col, n, k;
  if (get 2args(args,&from,&to) == ERR) {
    return;
  }
  /* Get search and change masks into oldpat, newpat. */
  fmtsout("search mask ? ",0);
  getcmnd(oldpat,15);
  fmtcrlf();
  if (oldpat [0] == EOS) {
    return;
  }
  pmtline();
  fmtsout("change mask ? ",0);
  getcmnd(newpat,15);
  fmtcrlf();
  /* Make substitution for lines between from, to. */
  while (from <= to) {
    if (chkkey() == YES) {
    break;
  }
  if (bufgo(from++) == ERR) {
    break;
  }
  if (bufatbot() == YES) {
    break;
  }
  n=bufgetln(oldline,MAXLEN);
  n=min(n,MAXLEN);
  oldline [n]=EOS;
  /* '^' anchors search */
  if (oldpat [0] == '^') {
    if (amatch(oldline,oldpat+1,0) == YES) {
      k=replace(oldline,newline,
```

```
            oldpat+1,newpat,0);
        if (k == ERR) {
          return;
        }
        fmtcrlf();
        putdec(bufln(),5);
        fmtsout(newline,5);
        outdeol();
        bufrepl(newline,k);
      }
      continue;
    }
    /* Search oldline for oldpat. */
    col=0;
    while (col < n) {
      if (amatch(oldline,oldpat,col++) == YES){
        k=replace(oldline,newline,
          oldpat,newpat,col-1);
        if (k == ERR) {
          return;
        }
        fmtcrlf();
        putdec(bufln(),5);
        fmtsout(newline,5);
        outdeol();
        bufrepl(newline,k);
        break;
      }
    }
  }
  fmtcrlf();
}
/* Clear main buffer and file name. */
clear()
{
  /* Make sure it is ok to clear buffer. */
  if (chkbuf() == YES) {
    filename [0]=0;
```

```c
        pmtfile("");
        outclr();
        outxy(O,SCRNL1);
        bufnew();
        message("buffer cleared");
    }
}
/* multiple line delete command */
delete(args) char *args;
{
int from, to;
    if(get2args(args,&from,&to) == ERR) {
        return;
    }
    if (from > to) {
        return;
    }
    /* Go to first line to be deleted. */
    if (bufgo(from) == ERR) {
        return;
    }
    /* Delete all line between from and to. */
    if (bufdeln(to-from+1) == ERR) {
        return;
    }
    /* Redraw the screen. */
    bufout(bufln(),1,SCRNL1);
}
/* Search all lines below the current line for a pattern. */
/* Return -1 if pattern not found. */
/* Otherwise, return column number of start of pattern. */
find()
{
    return(search1(bufln()+1,HUGE,YES));
}
/* List lines to list device. */
list(args) char *args;
{
```

```c
char linebuf [MAXLEN1];
int n;
int from, to, line, oldline;
    /* Save the buffer's current line. */
    oldline=bufln();
    /* Get starting, ending lines to print. */
    if (get2args(args,&from,&to) == ERR) {
        return;
    }
    /* Print lines one at a time to list device. */
    line=from;
    while (line <= to) {
        /* Make sure prompt goes to console. */
    fmtassn(NO);
    /* Check for interrupt. */
    if (chkkey() == YES) {
        break;
        }
        /* Print line to list device. */
        fmtassn(YES);
        if (bufgo(line++) != OK) {
            break;
        }
        if (bufatbot()) {
            break;
        }
        n=bufgetln(linebuf,MAXLEN1);
        n=min(n,MAXLEN);
        linebuf [n]=CR;
        fmtsout(linebuf,0);
        fmtcrlf();
    }
    /* Redirect output to console. */
    fmtassn(NO);
    /* Restore cursor. */
    bufgo(oldline);
}
/* Load file into buffer. */
```

```
load (args) char *args;
{
char buffer [MAXLEN]; /* Disk line buffer. */
char locfn [SYSFNMAX]; /* File name until we check it. */
int n;
int file;
int topline;
   /* Get filename following command. */
   if (name1(args,locfn) == ERR) {
      return;
   }
   if (locfn [0] == EOS) {
      message("no file argument");
      return;
   }
   /* Give user a chance to save the buffer. */
   if (chkbuf( ) == NO) {
      return;
   }
   /* Open the new file. */
   if ((file=sysopen(locfn,"r")) == ERR) {
      message("file not found");
      return;
   }
   /* Update file name. */
   syscopfn(locfn, filename);
   pmtfile(filename);
   /* Clear the buffer. */
   bufnew();
   /* Read the file into the buffer. */
   while ((n=readline(file,buffer,MAXLEN)) >= 0) {
      if (n > MAXLEN) {
         message("line truncated");
         n=MAXLEN;
      }
      if (bufins(buffer,n) == ERR) {
         break;
      }
```

```
   if (bufdn( ) == ERR) {
      break;
   }
}
/* Close the file. */
sysclose(file);
/* Indicate that the buffer is fresh. */
bufsaved( );
/* Set current line to line 1. */
bufgo(1);
/* Redraw the screen so that topline will be */
/* on line 1 after command( ) does a CR/LF. */
topline=max(1,bufln( )-SCRNL2);
bufout(topline,2,SCRNL2);

   bufgo(topline);
}
/* Change current file name. */
name(args) char *args;
{
   name1(args,filename);
   pmtfile(filename);
}
/* Check syntax of args. */
/* Copy to filename. */
/* return OK if the name is valid */
name1(args,filename) char *args, *filename;
{
   /* Skip command. */
   args=skiparg(args);
   args=skipbl(args);
   /* Check file name syntax. */
   if (syschkfn(args) == ERR) {
      return(ERR);
   }
   /* Copy filename. */
   syscopfn(args,filename);
   return(OK);
```

```
}
/* Save the buffer in an already existing file. */
resave()
{
char linebuf [MAXLEN];
int file, n, oldline;
  /* Make sure file has a name. */
  if (filename [0] == EOS) {
    message("file not named");
    return;
  }
  /* The file must exist for resave. */
  if ((file=sysopen(filename,"r")) == ERR) {
    message("file not found");
    return;
  }
  if (sysclose(file) == ERR) {
    return;
  }
  /* Open the file for writing. */
  if ((file=sysopen(filename,"w")) ==ERR) {
    return;
  }
  /* Save the current position of file. */
  oldline=bufln();
  /* Write out the whole file. */
  if (bufgo(1) == ERR) {
    sysclose(file);
    return;
  }
  while (bufatbot() == NO) {
    n=bufgetln(linebuf,MAXLEN);
    n=min(n,MAXLEN);
    if (pushline(file,linebuf,n) == ERR) {
      break;
    }
    if (bufdn() == ERR) {
      break;
```

```
      }
   }
   /* Indicate if all buffer was saved. */
   if (bufatbot( )){
      bufsaved( );
   }
   /* Close file and restore line number. */
   sysclose(file);
   bufgo(oldline);
}
/* Save the buffer in a new file. */
save( )
{
char linebuf [MAXLEN];
int file, n, oldline;
   /* Make sure the file is named. */
   if (filename [0] == EOS) {
      message("file not named");
      return;
   }
   /* File must NOT exist for save. */
   if ((file=sysopen(filename,"r")) != ERR) {
      sysclose(file);
      message("file exists");
      return;
   }
   /* Open file for writing. */
   if ((file=sysopen(filename,"w")) == ERR) {
      return;
   }
}
/* Remember current line. */
oldline=bufln( );
/* Write entire buffer to file. */
if (bufgo(1) == ERR) {
   sysclose(file);
   return;
}
while (bufatbot( ) == NO) {
```

```
      n=bufgetln(linebuf,MAXLEN);
      n=min(n,MAXLEN);
      if (pushline(file,linebuf,n) == ERR) {
        break;
      }
      if (bufdn() == ERR) {
        break;
      }
    }
  /* Indicate buffer saved if good write. */
  if (bufatbot()) {
    bufsaved();
  }
  /* Restore line and close file. */
  bufgo(oldline);
  sysclose(file);
}
/* global search command */
search(args) char *args;
{
int from, to;
  if (get2args(args,&from,&to) == ERR) {
    return;
  }
  search1(from, to, NO);
}
/* Search lines for a pattern. */
/* If flag == YES: stop at the first match. */
/* Return -1 if no match. */
/* Otherwise return column number of match. */
/* If flag == NO: print all matches found. */
search1(from, to, flag) int from, to, flag;
{
char pat [MAXLEN1]; /* Reserve space for EOS. */
char line [MAXLEN1];
int col, n;
  /* Get search mask into pat. */
  fmtsout("search mask ? ",0);
```

```
getcmnd(pat,15);
fmtcrlf();
if (pat, [0] == EOS) {
   return (-1) /* Dr. Dobb's Jrnl bug fix May, 1982; p. 4 */;
}
/* Search all lines between from and to for pat. */
while (from <= to) {
   if (chkkey() == YES) {
      break;
   }
   if (bufgo(from++) == ERR) {
      break;
   }
   if (bufatbot() == YES) {
      break;
   }
   n=bufgetln(line,MAXLEN);
   n=min(n,MAXLEN);
   line [n]=EOS;
   /* ^ anchors search */
   if (pat [0] == '^') {
      if (amatch(line,pat+1,0) == YES) {
         if (flag == NO) {
            fmtcrlf();
            putdec(bufln(),5);
            fmtsout(line,5);
            outdeol();
         }
         else {
            return(0);
         }
      }
      continue;
   }
   /* Search whole line for match. */
   col=0;
   while (col < n) {
      if (amatch(line,pat,col++) == YES) {
```

```
        if (flag == NO) {
          fmtcrlf( );
          putdec(bufln( ),5);
          fmtsout(line,5);
          outdeol( );
          break;
        }
        else {
          return(col-1);
        }
      }
    }
  }
  /* All searching is finished. */
  if (flag == YES) {
    return(-1);
  }
  else {
    fmtcrlf( );
  }
}
/* Set tab stops for fmt routines. */
tabs(args) char *args;
{
int n, junk;
  if (get2args(args,&n,&junk) == ERR) {
    return;
  }
  fmtset(n);
}
/* Return YES if buffer may be drastically changed. */
chkbuf( )
{
  if (bufchng( ) == NO) {
    /* Buffer not changed. No problem. */
    return(YES);
  }
  fmtsout("buffer not saved. proceed ? " ,0);
```

```
    pmtline();
    if (tolower(syscout(syscin())) != 'y') {
      fmtcrlf();
      message("cancelled");
      return(NO);
    }
    else {
      fmtcrlf();
      return(YES);
    }
  }
/* Print message from a command. */
message(s) char *s;
{
    fmtsout(s,0);
    fmtcrlf();
  }
  /* Get two arguments. */
  /* No arguments implies 1 HUGE. */
  /* One argument implies both args the same. */
  get2args(args,val1,val2) char *args; int *val1, *val2;
  {
    /* Skip over the command. */
    args=skiparg(args);
    args=skipbl(args);
    if (*args == EOS) {
      *val1=1;
      *val2=HUGE;
      return(OK);
    }
    /* Check first argument. */
    if (number(args,val1) == NO) {
      message("bad argument");
      return(ERR);
    }
    /* Skip over first argument. */
    args=skiparg(args);
    args=skipbl(args);
```

```
    /* 1 arg: arg 2 is HUGE */
    if (*args == EOS) {
      *val2=HUGE;
      return(OK);
    }
    /* Check second argument. */
    if (number(args,val2) == NO) {
      message("bad argument");
      return(ERR);
    }
    else {
      return(OK);
    }
}
/* Skip over all except EOS and blanks. */
skiparg(args) char *args;
{
    while (*args != EOS && *args!=' ') {
      args++;
    }
    return(args);
}
/* Skip over all blanks. */
skipbl(args) char *args;
{
    while (*args == ' ') {
      args++;
    }
    return(args);
}
/* Return YES if the user has pressed any key. */
/* Blanks cause a transparent pause. */
chkkey()
{
int c;
    c=syscstat();
    if (c == -1) { /* Dr. Dobb's Jrnl bug fix May, 1982; p. 6 */
      /* No character at keyboard. */
```

```
      return(NO);
    }
  else if (c == ' ') {
    /* Pause. Another blank ends pause. */
    pmtline();
    if (syscin() == ' ') {
      return(NO);
    }
  }
  /* We got a nonblank character. */
  return(YES);
}
/* Anchored search for pattern in text line at column col. */
/* Return YES if the pattern starts at col. */
amatch(line,pat,col) char *line, *pat; int col;
{
int k;
  k=0;
  while (pat [k] != EOS) {
    if (pat [k] == line[col]) {
      k++;
      col++;
    }
    else if (pat [k] == '?' && line[col] != EOS) {
      /* Question mark matches any char. */
      k++;
      col++;
    }
    else {
      return(NO);
    }
  }
  /* The entire pattern matches */
  return(YES).
}
/* Replace oldpat in oldline by newpat starting at col. */
/* Put result in newline. */
/* Return number of characters in newline. */
```

```
replace(oldline,newline,oldpat,newpat,col)
char *oldline, *newline, *oldpat, *newpat; int col;
{
int k;
char *tail, *pat;
/* Copy oldline preceding col to newline. */
k=0;
while (k < col) {
   newline [k++]=*oldline++;
}
/* Remember where end of oldpat in oldline is. */
tail=oldline;
pat=oldpat;
while (*pat++ != EOS) {
   tail++;
}
/* Copy newpat to newline. */
/* Use oldline and oldpat to resolve question marks */
/* in newpat. */
while (*newpat != EOS) {
  if (k > MAXLEN-1) {
     message("new line too long");
     return(ERR);
  }
  if (*newpat != '?') {
     /* Copy newpat to newline. */
     newline [k++]=*newpat++;
     continue;
  }
  /* Scan for '?' in oldpat. */
  while (*oldpat != '?') {
     if (*oldpat == EOS) {
     message(
     "too many ?'s in change mask"
     );
     return(ERR);
  }
  oldpat++;
```

```
      oldline++;
    }
    /* Copy char from oldline to newline. */
    newline [k++]=*oldline++;
    oldpat++;
    newpat++;
  }
  /* Copy oldline after oldpat to newline. */
  while (*tail != EOS) {
    if (k >= MAXLEN-1) {
      message("new line too long");
      return(ERR);
    }
    newline [k++]=*tail++;
  }
  newline [k]=EOS;
  return(k);
}
```

MODULE NAME: ed4.bds

Function: Window Module

C Function	Purpose/Function
edabt()	Abort any changes made to the current line.
edbegin()	Put cursor at beginning (left margin) of current line.
edchng(c)	Change the edit buffer editbuf[editp] to c, check for line length problems. If line becomes too long, ignore change request.
eddel()	Delete the character to the left of the cursor if it exists.
eddn()	Edit the next line; do not go beyond the end of the buffer.

edend( )	Put cursor at end of the current line.
edgo(n, p)	Start editing line number n with the cursor at column position p.
edins(c)	Insert character c into buffer (if possible without overflow).
edjoin( )	Join (concatenate) the current line with the line above it.
edkill(c)	Delete characters until the end of line is reached or until character c is found.
edleft( )	Move cursor left one column. Never move the cursor off the current line.
ednewdn( )	Insert a new blank line below the current line.
ednewup( )	Insert a new blank line above the current line.
edright( )	Move the cursor right one character. Do not move the cursor off the current line.
edsplit( )	Split the current line into two parts. Scroll the first half of the line up.
edsrch(c)	Move cursor right until the end of line or until character c is found.
edup( )	Move cursor up one line (if possible).
edzap( )	Delete (in programmer's parlance, "zap") the current line.
edatbot( )	Check for line at the bottom of the screen. Return TRUE if the current edit line is being displayed on the bottom line of the screen.
edattop( )	Check for line at the bottom of the screen. Return TRUE if the current edit line is being displayed on the top line of the screen.
edredraw( )	Redraw the edit line from index to the end of line. Reposition the cursor.
edxpos( )	Return the x position of the cursor on the screen.
edgetln( )	Fill the edit buffer from the current main buffer line. Before calling this function, the caller must check to make sure that the main buffer is available.

edrepl	Replace the current main buffer line by edit buffer. The edit buffer is not changed or cleared. Returns ERR if something goes wrong.
edscan(xpos)	Set editp (the edit pointer) to the largest index such that buf[editp] will be printed <= xpos.
edsup(topline)	Scroll the screen up. The new top line will be topline.
edsdn(topline)	Scroll the screen down. The new top line will be topline.

ed4.bds—Window Module

```
/* Screen editor: window module */
/* Module name: ed4.bds */
/* Define global constants, variables. */
#include ed2.h
#include bdscio.h
#include ed1.ccc
#include edext.cc
/* data global to this module ----- */
/* char editbuf[MAXLEN];    the edit buffer */
/* int editp;               cursor: buffer index */
/* int editpmax;            length of buffer */
/* int edcflag;             buffer change flag */
/* ----- */
/* Abort any changes made to current line. */
edabt()
{
    /* Get unchanged line and reset cursor. */
    edgetln();
    edredraw();
    edbegin();
    edcflag = NO;
```

```
}
/* Put cursor at beginning of current line. */
edbegin()
{
   editp = 0;
   outxy(0,outgety());
}
/* Change editbuf[editp] to c. */
/* Don't make change if line would become too long. */
edchng(c) char c;
{
char oldc;
int k;
   /* If at right margin then insert char. */
   if (editp >= editpmax) {
      edins(c);
      return;
   }
/* Change char and print length of line. */
oldc = editbuf[editp];
   editbuf[editp] = c;
   fmtadj(editbuf,editp,editpmax);
   k = fmtlen(editbuf,editpmax);
   if (k > SCRNW1) {
      /* Line would become too long. */
      /* Undo the change. */
      editbuf[editp] = oldc;
      fmtadj(editbuf,editp,editpmax);
   }
   else {
      /* Set change flag, redraw line. */
      edcflag = YES;
      editp++;
      edredraw();
   }
}
/* Delete the char to left of cursor if it exists. */
```

```
eddel()
{
int k;
  /* Just move left one column if past end of line. */
  if (edxpos() < outgetx()) {
    outxy(outgetx()-1, outgety());
    return;
  }
  /* Do nothing if cursor is at left margin. */
  if (editp == 0) {
    return;
  }
  edcflag = YES;
  /* Compress buffer (delete char). */
  k = editp;
  while (k < editpmax) {
    editbuf[k-1] = editbuf[k];
    k++;
  }
  /* Update pointers, redraw line. */
  editp--;
  editpmax--;
  edredraw();
}
/* Edit the next line. Do not go to end of buffer. */
eddn()
{
int oldx;
  /* Save visual position of cursor. */
  oldx = outgetx();
  /* Replace current edit line. */
  if (edrepl() != OK) {
    return(ERR);
  }
  /* Do not go past last nonnull line. */
  if (bufnrbot()) {
    return(OK);
```

```c
    }
    /* Move down one line in buffer. */
    if (bufdn() != OK) {
        return(ERR);
    }
    edgetln();
    /* Put cursor as close as possible on this */
    /* new line to where it was on the old line. */
    editp = edscan(oldx);
    /* Update screen. */
    if (edatbot()) {
        edsup(bufln()-SCRNL2);
        outxy(oldx, SCRNL1);
    }
    else {
        outxy(oldx, outgety()+1);
    }
    return(OK);
}
/* Put cursor at the end of current line. */
edend()
{
    editp = editpmax;
    outxy(edxpos(),outgety());
    /* Comment out ----- put cursor at end of screen. */
    /* outxy(SCRNW1, outgety()); */
    /* ----- end comment out */
}
/* Start editing line n. */
/* Redraw the screen with cursor at position p. */
edgo(n, p) int n, p;
{
    /* Replace current line. */
    if (edrepl() == ERR) {
        return(ERR);
    }
    /* Go to new line. */
    if (bufgo(n) == ERR) {
```

```
      return(ERR);
   }
   /* Prevent going past end of buffer. */
   if (bufatbot()) {
      if (bufup() == ERR) {
         return(ERR);
      }
   }
   /* Redraw the screen. */
   bufout(bufln(),1,SCRNL1);
   edgetln();
   editp = min(p, editpmax);
   outxy(edxpos(), 1);
   return(OK);
}
/* Insert c into the buffer if possible. */
edins(c) char c;
{
int k;
   /* Do nothing if edit buffer is full. */
   if (editpmax >= MAXLEN) {
      return;
   }
   /* Fill out line if we are past its end. */
   if (editp == editpmax && edxpos() < outgetx()) {
      k = outgetx() - edxpos();
      editpmax = editpmax + k;
      while (k-- > 0) {
         editbuf [editp++] = ' ';
      }
      editp = editpmax;
   }
   /* Make room for inserted character. */
   k = editpmax;
   while (k > editp) {
      editbuf[k] = editbuf[k-1];
      k--;
   }
```

```
    /* Insert character. Update pointers. */
    editbuf[editp] = c;
    editp++;
    editpmax++;
    /* Recalculate print length of line. */
    fmtadj(editbuf,editp-1,editpmax);
    k = fmtlen(editbuf,editpmax);
    if (k > SCRNW1) {
        /* Line would become too long. */
        /* Delete what we just inserted. */
        eddel( );
    }
    else {
        /* Set change flag, redraw line. */
        edcflag = YES;
        edredraw( );
    }
}
/* Join (concatenate) the current line with the one above it. */
edjoin( )
{
int k;
    /* Do nothing if at top of file. */
    if (bufattop( )) {
        return;
    }
    /* Replace lower line temporarily. */
    if (edrepl( ) != OK) {
        return;
    }
    /* Get upper line into buffer. */
    if (bufup( ) != OK) {
        return;
    }
    k = bufgetln(editbuf, MAXLEN);
    /* Append lower line to buffer. */
    if (bufdn( ) != OK) {
        return;
```

```
  }
  k = k + bufgetln(editbuf+k, MAXLEN-k);
  /* Abort if the screen isn't wide enough. */
  if (k > SCRNW1) {
    /* bug fix */
    bufgetln(editbuf,MAXLEN);
    return;
  }
  /* Replace upper line. */
  if (bufup() != OK) {
    return;
  }
  editpmax = k;
  edcflag = YES;
  if (edrepl() != OK) {
    return;
  }
  /* Delete lower line. */
  if (bufdn() != OK) {
    return;
  }
  if (bufdel() != OK) {
    return;
  }
  if (bufup() != OK) {
    return;
  }
  /* Update screen. */
  if (edattop()) {
    edredraw();
  }
  else {
    k = outgety() - 1;
    bufout(bufln(),k,SCRNL-k);
    outxy(0,k);
    edredraw();
  }
}
```

```
/* Delete chars until end of line or c found. */
edkill(c) char c;
{
int k,p;
    /* Do nothing if at right margin. */
    if (editp == editpmax) {
        return;
    }
    edcflag = YES;
    /* Count number of deleted chars. */
    k = 1;
    while ((editp+k) < editpmax) {
        if (editbuf[editp+k] == c) {
            break;
        }
        else {
            k++;
        }
    }
    /* Compress buffer (delete chars). */
    p = editp+k;
    while (p < editpmax) {
        editbuf[p-k] = editbuf[p];
        p++;
    }
    /* Update buffer size, redraw line. */
    editpmax = editpmax-k;
    edredraw();
}
/* Move cursor left one column. */
/* Never move cursor off the current line. */
edleft()
{
int k;
    /* If past right margin, move left one column. */
    if (edxpos() < outgetx()) {
        outxy(max(0, outgetx()-1), outgety());
    }
```

```
    /* Inside the line. Move left one character. */
    else if (editp != 0) {


        editp--;
        outxy(edxpos(),outgety());
    }
}
/* Insert a new blank line below the current line. */
ednewdn()
{
int k;
    /* Make sure there is a current line and */
    /* put the current line back into the buffer. */
    if (bufatbot()) {
        if (bufins(editbuf,editpmax) != OK) {
            return;
        }
    }
    else if (edrepl() != OK) {
        return;
    }
    /* Move past current line */
    if (bufdn() != OK) {
        return;
    }
    /* Insert place holder: zero length line. */
    if (bufins(editbuf,0) != OK) {
        return;
    }
    /* Start editing zero length line. */
    edgetln();
    /* Update the screen. */
    if (edatbot()) {
        /* note: bufln() >= SCRNL */
        edsup(bufln()-SCRNL2);
        outxy(edxpos(),SCRNL1);
    }
```

```
    else {
      k = outgety();
      bufout(bufln(),k+1,SCRNL1-k);
      outxy(edxpos(),k+1);
    }
}
/* Insert a new blank line above the current line. */
ednewup()
{
int k;
  /* Put current line back in buffer. */
  if (edrepl() != OK) {
    return;
  }
  /* Insert zero length line at current line. */
  if (bufins(editbuf,0) != OK) {
    return;
  }
  /* Start editing the zero length line. */
  edgetln();
  /* Update the screen. */
  if (edattop()) {
    edsdn(bufln());
    outxy(edxpos(),1);
  }
  else {
    k = outgety();
    bufout(bufln(),k,SCRNL-k);
    outxy(edxpos(),k);
  }
}
/* Move cursor right one character. */
/* Never move the cursor off the current line. */
edright()
{
    /* If outside the line move right one column. */
    if (edxpos() < outgetx()) {
      outxy (min(SCRNW1, outgetx()+1), outgety());
```

```
    }
    /* If inside a tab move to the end of it. */
    else if (edxpos( ) > outgetx( )) {
        outxy (edxpos( ), outgety( ));
    }
    /* Move right one character if inside line. */
    else if (editp < editpmax) {
        editp++;
        outxy(edxpos( ),outgety( ));
    }
    /* Else move past end of line. */
    else {
        outxy (min(SCRNW1, outgetx( )+1), outgety( ));
    }
}
/* Split the current line into two parts. */
/* Scroll the first half of the old line up. */
edsplit( )
{
int p, q;
int k;
    /* Indicate that edit buffer has been saved. */
    edcflag = NO;
    /* Replace current line by the first half of line. */
    if (bufatbot( )) {
        if (bufins(editbuf, editp) != OK) {
            return;
        }
    }
    else {
        if (bufrepl(editbuf, editp) != OK) {
            return;
        }
    }
    /* Redraw the first half of the line. */
    p = editpmax;
    q = editp;
    editpmax = editp;
```

```
      editp = 0;
      edredraw();
      /* Move the second half of the line down. */
      editp = 0;
      while (q < p) {
         editbuf[editp++] = editbuf[q++];
      }
      editpmax = editp;
      editp = 0;
      /* Insert second half of the line below the first. */
      if (bufdn() != OK) {
         return;
      }
      if (bufins(editbuf, editpmax) != OK) {
         return;
      }
      /* Scroll the screen up and draw the second half. */
      if (edatbot()) {
         edsup(bufln()-SCRNL2);
         outxy(1,SCRNL1);
         edredraw();
      }
      else {
         k = outgety();
         bufout(bufln(), k+1, SCRNL1-k);
         outxy(1, k+1);
         edredraw();
      }
   }
}
/* Move cursor right until end of line or */
/* character c found. */
edsrch(c) char c;
{
   /* Do nothing if at right margin. */
   if (editp == editpmax) {
      return;
   }
   /* Scan for search character. */
```

```
  editp++;
  while (editp < editpmax) {
    if (editbuf[editp] == c) {
      break;
    }
    else {
      editp++;
    }
  }
  /* Reset cursor. */
  outxy(edxpos(),outgety());
}
/* Move cursor up one line if possible. */
edup()
{
int oldx;
  /* Save visual position of cursor. */
  oldx = outgetx();
  /* Put current line back in buffer. */
  if (edrepl() != OK) {
    return(ERR);
  }
  /* Done if at top of buffer. */
  if (bufattop()) {
    return(OK);
  }
  /* Start editing the previous line. */
  if (bufup() != OK) {
    return(ERR);
  }
  edgetln();
  /* Put cursor on this new line as close as */
  /* possible to where it was on the old line. */
  editp = edscan(oldx);
  /* Update screen. */
  if (edattop()) {
    edsdn(bufln());
    outxy(oldx, 1);
```

```
    }
  else {
     outxy(oldx, outgety( )-1);
  }
  return(OK);
}
/* Delete the current line. */
edzap( )
{
int k;
  /* Delete the line in the buffer. */
  if (bufdel( ) != OK) {
    return;
  }
  /* Move up one line if now at bottom. */
  if (bufatbot( )) {
    if (bufup( ) != OK) {
      return;
    }
    edgetln( );
    /* Update screen. */
    if (edattop( )) {
      edredraw( );
    }
    else {
      outdelln( );
      outxy(0,outgety( )-1);
    }
    return;
  }
  /* Start editing new line. */
  edgetln( );
  /* Update screen. */
  if (edattop( )) {
    edsup(bufln( ));
    outxy(0,1);
  }
  else {
```

```
  k = outgety();
  bufout(bufln(),k,SCRNL-k);



    outxy(0,k);
  }
}
/* Return true if the current edit line is being */
/* displayed on the bottom line of the screen. */
edatbot()
{
  return(outgety() == SCRNL1);
}
/* Return true if the current edit line is being */
/* displayed on the top line of the screen. */
edattop()
{
  return(outgety() == 1);
}
/* Redraw edit line from index to end of line. */
/* Reposition cursor. */
edredraw()
{
  fmtadj(editbuf,0,editpmax);
  fmtsubs(editbuf,max(0,editp-1),editpmax);
  outxy(edxpos(),outgety());
}
/* Return the x position of the cursor on screen. */
edxpos()
{
  return(min(SCRNW1,fmtlen(editbuf,editp)));
}
/* Fill edit buffer from current main buffer line. */
/* The caller must check to make sure the main */
/* buffer is available. */
edgetln()
{
int k;
```

```
    /* Put cursor on left margin, reset flag. */
    editp = 0;
    edcflag = NO;
    /* Get edit line from main buffer. */
    k = bufgetln(editbuf,MAXLEN);
    if (k > MAXLEN) {
      error("line truncated");
      editpmax = MAXLEN;
    }
    else {
      editpmax = k;
    }
    fmtadj(editbuf,0,editpmax);
}
/* Replace current main buffer line by edit buffer. */
/* The edit buffer is NOT changed or cleared. */
/* Return ERR if something goes wrong. */
edrepl()
{
    /* do nothing if nothing has changed */
    if (edcflag == NO) {
      return(OK);
    }
    /* Make sure we don't replace the line twice. */
    edcflag = NO;
    /* Insert instead of replace if at bottom of file. */
    if (bufatbot()) {
      return(bufins(editbuf,editpmax));
    }
    else {
      return(bufrepl(editbuf,editpmax));
    }
}
/* Set editp to the largest index such that */
/* buf[editp] will be printed <= xpos. */
edscan(xpos) int xpos;
{
    editp = 0;
    while (editp < editpmax) {
```

```
      if (fmtlen(editbuf,editp) < xpos) {
        editp++;
      }
      else {
        break;
      }
    }
  return(editp);
  }
/* Scroll the screen up. Topline will be new top line. */
edsup(topline) int topline;
{
    if (outhasup() == YES) {
      /* hardware scroll */
      outsup();
      /* Redraw bottom line. */
      bufout(topline+SCRNL2,SCRNL1,1);
    }
    else {
      /* Redraw whole screen. */
      bufout(topline,1,SCRNL1);
    }
}
/* Scroll screen down. Topline will be new top line. */
edsdn(topline) int topline;
{
    if (outhasdn() == YES) {
      /* hardware scroll */
      outsdn();
      /* Redraw top line. */
      bufout(topline,1,1);
    }
    else {
      /* Redraw whole screen. */
      bufout(topline,1,SCRNL1);
      }
}
```

MODULE NAME: ed5.bds

Function: Output Format Module

C Function	Purpose/Function
fmtassn(listflag)	Assign output format to either console or list device.
fmtadj(buf,minind,maxind)	Adjust fmtcol[ ] prior to calls to fmtout( ) or fmtlen( ).
fmtlen(buf,i)	Return column at which buf[i] will be printed.
fmtsubs(buf,i,j)	Print buf[i] . . . buf[j–1] on current device. No characters will be printed in last column.
fmtsout(buf,offset)	Print string that ends with carriage return or end-of-string (EOS) to current device. Output is truncated if string is too long.
fmtlench(c,col)	Return length of char c at column col (control characters have a length of 2).
fmtoutch(c,col)	Output one character c to current device at column col. Tabs are converted to blanks.
fmtdevch(c)	Output character to current device.
fmtcrlf( )	Standardized routine to output a carriage return (CR) line-feed (LF) pair to the currently assigned device.
fmtset(n)	Set tabs at every n column.

ed5.bds—Output Format Module

```
/* Screen editor: output format module */
/* Module name: ed5.bds */
/* Define globals. */
#include ed2.h
#include bdscio.h
#include ed1.ccc
#include edext.cc
```

```
/* variables global to this module ----- */
/* int fmttab;      maximal tab length */
/* int fmtdev;      device flag -- YES/NO = LIST/CONSOLE */
/* int fmtwidth;        device width. LISTW/SCRNW1 */
/* Fmtcol[i] is the first column at which buf[i] is printed. */
/* Fmtsub() and fmtlen() assume fmtcol[] is valid on entry. */
/* int fmtcol[MAXLEN1]; */
/* ----- */
/* Direct output from this module to either the console or */
/* the list device. */
fmtassn(listflag) int listflag;
{
  if (listflag==YES) {
    fmtdev=YES;
    fmtwidth=LISTW;
  }
  else {
    fmtdev=NO;
    fmtwidth=SCRNW1;
  }
}
  /* Adjust fmtcol[] to prepare for calls on */
  /* fmtout() and fmtlen(). */
  /* NOTE: This routine is needed as an efficiency */
  /*         measure. Without fmtadj(), calls on */
  /*         fmtlen() become too slow. */
fmtadj(buf,minind,maxind) char *buf; int minind,maxind;
  {
  int k;
    /* Line always starts at left margin. */
    fmtcol[0]=0;
    /* Start scanning at minind. */
    k=minind;
    while (k<maxind) {
      if (buf[k]==CR) {
        break;
      }
```

```
      fmtcol[k+1]=fmtcol[k]+fmtlench(buf[k],fmtcol[k]);
      k++;
    }
}
/* Return column at which buf[i] will be printed. */
fmtlen(buf,i) char *buf; int i;
{
    return(fmtcol[i]);
}
/* Print buf[i] ... buf[j-1] on current device so long as */
/* characters will not be printed in last column. */
fmtsubs(buf,i,j) char *buf; int i,j;
{
int k;
    if (fmtcol[i]>=fmtwidth) {
      return;
    }
    outxy(fmtcol[i],outgety()); /* Position cursor. */
    while (i<j) {
      if (buf[i]==CR) {
        break;
      }
      if (fmtcol[i+1]>fmtwidth) {
        break;
      }
      fmtoutch(buf[i],fmtcol[i]);
      i++;
    }
    outdeol(); /* Clear rest of line. */
}
/* Print string that ends with CR or EOS to current device. */
/* Truncate the string if it is too long. */
fmtsout(buf,offset) char *buf; int offset;
{
char c;
int col,k;
    col=0;
while (c=*buf++) {
```

MODULE NAME: ed6.ccc

Function: Terminal Output Module

C Function	Purpose/Function
outgetx( )	Return current x coordinate of cursor position. 0,0 is upper left corner.
outget(y)	Return current y coordinate of cursor position. 0,0 is upper left corner.
outchar(c)	Output one printable character to the screen.
outxy(x,y)	Position cursor to position x,y on the screen. Point 0,0 is the upper left corner (home position).
outclr( )	Erase the entire screen. Specifically output the character required to do a hardware screen clear.
outdelln( )	Delete the line on which the cursor rests. Cursor remains at left margin.
outdeol( )	Delete (erase) to end of line. Last column is assumed to be blank.
outhasup( )	Return YES if terminal has hardware scroll for scroll up.
outhasdn( )	Return YES if terminal has hardware scroll for scroll down.
outsup( )	Scroll screen up. Assumes cursor is on the bottom line.
outsdn( )	Scroll screen down. Assumes cursor is on the top line.

ed6.ccc—Terminal Output Model

```
/* Screen editor: terminal output module */
/* This file will need to be modified by the user for the */
/* screen hardware available. The public domain diskettes */
/* have a program "config" that can be used to create this */
```

```
/* module automatically. The public domain diskettes also */
/* include details of this automatic configuration process. */
/* Module name: ed6.ccc */
#include ed2.h
#include bdscio.h
#include ed1.ccc
#include edext.cc
/* Define the current coordinates of the cursor. */
/* Return the current coordinates of the cursor. */
outgetx()
{
   return(outx);
}
outgety()
{
   return(outy);
}
/* Output one printable character to the screen. */
outchar(c) char c;
{
   syscout(c);
   outx++;
   return(c);
}
/* Position cursor to position x,y on screen. */
/* 0,0 is the top left corner. */
outxy(x,y) int x,y;
{
   outx=x;            /* This code assumes that the process for */
   outy=y;            /* positioning the cursor is as follows: */
   syscout(27);       /* escape */
   syscout('=');      /* = */
   syscout(y+32);     /* y coordinate + 32 */
   syscout(x+32);     /* x coordinate + 32 */
}
/* Erase the entire screen. */
/* Make sure the rightmost column is erased. */
outclr()
```

```
{
  syscout(12);      /* character to erase entire screen */
  outxy(0,0);
}
/* Delete the line on which the cursor rests. */
/* Leave the cursor at the left margin. */
outdelln( )
{
  outxy(0,outy);
  outdeol( );
}
/* Delete to end of line. */
/* Assume the last column is blank. */
outdeol( )
{
int k;
  k=outx;
  while (k++<SCRNW1) {
    syscout (' ');
  }
  outxy(outx,outy);
}
/* Return YES if terminal has indicated hardware scroll. */
/* Otherwise return NO. */
/* Modify appropriate version of outsup or outsdn below. */
outhasup( )
{
  return(YES);
}
outhasdn( )
{
  return(NO);
}
/* Scroll the screen up. Assume the cursor is on the bottom line. */
/* Only one of the following two versions of outsup should be used. */
/* Depending upon your hardware, one must be commented out or the */
/* editor will not compile. */
/* outsup( ) /* version for outhasup that returns (YES) */
```

```
/* { */
/* auto scroll */
/* outxy(0,SCRNL1); */
/* syscout(10); line feed to scroll up */
/* } */
/* outsup() /* outsup if hardware outhasup returns NO */
/* { */
/* } */
/* Scroll the screen down. Assume the cursor is on the top line. */
/* Only one of the following two versions of outsdn should be used. */
/* Depending upon your hardware, one must be commented out or the */
/* editor will not compile. */
/* outsdn() /* version for outhasdn that returns (YES) */
/* { */
/* auto scroll */
/* outxy(0,0); */
/* syscout(27); */
/* syscout ('^');      scroll down with esc ^ sequence */
/* } */
/* outsdn() /* outsdn if hardware outhasdn returns NO */
/* { */
/* } */
```

MODULE NAME: ed7.bds

Function: Prompt Line Module

C Function	Purpose/Function
pmtmess(s1,s2)	Prompt line error message function. Put error message on prompt line, wait for response.
pmtmode(s)	Write new mode message upon prompt line.
pmtfile(s)	Update file name on the prompt line.
pmtedit()	Change mode message on prompt line to "edit:."

pmtline( )	Update line and column numbers on prompt line.
pmtcol( )	Update column number only on the prompt line.
pmtcmnd(mode,buffer)	Update mode message. Call getcmnd to write on prompt line.
pmtmode1(s)	Update and print mode on prompt line.
pmtfile1(s)	Print the file name on prompt line.
pmtline1( )	Print the line number on prompt line.
pmtcol1( )	Print the column number of cursor's current position.

ed7.bds—Prompt Line Module

```
/* Screen editor: prompt line module */
/* Module name: ed7.bds */
/* Define globals. */
#include ed2.h
#include bdscio.h
#include ed1.ccc
#include edext.cc
/* globals used by this module ----- */
/* char pmtln[MAXLEN];     mode */
/* char pmtfn[SYSFNMAX];   file name */
/* ----- */
/* Put error message on prompt line. */
/* Wait for response. */
pmtmess(s1,s2) char *s1, *s2;
{
int x,y;
  /* Save cursor. */
  x=outgetx( );
  y=outgety( );
  outxy(0,0);
  /* Make sure line is correct. */
```

```
    outdelln();
    pmtline1();
    pmtcol1(x);
    /* Output error message. */
    fmtsout(s1,outgetx());
    fmtsout(s2,outgetx());
    /* Wait for input from console. */
    syscin();
    /* Redraw prompt line. */
    pmtline1();
    pmtcol1(x);
    pmtfile1(pmtfn);
    pmtmode1(pmtln);
    /* Restore cursor. */
    outxy(x,y);
}
/* Write new mode message on prompt line. */
pmtmode(s) char *s;
{
int x,y; /* Save cursor on entry. */
    /* Save cursor. */
    x=outgetx();
    y=outgety();
    /* Redraw whole line. */
    outxy(0,0);
    outdelln();
    pmtline1();
    pmtcol1(x);
    pmtfile1(pmtfn);
    pmtmode1(s);
    /* Restore cursor. */
    outxy(x,y);
}
/* Update file name on prompt line. */
pmtfile(s) char *s;
{
int x, y;
    /* Save cursor. */
```

```
    x=outgetx( );
    y=outgety( );
    /* Update whole line. */
    outxy(0,0);
    outdelln( );
    pmtline1( );
    pmtcol1(x);   /* Dr. Dobb's Jrnl bug fix May, 1982; p. 4 */
    pmtfile1(s);
    pmtmode1(pmtln);
    /* restore cursor */
    outxy(x,y);
}
/* Change mode on prompt line to edit:. */
pmtedit( )
{
    pmtmode("edit:");
}
/* Update line and column numbers on prompt line. */
pmtline( )
{
int x,y;
    /* Save cursor. */
    x=outgetx( );
    y=outgety( );
    /* Redraw whole line. */
    outxy(0,0);
    outdelln( );
    pmtline1( );
    pmtcol1(x);
    pmtfile1(pmtfn);
    pmtmode1(pmtln);
    /* Restore cursor. */
    outxy(x,y);
}
/* Update just the column number on prompt line. */
pmtcol( )
{
int x,y;
```

```c
    /* Save cursor. */
    x=outgetx();
    y=outgety();
    /* Update column number. */
    pmtcoll(x);
    /* Update cursor. */
    outxy(x,y);
}
/* Update mode. Call getcmnd() to write on prompt line. */
pmtcmnd(mode,buffer) char *mode, *buffer;
{
int x,y;
    /* Save cursor. */
    x=outgetx();
    y=outgety();
    pmtmodel(mode);
    /* User types command on prompt line. */
    getcmnd(buffer,outgetx());
    /* Restore cursor. */
}
/* Update and print mode. */
pmtmodel(s) char *s;
{
int i;
    outxy(40,0);
    fmtsout(s,40);
    i=0;
    while (pmtln[i++]=*s++) {
        ;
    }
}
/* Print the file name on the prompt line. */
pmtfilel(s) char *s;
{
int i;
    outxy(25,0);
    if (*s==EOS) {
        fmtsout("no file",25);
```

```
   }
   else {
      fmtsout(s,25);
   }
   i=0;
   while (pmtfn[i++]=*s++) {
      ;
   }
}
/* Print the line number on the prompt line. */
pmtline1()
{
   outxy(0,0);
   fmtsout("line: ",0);
   putdec(bufln(),5);
}
/* Print column number of the cursor. */
pmtcoll(x) int x;
{
   outxy(12,0);
   fmtsout("column: ",12);
   putdec(x,3);
}
```

MODULE NAME: ed8.bds

Function: Operating System Module (CP/M 2 or later)

C Function	Purpose/Function
syscstat()	Check for character at console input. Return −1 if not ready, else return character c.
syscin()	Wait for next character from the console. Do not echo it.
syscout(c)	Print character on the console.

syslout(c)   Print character on the printer (list device).
sysend( )   Return address of last usable memory
                                location.
sysopen(file,mode)   Open a file.
sysclose(file)   Close a file.
sysrdch(file)   Read next character from the file. Uses
                                function sysrdc1( ).
syspshch(c,file)   Write next character to file. Uses function
                                syspshc1(c,file).
syspopch(file)   Read one character from end of file.
                                Not currently implemented.
syschkfn(args)   Check file name specified for correct syntax.
syscopfn(args,buffer)   Copy file name from args to buffer.
sysmovdn(n,dest,source)   Move a block of n bytes down (in CP/M
                                toward HIGH addresses). Block to be
                                moved starts at source and the first byte
                                goes to dest.
sysmovup(n,dest,source)   Move a block of n bytes up (in CP/M
                                toward LOW addresses). Block to be moved
                                starts at source and the first byte goes to
                                dest.

ed8.bds—Operating System Module

```
/* Screen editor: operating system module — BDS C version */
/* Module name: ed8.bds */
/* Define globals. */
#include ed2.h
#include bdscio.h
#include ed1.ccc
#include edext.cc
/* globals used by this module ----- */
/* #define NSECTS 8 */
/* #define SECSIZ 128 */
/* #define BUFSIZ (NSECTS * SECSIZ + 6) */
```

```
/* int iormode; 'r' 'w' or 'c' */
/* char iobufl[BUFSIZ]; file buffer */
/* ----- */
/* All calls to the operating system are made here. */
/* Only this module will have to be */
/* rewritten for a new operating system. */
/* The routines syscstat( ), syscin( ), and syscout( ) come in */
/* two flavors: CP/M version 2.2 and CP/M version 1.4. */
/* Only the CP/M 2.2 version of these */
/* routines is shown below. The public domain diskettes */
/* contain both varieties of system functions. */
/* Return -1 if no character is ready from the console. */
/* Otherwise, return the character. */
syscstat( )
{
   c = bdos(6,-1); /* extensive bug fix from */
   if (c == 0) { /* Dr. Dobb's Jrnl May, 1982; p. 6 */
     return (-1);
   }
   else {
     return (c);
   }
/* Wait for next character from the console. Do not echo it. */
syscin( )
{
int c;
   while ((c=bdos(6,-1))==0) {
     ;
   }
   return(c);
}
/* Print character on the console. */
syscout(c) char c;
{
   bdos(6,c);
   return(c);
}
/* Print character on the printer. */
```

```
syslout(c) char c;
{
  bdos(5,c);
  return(c);
}
/* Return address of last usable memory location. */
sysend()
{
  return(topofmem());
}
sysopen(name,mode) char *name, *mode;
{
int file;
int m;
  m=tolower(mode[0]);
  if (m=='r') {
    if ((file=fopen(name,iobufl))==-1) {
      iormode='c';
      fclose(iobufl);
      return(ERR);
    }
    else {
      iormode=m;
      return(iobufl);
    }
  }
  else if (m=='w') {
    if ((file=fcreat(name,iobufl))==-1) {
      iormode='c';
      fclose(iobufl);
      return(ERR);
    }
    else {
      iormode=m;
      return(iobufl);
    }
  }
  else {
```

```
        iormode='c';
        syserr("fopen: bad mode");
        return(ERR);
    }
}
/* Close a file. */
sysclose(file) int file;
{
    if (iormode=='w') {
        /* Write end of file byte. */
        putc(0x1a,iobufl);
        fflush(iobufl);
    }
    iormode='c';
    fclose(iobufl);
    return(OK);
}
/* Read next char from file. */
sysrdch(file) int file;
{
int c;
    while ((c=sysrdcl())==LF) {
        ;
    }
    return(c);
}
sysrdcl()
{
int c;
    if (iormode!='r') {
        error ("sysrdch: read in w mode");
        return(ERR);
    }
    if ((c=getc(iobufl))==-1) {
        return(EOF);
    }
    else if (c==0x1a) {
        return(EOF);
```

```
    }
  else {
    return(c);
  }
}
/* Write next char to file. */
syspshch(c,file) char c; int file;
{
    if (c!=CR) {
    return(syspshcl(c,file));
  }
  else if (syspshcl(c,file)==ERR) {
    return(ERR);
  }
  else {
    return(syspshcl(LF,file));
  }
}
syspshcl(c,file) char c; int file;
{
  if (iormode!='w') {
    error("syspshch: write in r mode");
    return(ERR);
  }
  if (putc(c,iobufl)==-1) {
    error("disk write failed");
    return(ERR);
  }
  else {
    return(c);
  }
}
/* Read one char from END of file. */
syspopch(file) int file;
{
  error("syspopch() not implemented");
  return(ERR);
}
```

```
/* Check file name for syntax. */
syschkfn(args) char *args;
{
  return(OK);
}
/* Copy file name from args to buffer. */
syscopfn(args,buffer) char *args, *buffer;
{
int n;
  n=0;
  while (n<(SYSFNMAX-1)) {
    if (args[n]==EOS) {
      break;
    }
    else {
      buffer[n]=args[n];
      n++;
    }
  }
  buffer[n]=EOS;
}
/* Move a block of n bytes down (towards HIGH addresses). */
/* Block starts at source and the first byte goes to dest. */
/* This routine is only called from bufmovdn() as follows: */
/* sysmovdn( n=to-from+1, dest=to+length, source=to); */
sysmovdn(n,dest,source) int n; char *dest, *source;
{
  if (n>0) {
    movmem(source-n+1,dest-n+1,n);
  }
}
/* Move a block of n bytes up (towards LOW addresses). */
/* The block starts at source and the first byte goes to dest. */
/* This routine is called only from bufmovup() as follows: */
/* sysmovup( n=to-from+1, dest=from-length, source=from); */
sysmovup(n,dest,source) int n; char *dest, *source;
{
```

```
if (n>0) {
   movmem(source,dest,n);
 }
}
```

MODULE NAME: ed9.bds

Function: General Utilities for ed2 Editor

C Function	Purpose/Function
number(args,val)	Return YES if the first token in args is a number and value of number is returned in *val.
ctoi(buf,index)	Convert character buffer to numeric (integer) values.
putdec(n,w)	Put decimal integer n in field width >= w. The number is left justified in the field.
itoc(n,str,size)	Convert integer n to character string in str.
syserr(s)	System error function.
error(s)	User error function.
diskerr(s)	Disk error function.
readline(file,p,n)	Read the next line of the file into the buffer of size n that p points to. Successive calls to the function readline() will read the file from front to back.
pushline(file,p,n)	Write (push) line to the file. Line is in the buffer of size n that p points to. Lines written by this function may be read by either the readline() or popline() functions.
popline(file,p,n)	Pop a line from the back of the file. The line should have been written (pushed) using the above function pushline().

ed9.bds—General Utilities

```
/* Screen editor: general utilities — BDS C version */
/* Module name: ed9.bds */
/* Define global constants and variables. */
#include ed2.h
#include bdscio.h
#include ed1.ccc
#include edext.cc
/* Return: Is first token in args a number ? */
/* Return value of number in *val. */
number(args,val) char *args; int *val;
{
char c;
  c=*args++;
  if ((c<'0')||(c>'9')) {
    return(NO);
  }
  *val=c-'0';
  while (c=*args++) {
    if ((c<'0')||(c>'9')) {
      break;
    }
    *val=(*val*10)+c-'0';
  }
  return(YES);
}
/* Convert character buffer to numeric. */
ctoi(buf,index) char *buf; int index;
{
int k;
  while ( (buf[index]==' ')||
    (buf[index]==TAB) ) {
    index++;
  }
  k=0;
```

```
  while ((buf[index]>='0')&&(buf[index]<='9')) {
    k=(k*10)+buf[index]-'0';
    index++;
  }
  return(k);
}
/* Put decimal integer n in field width >= w. */
/* Left justify the number in the field. */
putdec(n,w) int n,w;
{
char chars[10];
int i,nd;
  nd=itoc(n,chars,10);
  i=0;
  while (i<nd) {
    syscout(chars[i++]);
  }
  i=nd;
  while (i++<w) {
    syscout(' ');
  }
}
/* Convert integer n to character string in str. */
itoc(n,str,size) int n; char *str; int size;
{
int absval;
int len;
int i,j,k;
  absval=abs(n);
  /* Generate digits. */
  str[0]=0;
  i=1;
  while (i<size) {
    str[i++]=(absval%10)+'0';
    absval=absval/10;
    if (absval==0) {
      break;
    }
}
```

```
    }
    /* Generate sign. */
    if ((i<size)&&(n<0)) {
      str[i++]='-';
    }
    len=i-1;
    /* Reverse sign, digits. */
    i--;
    j=0;
    while (j<i) {
      k=str[i];
      str[i]=str[j];
      str[j]=k;
      i--;
      j++;
    }
    return(len);
}
/* system error routine */
syserr(s) char *s;
{
    pmtmess("system error: ",s);
}
/* user error routine */
error(s) char *s;
{
    pmtmess("error: ",s);
}
/* disk error routine */
diskerr(s) char *s;
{
    pmtmess("disk error: ",s);
}
/* Read the next line of the file into */
/* the buffer of size n that p points to. */
/* Successive calls to readline() read the file */
/* from front to back. */
readline(file,p,n) int file; char *p; int n;
```

```c
{
int c;
int k;
  k=0;
  while (1) {
    c=sysrdch(file);
    if (c==ERR) {
      return(ERR);
    }
    if (c==EOF) {
      /* Ignore line without CR. */
      return (EOF);
    }
    if (c==CR) {
      return(k);
    }
    if (k<n) {
      /* Move char to buffer. */
      *p++=c;
    }
    /* Always bump count. */
    k++;
  }
}
/* Push (same as write) line to end of file. */
/* Line is in the buffer of size n that p points to. */
/* Lines written by this routine may be read by */
/* either readline( ) or popline( ). */
pushline(file,p,n) int file; char *p; int n;
{
  /* Write all but trailing CR. */
  while ((n--)>0) {
    if (syspshch(*p++,file)==ERR) {
      return(ERR);
    }
  }
  /* Write trailing CR. */
  return(syspshch(CR,file));
```

```
}
/* Pop a line from the back of the file. */
/* The line should have been pushed using pushline( ). */
popline(file,p,n) int file; char *p; int n;
{
int c;
int k, kmax, t;
/* First char must be CR */
  c=syspopch(file);
  if (c==EOF) {
    /* at START of file */
    return(EOF);
  }
  if (c==CR) {
  /* Put into buffer. */
  *p++=CR;
  k=1;
}
else {
  syserr("popline: missing CR");
  return(ERR);
}
/* Pop line into buffer in reverse order. */
while (1) {
  c=syspopch(file);
  if (c==ERR) {
    return(ERR);
  }
  if (c==EOF) {
    break;
  }
  if (c==CR) {
    /* This ends ANOTHER line. */
    /* Push it back. */
    if (syspshch(CR,file)==ERR) {
      return(ERR);
    }
  }
  break;
```

```
}
/* nonspecial case */
if (k<n) {
  /* Put into buffer. */
  *p++=c;
}
/* Always bump count. */
k++;
}
/* Remember if we truncated the line. */
kmax=k;
/* Reverse the buffer. */
k=min(k,n-1);
t=0;
while (k>t) {
  /* Swap p[t], p[k]. */
  c=p[k];
  p[k]=p[t];
  p[t]=c;
  k--;
  t++;
}
return(kmax);
}
```

MODULE NAME: ed10.bds

Function Buffer Module

C Function	Purpose/Function
bufnew()	Clear the main buffer.
bufln()	Return current line number.
bufchng()	Check if buffer has been changed since the last time file was saved. Return YES if the buffer (i.e., the file) has been changed.

bufsaved( )	The file has been saved. Clear the bufcflag.
buffree( )	Return number of bytes left in the buffer.
bufgo(line)	Position buffer pointers to the start of the indicated line.
bufup( )	Move one line closer to the front of the buffer. That is, set the buffer pointers to the start of the previous line.
bufdn( )	Move one line closer to the end of the buffer. That is, set the buffer pointers to the start of the next line.
bufins(p,n)	Insert a line before the current line. p points to a line of length n to be inserted. Note n does not include the trailing CR.
bufdel( )	Delete the current line.
bufdeln(n)	Delete n lines, starting with the current line.
bufrepl(p,n)	Replace the current line with the line that p points to. The new line is of length n.
bufgetln(p,n)	Copy the current line into buffer that p points to. The maximum size of the buffer is n. Return k, the length of the line in the main buffer. If the line length exceeds the buffer length (i.e., $k > n$) then truncate n–k characters and only return n characters in the caller's buffer.
bufmovdn(from,to,length)	Move buffer down (in CP/M towards HIGH addresses).
bufmovup(from,to,length)	Move buffer up (in CP/M towards LOW addresses).
bufatbot( )	Return true if at the bottom of the buffer. The last line of the buffer is always null and the last line number is always bufmaxln +1.
bufnrbot( )	Return TRUE if at bottom or at the last real line before the bottom.
bufattop( )	Return true if at the top of the buffer.
bufout(topline,topy,nlines)	Put nlines from the buffer starting with the line topline at position topy of the video screen.
bufoutln(line)	Print line of main buffer on the screen.

bufext(length)   Buffer extension. Create a "hole" in the
                            buffer at the current line location. Length is
                            the size of the hole created.

ed10.bds—Buffer Module

```
/* Screen editor: buffer module — BDS C version */
/* Module name: ed10.bds */
/* Define globals. */
#include ed2.h
#include bdscio.h
#include ed1.ccc
#include edext.cc
/* globals used by this module ----- */
/* int bufcflag;      main buffer changed flag */
/* char *bufp;        start of current line */
/* char *bufpmax;     end of last line */
/* char *bufend;      last byte of buffer */
/* int bufline;       current line number */
/* int bufmaxln;      number of lines in buffer */
/* char buffer[1];    start of buffer */
/* ----- */
/* This code is built around several invariable */
/* assumptions: */
/* First, the last line is always completely empty. */
/* When bufp points to the last line there is NO */
/* CR following it. */
/* Second, bufp points to the last line if and only if */
/* bufline==bufmaxln+1. */
/* Third, bufline is always greater than zero. */
/* Line zero exists only to make scanning for the */
/* start of line one easier. */
/* Clear the main buffer. */
bufnew()
{
```

```
    /* Point past line 0. */
    bufp=bufpmax=buffer+1;
    /* Point at last byte of buffer. */
    /* Allow space for stack */
    bufend=sysend()-1000;
    /* At line one. No lines in buffer. */
    bufline=1;
    bufmaxln=0;
    /* Line zero is always a null line. */
    buffer[0]=CR;
    /* Indicate no need to save file yet. */
    bufcflag=NO;
}
/* Return current line number. */
bufln()
{
    return(bufline);
}
/* Return YES if the buffer (i.e., file) has been */
/* changed since the last time the file was saved. */
bufchng()
{
    return(bufcflag);
}
/* The file has been saved. Clear bufcflag. */
bufsaved()
{
    bufcflag=NO;
}
/* Return number of bytes left in the buffer. */
buffree()
{
    return(bufend-bufp);
}
/* Position buffer pointers to start of indicated line. */
bufgo(line) int line;
{
    /* Put request into range. Prevent extension. */
```

```
    line=min(bufmaxln+1,line);
    line=max(1,line);
    /* Already at proper line? Return. */
    if (line==bufline) {
      return(OK);
    }
    /* Move through buffer one line at a time. */
    while (line<bufline) {
      if (bufup()==ERR) {
        return(ERR);
      }
    }
    while (line>bufline) {
      if (bufdn()==ERR) {
        return(ERR);
      }
    }
    /* We have reached the line we wanted. */
    return(OK);
}
/* Move one line closer to front of buffer, i.e., */
/* set buffer pointers to start of previous line. */
bufup()
{
char *oldbufp;
    oldbufp=bufp;
    /* Can't move past line 1. */
    if (bufattop()) {
      return(OK);
    }
    /* Move past CR of previous line. */
    if (*--bufp!=CR) {
      syserr("bufup: missing CR");
      bufp=oldbufp;
      return(ERR);
    }
    /* Move to start of previous line. */
```

```c
    while (*--bufp!=CR) {
        ;
    }
    bufp++;
    /* Make sure we haven't gone too far. */
    if (bufp<(buffer+1)) {
        syserr("bufup: bufp underflow");
        bufp=oldbufp;
        return(ERR);
    }
    /* Success! We ARE at previous line. */
    bufline--;
    return(OK);
}
/* Move one line closer to end of buffer, i.e., */
/* set buffer pointers to start of next line. */
bufdn()
{
char *oldbufp;
    oldbufp=bufp;
    /* Do nothing silly if at end of buffer. */
    if (bufatbot()) {
        return(OK);
    }
    /* Scan past current line and CR. */
    while (*bufp++!=CR) {
        ;
    }
    /* Make sure we haven't gone too far. */
    if (bufp>bufpmax) {
        syserr("bufdn: bufp overflow ");
        bufp=oldbufp;
        return(ERR);
    }
    /* Success! we are at next line. */
    bufline++;
    return(OK);
}
```

```
/* Insert a line before the current line. */
/* P points to a line of length n to be inserted. */
/* NOTE: n does not include trailing CR. */
bufins(p,n) char *p; int n;
{
int k;
  /* Make room in the buffer for the line. */
  if (bufext(n+1)==ERR) {
    return(ERR);
  }
  /* Put the line and CR into the buffer. */
  k=0;
  while (k<n) {
    *(bufp+k)=*(p+k);
    k++;
  }
  *(bufp+k)=CR;
  /* Increase number of lines in buffer. */
  bufmaxln++;
  /* SPECIAL CASE: Inserting a null line at */
  /* end of file is not a significant change. */
  if ((n==0)&&(bufnrbot())) {
    ;
  }
  else {
    bufcflag=YES;
  }
  return(OK);
}
/* Delete the current line. */
bufdel()
{
  return(bufdeln(1));
}
/* Delete n lines, starting with the current line. */
bufdeln(n) int n;
{
int oldline;
```

```
int k;
char *oldbufp;
   /* Remember current buffer parameters. */
   oldline=bufline;
   oldbufp=bufp;
   /* Scan for first line after deleted lines. */
   k=0;
   while ((n--)>0) {
     if (bufatbot()) {
        break;
     }
     if (bufdn()==ERR) {
        bufline=oldline;
        bufp=oldbufp;   /* Dr. Dobb's Jrnl bug fix May 1982; p. 6 */
        return(ERR);
     }
     k++;
   }
   /* Compress buffer. Update pointers. */
   bufmovup(bufp,bufpmax-1,bufp-oldbufp);
   bufpmax=bufpmax-(bufp-oldbufp);
   bufp=oldbufp;
   bufline=oldline;
   bufmaxln=bufmaxln-k;
   bufcflag=YES;
   return(OK);
}
/* Replace current line with the line that */
/* p points to. The new line is of length n. */
bufrepl(p,n) char *p; int n;
{
int oldlen, k;
char *nextp;
   /* Do not replace null line. Just insert */
   if (bufatbot()) {
     return(bufins(p,n));
   }
/* Point nextp at start of next line. */
```

```
if (bufdn( )==ERR) {
  return(ERR);
}
nextp=bufp;
if (bufup( )==ERR) {
  return(ERR);
}
/* Allow for CR at end. */
n=n+1;
/* See how to move buffer below us: */
/* up, down, or not at all. */
oldlen=nextp-bufp;
if (oldlen<n) {
  /* Move buffer down. */
  if (bufext(n-oldlen)==ERR) {
    return(ERR);
  }
  bufpmax=bufpmax+n-oldlen;
}
else if (oldlen>n) {
  /* Move buffer up. */
  bufmovup(nextp,bufpmax-1,oldlen-n);
  bufpmax=bufpmax-(oldlen-n);
}
/* Put new line in the hole we just made. */
 k=0;
 while(k<(n-1)) {
    bufp[k]=p[k];
    k++;
 }
 bufp[k]=CR;
 bufcflag=YES;
 return(OK);
}
/* Copy current line into buffer that p points to. */
/* The maximum size of that buffer is n. */
/* Return k=length of line in the main buffer. */
/* If k>n then truncate n-k characters and only */
```

```
/* return n characters in the caller's buffer. */
bufgetln(p,n) char *p; int n;
{
int k;
    /* Last line is always null. */
    if (bufatbot()) {
      return(0);
    }
    /* Copy line as long as it not too long. */
    k=0;
    while (k<n) {
      if (*(bufp+k)==CR) {
        return(k);
      }
        *(p+k)=*(bufp+k);
        k++;
    }
      /* Count length but move no more chars. */
      while (*(bufp+k)!=CR) {
        k++;
      }
      return(k);
    }
    /* Move buffer down (towards HIGH addresses). */
    bufmovdn(from,to,length) char *from, *to; int length;
    {
      /* This code needs to be very fast. */
      /* Use an assembly language routine. */
      sysmovdn(to-from+1,to+length,to);
    }
    /* The call to sysmovdn() is equivalent to the following code: */
    /*      int k; */
    /*        k=to-from+1; */
    /*        while ((k--)>0) { */
    /*          *(to+length)=*to; */
    /*          to--; */
    /*        } */
    /* Move buffer up (towards LOW addresses). */
```

```
bufmovup(from,to,length) char *from, *to; int length;
{
    /* This code must be very fast. */
    /* Use an assembly language routine. */
    sysmovup(to-from+1,from-length,from);
}
/* The call to sysmovup() is equivalent to the following code: */
/*      int k; */
/*      k=to-from+1; */
/*      while ((k--)>0) { */
/*          *(from-length)=*from; */
/*          from++; */
/*          } */
/* Return true if at bottom of buffer. */
/* NOTE 1: The last line of the buffer is always null. */
/* NOTE 2: The last line number is always bufmaxln+1. */
bufatbot()
{
    return(bufline>bufmaxln);
}
/* Return true if at bottom or at the last */
/* real line before the bottom. */
bufnrbot()
{
    return(bufline>=bufmaxln);
}
/* Return true if at top of buffer. */
bufattop()
{
    return(bufline==1);
}
/* Put nlines lines from buffer starting with */
/* line topline at position topy of the screen. */
bufout(topline,topy,nlines) int topline, topy, nlines;
{
int l,p;
    /* Remember buffer's state. */
```

```
    l=bufline;
    p=bufp;
    /* Write out one line at a time. */
    while ((nlines--)>0) {
      outxy(0,topy++);
      bufoutln(topline++);
    }
    /* Restore buffer's state. */
    bufline=l;
    bufp=p;
}
/* Print line of main buffer on screen. */
bufoutln(line) int line;
{
    /* Error message does NOT go on prompt line. */
    if (bufgo(line)==ERR) {
      fmtsout("disk error: line deleted",0);
      outdeol();
      return;
    }
    /* Blank out lines below last line of buffer. */
    if (bufatbot()) {
      outdeol();
    }
    /* Write one formatted line out. */
    else {
      fmtsout(bufp,0);
      outdeol();
    }
}
/* Simple memory version of bufext. */
/* Create a hole in buffer at current line. */
/* Length is the size of the hole. */
bufext(length) int length;
{
/* Make sure there is room for more. */
if ((bufpmax+length)>=bufend) {
```

```
        error("main buffer is full");
        return(ERR);
    }
    /* Move lines below current line down. */
    bufmovdn(bufp,bufpmax-1,length);
    bufpmax=bufpmax+length;
    return(OK);
}
```

7

Text Formatting

INTRODUCTION

A particularly common type of software used today is the text processor or text formatter. Text formatting is the technique by which rough text (e.g., text containing uneven margins or uncentered text) is transformed into a finished document with a neatly formatted style. This chapter will present only one tool, but the lack of tool quantity is compensated for by an abundance of computing tool power. The formatting tool is an entire, working text processor. Because the complete listing is included and because of its modular nature, the text formatter can be expanded at will by the interested reader.

The process of generating a document can be divided into two parts. The first step is the process of defining the content and structures of the document. At this stage, we might enter text and decide what will be presented in paragraph form and what will be presented in tabular format, for example. This process is accomplished with the aid of a text editor or word processor and the results reside on our disk file for later use.

The second step in the document preparation process involves the translation of this internal representation of the document into its real, printed format. This entire process, from initial conception of document to eventual printing is presented in schematic style:

THE DOCUMENT PREPARATION PROCESS

1. *Initial document conception* is transformed by a text editor into
2. *document description* (interspersed text and format commands), which is transformed by a formatter into
3. *formatted output,* which is directed to a specific output device to produce
4. *printed page of document.*

The process of document preparation proceeds by means of the four steps shown above. Initially, the conception of the document (1) is entered into the machine using an editor to become the specific document description (2). This description of the document includes the actual text and the formatting commands. The formatter then takes this file and produces a formatted output (3) that may then be interpreted by the actual physical printing device to produce the specific printed page (4).

As can be seen, the formatting process is not necessarily accomplished in conjunction with the editing function. This relationship between editor and formatter provides the first basis for classifying formatting schemes.

The original, or first-generation, text formatters could be called pure formatters or "batch-oriented" systems. In this type of text formatter, the text is interspersed with text formatting commands and stored as a simple text file. The formatting commands are generally distinguished by a unique character. For example, our formatter uses a dot command (e.g., ".nf") to distinguish formatting commands from simple text lines. Other formatters use such things as the ampersand (&) or some other unique character sequence to distinguish commands from text.

This first-generation formatter is perhaps best exemplified by the RUNOFF class of document preparation software. In fact, RUNOFF is quite similar in operation to the simplified formatter that we have included in this chapter.

The second generation of text formatters (such as ROFF or NROFF) are essentially similar to the pure formatters of the first generation but have more advanced features. The new capabilities typically include macro capabilities or repetitive command loops. This book has been prepared using a sophisticated variant of the formatter presented below. It includes such advanced features as a programmable mode, alternating header and footer lines, and macro capabilities.

An entirely different class of text formatters are those that combine the editing and formatting functions. In the microcomputer world, WordStar is perhaps the most well known of the integrated formatters. This type of formatter is often called a "what-you-see-is-what-you-get" type of word processor. When WordStar centers a line, for example, the screen display and disk file are adjusted accordingly. When text is to be justified, WordStar adjusts the text, and the display appears with aligned right margins.

While this style of document processing has its advantages (the sales of WordStar attest to this), there are several possible problem areas. The integrated editor/formatter is configuration specific. For WordStar to adjust text correctly, it must know the characteristics of the specific terminal or display unit that is being used. The pure formatter, on the other hand, does not care what editor is used in preparing the text and command file.

Also, the integrated editor/formatter offers fewer formatting options. For example, sophisticated pure formatters often operate on large chunks of text such as chapters or subchapters, which are distinguished by specific dot-commands. Generally, the integrated software product does not have this writer-oriented capability. Also, the creation of indices, concordances, and tables of contents is fairly simple with a pure formatter. The preparation of these larger units of text is generally not possible with a WordStar-like editor.

Because of these factors, this chapter presents a pure text formatter. The user of text formatting software will find that this program provides a starting point for a customized text preparation system.

This particular formatter traces its lineage to the initial RATFOR-based FORMAT program of Kernighan and Plauger (KERN76, Appendix D), as does an entire set of excellent C-based text formatters. These formatters can meet virtually all text formatting needs, and with the inclusion of the source code, they can provide the basis for any customized program. A directory of the available C-based text formatters follows.

C-BASED TEXT FORMATTERS

Name	Features/Source
ROFF	Similar to the fmt program of this chapter, ROFF includes macro facilities and enhanced footer/header capabilities.
	C Users Group ("Just Like Mom's" disk) 415 E. Euclid McPherson, KS 67460
RAP	Roff and Print enhances the ROFF editor by implementing improved macro capabilities

and printer control protocols such as XON/XOFF for increased printing speed.

Eric Martz
48 Hunter's Hill Circle
Amherst, MA 01002
or C Users Group (see above)

NRO

Improved underlining capabilities, headings enhanced with subheader functions and command-line options are just a few of the enhancements in this formatter. It is particularly useful for the preparation of standardized program documentation.

Stephen L. Browning
5723 North Parker Avenue
Indianapolis, IN 46220
or C Users Group Utilities V diskette (see above)

TEX

Based on Donald Knuth's exceptionally sophisticated typesetting system of the same name, TEX improves the formatter at the formatted document/printer interface. TEX is designed to take full advantage of an Epson MX-80 printer with Graftrax, and it provides for a mathematics symbol mode as well as other alternate character sets.

Mike Meyer
P.O. Box 1479
Norman, OK 73070
or C Users Group (see above)

ROFF4

Designed for technical document preparation, ROFF4 includes enhanced overstrike and directed I/O features.

Ernest E. Bergmann
Physics Building #16

Lehigh University
Bethlehem, PA 18015
or
C Users Group (see above)

format   format is a version of the text formatter for *Software Tools* implemented in small-C. It is optimized for use with the Epson series of printers (italics, boldface, etc.). format is included in a very comprehensive set of software tools known as small-tools. The *small* refers to their price and to the C compiler used in their preparation. The small-tools are in fact quite powerful and inexpensive software products. Recommended to any user of C.

J. E. Hendrix
Box 8378
University, MS 38677-8378

WS2ROFF   This unique program takes WordStar files and converts them into the corresponding ROFF-type file.

Algorithmic Technology, Inc.
P.O. Box 278
Exton, PA 19341-0278

SCRIBBLE   Unlike the other formatters, SCRIBBLE is a commercial product. However, it is modifiable by any user with access to the BDS C compiler. It includes very sophisticated capabilities for virtually any text processing need. Currently sells for approximately $125.00.

Mark of the Unicorn
222 Third Street
Cambridge, MA 02142

Utility/Tool

fmt.c   text formatter

Usage

fmt <input-file> <output-file or destination>

Function

fmt is a pure, or batch-oriented, text formatter that takes an input file with interspersed text and formatting commands and produces a formatted output file or document. The destination for the formatted output may be either a disk file or a physical device, such as the printer or console.

Example

To take the text and formatting commands in the file document.doc and produce the output file document.out, we would use the following command line:

A> fmt document.doc document.out

To send the output directly to the printer (i.e., the CP/M LST: device) we would use the following command:

A> fmt document.doc lst:

Theory of Operation

The text formatting utility fmt.c can be outlined in pseudocode (an English-like description of program operation) as shown below:

```
defines for commands
initialize
check syntax (abort on error)
while there is text
    get text
```

```
        expand tabs
        if command execute command
        else process text
until done
```

C Function	Purpose/Function
command(buf)	Function to interpret valid fmt commands. Extension to the formatter would involve adding additional valid commands to the case statement in this function.
text(inbuf)	Function to process text (e.g., underline, center text).
comtyp(buf)	Function to return command type. Extensions to fmt would also need to modify the if . . . else construct within this function.
getval(buf,argtyp)	Get a parameter value (such as the value to be used for page length) from the command line within the file. Determine whether the parameter is an absolute or a relative (+/–) value.
set(param,argtyp,defval,minval,maxval)	Set the parameter to the value or to the minimum or maximum value if out of range.
underl(buf,tbuf,size)	Underline function. Replaces nonwhite space with underline character ("_"); backspaces one character ("\b"), and outputs character.
center(buf)	Function to center text. Text is centered by calculating and setting a temporary indent.
spread(buf,outp,nextra,outwds)	Justify right margin function. Spreads words out to justify text.
putwrd(wrdbuf)	Put word into output buffer.
brk( )	End current filled line (break function).
width(buf)	Return width of printed line.
xpndtab(inbuf)	Expand tabs in the input buffer. Assumes CP/M tab set of 8 column intervals.
gettl(buf,ttl)	Copy title line from buffer buf to ttl.
space(n)	Space n lines or to the bottom of the page.

put(buf)	Put out a line with proper characteristics (e.g., spacing, indenting, underlining).
leadbl(buf)	Delete leading blanks and set temporary indent value.
phead( )	Print out page header.
pfoot( )	Print out page footer.
puttl(buf,pageno)	Put out title line with optional page number.
getwrd(in,i,out)	Get a nonblank word from in[i] to out [i] and increment i. Return length of out[ ].
skip(n)	Output n blank lines.
min(a,b)	Returns minimum of two arguments.
max(a,b)	Returns maximum of two arguments.
samestr(str1,str2)	Check for string equivalence. Upper and lower case are considered equivalent.
index(s,t)	Returns the index in string s where string t begins. Returns –1 if string does not contain t. String s is assumed to start at 0.

IMPLEMENTATION NOTES

1. User guide to fmt. fmt is a pure, text formatter. It is invoked as:

fmt <input-file> <output-file or device>

This means accept text with embedded commands from the file named <input-file> and send the processed text to <output-file>. These files are normally CP/M disk files. However, if the output file is specified to be LST: CON: or PUN: then the output is sent to the list device (printer), the console device (crt), or the punch device, respectively. An example of an invocation to send the output of the file fmt.doc to the line printer is:

fmt fmt.doc lst:

The text formatter accepts several commands to justify, center, or simply pass through text. In addition it allows both a header title at the beginning of each page and a footer title at the bottom of each page. These both default to an empty line. Each fmt command consists of three characters in the leftmost column and (in most cases) an optional parameter. Parameters are strings in the case of header and footer titles and numbers in all other cases.

In the header and footer strings, leading spaces are ignored and all occurrences of # are replaced in the output text by the current page number. If the first nonspace or tab character in a header or footer string is " or ' it will be discarded. This is a means to allow leading spaces in the string, since all spaces after the initial " or ' are significant.

The numeric parameters can be in one of two forms. An absolute number sets the associated parameter to that number, or if out of legal range, to the parameter limit. A signed (i.e., + or –) number sets the parameter to its current value offset by the value of the number. This latter technique allows a paragraph indent margin to be inset from the normal indent without the user remembering where the current indent is set. This technique could also be used in constructing tables of textual material.

The default mode is "fill." That is, fit as many words as possible on a line to fill out the line width. However, any input lines of text that start with space characters or tabs maintain that number of columns of leading space. In any case, these lines with leading whitespace cause a break, i.e., they cause the following text to begin on a new line. Several commands also cause a break (see table below).

In the function categories below the lines referred to are input lines. Therefore to cause a single word to be underlined, place it on a separate input line. Likewise, to avoid the need to count lines, centering and underlining may be made continuous by setting the number of lines to something huge (e.g., 4000) until you wish to disable them again, at which point specifying 0 will cause an immediate disable.

DEFINED COMMANDS

Command	Function	Default	Break
.bp n	begin page numbered n	n = +1	yes
.br	cause a break		yes
.ce n	center the next n lines	n = 1	yes

.fi	enable filling		yes
.fo s	set footer title to s	empty	no
.he s	set header title to s	empty	no
.in n	set indent to n	n = 0	no
.ls n	set line spacing to n	n = 1	no
.nf	disable filling		yes
.pl n	set page length to n	n = 66	no
.rm n	set right margin to n	n = 60	no
.sp n	space n lines	n = 1	yes
.ti n	set temporary indent to n	n = 0	yes
.ul n	underline* the next n lines	n = 1	yes

*Underlining works only for printers that can back up the print head one char position at a time.

2. This formatter is quite simple and unsophisticated. However, with this as the starting point, more sophisticated features can be added. The formatters listed in the directory at the end of the previous section are generally enhanced versions of the present fmt editor.

/* fmt.c—Text Formatter */

```
/* Text Formatter commands */
#define UNKNOWN -1
#define BP 1        /* begin page */
#define BR 2        /* break */
#define CE 3        /* center */
#define FI 4        /* fill */
#define FO 5        /* footer title */
#define HE 6        /* header title */
#define IN 7        /* indent */
#define LS 8        /* line spacing */
#define NF 9        /* no fill */
#define PL 10       /* page length */
#define RM 11       /* right margin */
#define SP 12       /* space by lines */
```

```
#define TI 13        /* temporary indent */
#define UL 14        /* underline */
/* array dimensions */
#define MAXLINE 200    /* title buffer size */
#define INSIZE 200     /* input buffer size */
#define MAXOUT 200     /* output buffer size */
#define PAGELEN 66     /* default page length */
#define PAGEWIDTH 60   /* default page width */
/* convenience definitions */
#define HUGE 2000
#define NOFILE -1
#define EOFF -1
#define YES 1
#define NO 0
#define COMMAND '.'
/* globals */
  int curpag; /* current output page number (init 0) */
  int newpag; /* next output page number (init 1) */
  int lineno; /* next line to be printed (init 0) */
  int plval; /* page length in lines (init PAGELEN) */
  int m1val; /* margin before and including header */
  int m2val; /* margin after header */
  int m3val; /* margin after last text line */
  int m4val; /* bottom margin including footer */
  int bottom; /* last live line on page */
  char header[MAXLINE]; /* (init '\n') */
  char footer[MAXLINE]; /* (init '\n') */
  char wrdbuf[INSIZE]; /* Should be static in text(). */
  char fill; /* Fill if YES (init YES). */
  int lsval; /* current line spacing (init 1) */
  int inval; /* current indent >= 0 (init 0) */
  int rmval; /* current right margin (init PAGEWIDTH) */
  int tival; /* current temporary indent (init 0) */
  int ceval; /* # of lines to be centered (init 0) */
  int ulval; /* # of lines to be underlined (init 0) */
  char argtyp; /* '+', '-' or '0' argument type */
  int outp; /* last char pos in outbuf (init 0) */
  int outw; /* width of outbuf */
```

```
    int outwds; /* # of words in outbuf */
    char outbuf[MAXOUT]; /* lines to be filled collect here */
    char dir; /* direction from which to add blanks */
    char *outfile; /* buffered output file structure pointer */
/* Initialize global variables. */
initialize()
    {
    lineno = curpag = 0;
    newpag = 1;
    plval = PAGELEN;
    m1val = m2val = m3val = m4val = 2;
    bottom = plval - m3val - m4val;
    strcpy(header,"\n");
    strcpy(footer,"\n");
    *outbuf = '\0';   /* initially empty output buffer */
    fill = YES;
    lsval = 1;
    rmval = PAGEWIDTH;
    inval = tival = ceval = ulval = 0;
    outp = outw = outwds = 0;
    dir = 0;
    }
/* text formatting main program */
main(argc,argv)
    int argc;
    char *argv[];
    {
    char *fgets();
    char ifile[134];
    char ofile[134];
    int ofd;
    char inbuf[INSIZE]; /* input line buffer */
    if( argc != 3 )
      exit(puts("\nusage: FMT <infile> <outfile>"));
    if( fopen(argv[1],ifile) == NOFILE )
      exit(printf("\nNO such file : %s",argv[1]));
    if( samestr(argv[2],"CON:") )
      outfile = 1;
```

```
    else if( samestr(argv[2],"LST:") )
        outfile = 2;
    else if( samestr(argv[2],"PUN:") )
        outfile = 3;
    else { /* output sent to disk */
        if( (ofd = fcreat(argv[2],ofile)) ==NOFILE )
            exit(printf("\nCan't open : %s",argv[2]));
        else
            outfile = ofile;
    }
    initialize();
    while( fgets(inbuf,ifile) ) {
        xpndtab(inbuf);
        if( inbuf[0] == COMMAND )
            command(inbuf);
        else
            text(inbuf);
    }
    brk(); /* Flush any remaining text. */
    if( lineno > 0 )
        space(HUGE);
    if( outfile == 2 ) /* lineprinter */
        putc('\f',outfile);
    else if( outfile > 3 ) { /* diskfile */
        putc(0x1a,outfile);
        fflush(outfile);
        if( close(ofd) == NOFILE )
        printf("\nCan't close : %s",argv[2]);
    }
}
/*        */
/* command handler */
/* defined commands: */
/* BP  .bp  {+,-}{<n>}  *  begin page and set page number */
/* BR  .br              *  break */
/* CE  .ce  {<n>}       *  center n lines (default 1) */
/* FI  .fi              *  fill */
/* FO  .fo  {<text>}       footer title */
```

```
/* HE   .he  {<text>}        header title */
/* IN   .in  {+,-}<n>        indent n columns */
/* LS   .ls  {+,-}<n>        line spacing */
/* NF   .nf              *   no fill */
/* PL   .pl  {+,-}<n>        page length of n lines */
/* RM   .rm  {+,-}<n>        right margin n columns */
/* SP   .sp  {<n>}       *   space n lines (default 1 ) */
/* TI   .ti  {+,-}<n>    *   temporary indent n columns */
/* UL   .ul  {<n>}           underline n lines (default 1) */
/* note: * => causes a break */
/*          */
command(buf)
    char *buf;
    {
    int comtyp(),getval(),max();
    char argtyp;
    int ct;
    int spval;
    int val;
    val = getval(buf,&argtyp);
    switch( ct = comtyp(buf) ) {
      case BP:   if( lineno > 0 )
                     space(HUGE);
                 set(&curpag,val,argtyp,curpag+1,-HUGE,HUGE);
                 newpag = curpag;
                 break;
      case BR:   brk();
                 break;
      case CE:   brk();
                 set(&ceval,val,argtyp,1,0,HUGE);
                 break;
      case FI:   brk();
                 fill = YES;
                 break;
      case FO:   gettl(buf,footer);
                 break;
      case HE:   gettl(buf,header);
                 break;
```

```
        case IN:    set(&inval,val,argtyp,0,0,rmval-1);
                    tival = inval;
                    break;
        case LS:    set(&lsval,val,argtyp,1,1,HUGE);
                    break;
        case NF:    brk();
                    fill = NO;
                    break;
        case PL:    set(&plval,val,argtyp,PAGELEN,
                        (m1val+m2val+m3val+m4val+1),HUGE);
                    bottom = plval - m3val - m4val;
                    break;
        case RM:    set(&rmval,val,argtyp,PAGEWIDTH,tival+1,HUGE);
                    break;
        case SP:    set(&spval,val,argtyp,1,0,HUGE);
                    space(spval);
                    break;
        case TI:    brk();
                    set(&tival,val,argtyp,0,0,rmval);
                    break;
        case UL:    set(&ulval,val,argtyp,0,1,HUGE);
                    break;
        default:    break; /* Ignore unknown commands. */
        }
    }
}
/* Process text. */
text(inbuf)
    char inbuf[];
    {
    int i;
    if( inbuf[0] == ' ' || inbuf[0] == '\n' )
        leadbl(inbuf);
    if( ulval > 0 ) { /* underlining */
        underl(inbuf,wrdbuf,INSIZE);
        ulval--;
        }
    if( ceval > 0 ) { /* centering in effect */
        center(inbuf);
```

```
      put(inbuf);
      ceval--;
      }
  else if( inbuf[0] == '\n' ) /* all blank line */
      put(inbuf);
  else if( fill == NO ) /* unfilled text */
      put(inbuf);
  else /* filled text */
      for( i=0; getwrd(inbuf,&i,wrdbuf) > 0; )
          putwrd(wrdbuf);
      }
/* command type */
comtyp(buf)
  char *buf;
  {
  int index();
  char cmd[2];
  int i;
  for(i=0; i < 2; i++ )
      cmd[i] = tolower(buf[i+1]);
  cmd[2] = '\0';
  if( samestr(cmd,"bp") )
      return BP;
  else if( samestr(cmd,"br") )
      return BR;
  else if( samestr(cmd,"ce"))
      return CE;
  else if( samestr(cmd,"fi") )
      return FI;
  else if( samestr(cmd,"fo") )
      return FO;
  else if( samestr(cmd,"he") )
      return HE;
  else if( samestr(cmd,"in") )
      return IN;
  else if( samestr(cmd,"ls") )
      return LS;
```

```
      else if( samestr(cmd,"nf") )
          return NF;
      else if( samestr(cmd,"pl") )
          return PL;
      else if( samestr(cmd,"rm") )
          return RM;
      else if( samestr(cmd,"sp") )
          return SP;
      else if( samestr(cmd,"ti") )
          return TI;
      else if( samestr(cmd,"ul") )
          return UL;
      else
          return UNKNOWN;
      }
/* Get a parameter value from a command line and determine whether */
/* it is an absolute or relative value. */
getval(buf,argtyp)
      char *buf;
      char *argtyp; /* pointer to single char */
      {
      int abs( ),atoi( );
      while( ! isspace(*buf) )   /* skip command */
        buf++;
      while( isspace(*buf) )      /* skip whitespace separator */
        buf++;
      *argtyp = *buf;             /* argument type: +, - or digit */
      if( isdigit(*argtyp) )
        *argtyp = 'O';
      if( *argtyp == '+' )
        ++buf;
      return abs(atoi(buf));
      }
/* Set parameter and saturate on out of valid range. */
set(param,val,argtyp,defval,minval,maxval)
      int *param;      /* address of parameter to be set */
      int val;         /* value from command line */
```

```
        char argtyp;      /* +, -, or 0 */
        int defval;       /* default value */
        int minval;       /* minimum allowable value */
        int maxval;       /* maximum allowable value */
        {
        switch( argtyp ) {
           case '+':   *param += val;
                       break;
           case '-':   *param -= val;
                       break;
           case '0':   *param = val;
                       break;
           default:    *param = defval;
           }
        if( *param > maxval )
           *param = maxval;
        if( *param < minval )
           *param = minval;
        }
/* Underline: Replace nonwhitespace chars with '_', '\b',char */
underl(buf,tbuf,size)
        char buf[ ];
        char tbuf[ ];
        int size;
        {
        int i,j;
        char c;
        j = 0;
        for( i = 0; buf[i] != '\n' && j < size-1; i++ ) {
           tbuf[j++] = buf[i];
           if( buf[i] != ' ' && buf[i] != '\t' && buf[i] != '\b' ) {
              c = tbuf[--j];
              tbuf[j++] = '_';
              tbuf[j++] = '\b';
              tbuf[j++] = c;
              }
           }
        tbuf[j++] = '\n';
```

```
        tbuf[j] = '\0';
        strcpy(buf,tbuf);
        }
/* Center — fakeout by setting temporary indent. */
center(buf)
        char *buf;
        {
        int width( );
        int temp;
        temp = (rmval + tival - width(buf))/2;
        tival = max(temp,0);
        }
/* Spread words to justify right margin. */
spread(buf,outp,nextra,outwds)
        char buf[ ];
        int outp;
        int nextra;
        int outwds;
        {
        int i,j,nb,nholes;
        int kk;
        if( nextra <= 0 || outwds <= 1 )
           return;
        dir = ++dir & 1; /* toggle bias direction */
        nholes = outwds - 1;
        i = outp - 1; /* Point at final nonblank. */
        j = min(i + nextra,(MAXOUT-2));
        while( i < j ) {
           buf[j] = buf[i];
           if( buf[i] == ' ' ) {
              if( dir )
                 nb = nextra / nholes; /* truncated */
              else
                 nb = (nextra - 1) / nholes + 1; /* rounded */
              nextra -= nb;
              nholes--;
              for( ; nb > 0; nb-- )
                 buf[--j] = ' ';
```

```
                }
            --i;
            --j;
            }
        }
/* Put a word in outbuf including margin justification. */
putwrd(wrdbuf)
        char *wrdbuf;
        {
        int width();
        int last;
        int llval;
        int nextra;
        int w;
        int i; /* Debug only. */
        w = width(wrdbuf); /* printable width of wrdbuf[] */
        last = strlen(wrdbuf) + outp;
        llval = rmval - tival; /* printable line length */
        if( outp > 0 && ( (outw+w) > llval || last >= (MAXOUT-2) ) ) {
           last -= outp;        /* too big */
           nextra = llval - (outw - 1); /* # blanks needed to pad */
           if( nextra > 0 && outwds > 1 ) {
              outp--;        /* Back up to final blank. */
              spread(outbuf,outp,nextra,outwds);
              outp += nextra;
              }
           brk(); /* Flush previous line. */
           }
        strcpy(outbuf+outp,wrdbuf); /* Add new word to outbuf[]. */
        outp = last;
        outbuf[outp++] = ' '; /* Add a blank behind it. */
        outw += (w + 1); /* Update output width. */
        outwds++; /* Increment the word count. */
        }
/* brk — end current filled line */
brk()
        {
        if( outp > 0 ) {
```

```
            outbuf[outp] = '\n';
            outbuf[++outp] = '\0';
            put(outbuf);
            }
        outp = outw = outwds = 0;
        }
/* width of a printed line */
width(buf)
        char *buf;
        {
        int wid;
        char c;
        wid = 0;
        while ( c = *buf++ )
          if( c == '\b' )
            wid--;
          else if( c != '\n' )
            wid++;
        return wid;
        }
/* Expand tabs in the input buffer since */
/* the word processor doesn't really know how */
/* to handle them. */
xpndtab(inbuf)
        char *inbuf;
        {
        char tbuf[300];
        char *i,*t;
        int col;
        char c;
        col = 0;
        i = inbuf;
        t = tbuf;
        while( c=*i++ ) {
          if( c == '\t' )
            do {
              *t++ = ' ';
              } while( ++col & 7 );
```

```
        else
          *t++ = c;
        }
      *t = '\0';
      strcpy(inbuf,tbuf);
      }
/* utility functions for text formatter */
/* Copy title from buf to ttl. */
gettl(buf,ttl)
      char *buf;
      char *ttl;
      {
      while ( ! isspace(*buf) )
        buf++;
      while ( isspace(*buf) )
        buf++;
      if ( *buf == '\" || *buf == '"' )
        buf++;
      strcpy(ttl,buf);
      }
/* Space n lines or to bottom of page. */
space(n)
      int n;
      {
      brk();
      if ( lineno > bottom )
        return;
      if( lineno == 0 )
        phead();
      skip( min(n,bottom+1-lineno));
      lineno += n;
      if ( lineno > bottom )
        pfoot();
      }
/* Put out a line with proper spacing and indenting. */
put(buf)
      char buf[ ];
      {
```

```
        int i;
        if ( lineno == 0 || lineno > bottom )
            phead();
        for ( i=0; i < tival; i++ )
            putc(' ',outfile);
        tival = inval;
        fputs(buf,outfile);
        skip( min(lsval-1,bottom-lineno));
        lineno += lsval;
        if ( lineno > bottom )
            pfoot();
        }
/* Delete leading blanks and set tival. */
leadbl(buf)
        char buf[ ];
        {
        int i;
        brk();
        for ( i = 0; buf[i] == ' '; i++ )
            ;
        if ( buf[i] != '\n' )
            tival = i;
        strcpy(buf,&buf[i]);
        }
/* Put out page header. */
phead()
        {
        curpag = newpag++;
        if ( m1val > 0 ){
            skip(m1val-1);
            puttl(header,curpag);
            }
        skip(m2val);
        lineno = m1val + m2val + 1;
        }
/* Put out page footer. */
pfoot()
        {
```

```
      skip(m3val);
      if ( m4val > 0 )
        puttl(footer,curpag);
      skip(m4val-1);
      lineno = 0;
      }
/* Put out title line with optional page number. */
puttl(buf,pageno)
      char *buf;
      int pageno;
      {
      char c;
      while ( c = *buf++ )
        if ( c == '#' )
          fprintf(outfile,"%4d",pageno);
        else
          putc(c,outfile);
      }
/* Get a nonblank word from in[i] to out[ ] */
/* and advance i. */
/* Return length of out[ ]. */
getwrd(in,i,out)
      char in[ ];
      int *i;
      char out[ ];
      {
      int ii;
      int j;
      char c;
      ii = *i;
      while ( (c=in[ii]) == ' ' || c == '\t' )
        ++ii;
      j = 0;
      while ( (c=in[ii]) != ' ' && c != '\t' && c != '\n' && c != '\0' )
        out[j++] = in[ii++];
      out[j] = '\0';
      *i = ii;
      return j;
```

```
      }
/* Output n blank lines. */
skip(n)
      int n;
      {
      int i;
      for ( i = 0; i < n; i++ ) {
         putc('\r',outfile);
         putc('\n',outfile);
         }
      }
/* minimum of two arguments */
min(a,b)
      int a;
      int b;
      {
      return a < b ? a : b;
      }
/* maximum of two arguments */
max(a,b)
      int a;
      int b;
      {
      return a > b ? a : b;
      }
/* Compare strings for equality. */
/* Make upper and lower case equivalent. */
samestr(str1,str2)
      char *str1,*str2;
      {
      while ( *str1 )
         if ( toupper(*str1++) != toupper(*str2++) )
            return 0;
      if ( *str2 != '\0' )
         return 0;
      return 1;
      }
/* Return the index in string s where string t begins, or */
```

```
/* -1 if s doesn't contain t. s starts at 0. */
index(s, t)
      char s[ ], t[ ];
      {
      int i, j, k;
      for (i = 0; s[i] != '\0'; i++) {
         for (j=i, k=0; t[k]!='\0' && s[j]==t[k]; j++, k++)
            ;
         if (t[k] == '\0')
            return(i);
            }
      return -1;
}
```

8

Microcomputer Telecommunications

One of the fastest growing areas of interest in the microcomputer world is telecommunications. On the national level, we have users groups and bulletin boards with their massive data bases like the SOURCE or COMPUSERVE. Locally, we have microcomputers talking across town to the local university mainframe and to each other. This chapter presents a program, teledit, that is a complete telecommunications program/editor system that utilizes a type of error checking and correcting system that allows flawless transmission of information to and from microcomputers. This virtually standard error-control software is known as the MODEM7/XMODEM protocol and was developed by Ward Christensen in the very early days of public domain software. This protocol makes available a simple, yet effective means of error checking via the generation of checksums and the capability of retrying the transmission upon detection of an error. The basic file transmission process for an XMODEM-type system is shown below under "Theory of Operation."

In addition to being effective, the XMODEM system is available at minimal cost from any computer bulletin board system. Any machine-specific users group (such as the First Osborne Group) generally also has the software specially configured for their machine of interest. In the micro to micro communications arena there is simply no excuse for not using XMODEM or an XMODEM-type telecommunications program. If this isn't encouragement enough, a recent *Byte* article (David D. Clark, "Lmodem: A Small Remote-Communication Program," November 1983, pp. 410–428) provides a completely documented and annotated source code listing (in BDS C) for an XMODEM-type communications system. While not as sophisticated as the program presented in this chapter, it nevertheless may be of interest to readers as another example of fine public domain C software.

Teledit is a communications program for transmitting files and connecting microcomputers to other computer systems or networks as an ASCII terminal. It includes a simple text editor that can manipulate lines of text collected during a telecommunications session with a remote computer. The file transmission modes allow sending and receiving either binary or text files. The modes selected from the menu are:

T: Terminal Mode—No Text Collection   Teledit behaves like an ASCII terminal (specifically, a "dumb" ASCII terminal). Eight-bit characters are sent and received. No parity bits are checked, inserted, or removed. To return to the selection menu the SPECIAL character is typed. The SPECIAL character of <control> shift up-arrow was chosen because it is unlikely to be struck accidentally. The SPECIAL character can be modified by recompiling teledit and changing the #define of SPECIAL to the appropriate, new SPECIAL character sequence.

X: Terminal Mode—with Text Collection   This is the same as terminal mode above, except that any printing text characters received on the communication link are saved in a text buffer. The tab, newline, and formfeed characters are also placed into the buffer; any other characters are discarded. While in terminal mode X, the editor is entered by holding down the control key while typing the letter "E" (i.e., the ctrl E). X mode prompts the user for a filename to be used for the gathered text. After 500 lines of text have been collected and saved in the text buffer, each additional line of text collected causes the console bell (alarm) to sound. When this happens, the user should find a convenient time to suspend communication with the remote station so that the accumulated text can be saved (flushed) onto a disk file as described below.

G: Toggle Echo Mode (Currently Set to Echo)   This mode should *not* be toggled if the user is communicating in full duplex mode and receiving an echo from the remote station or the user is in half duplex mode. Use this option to talk to another person using teledit, typically between file transfers to inform the person of the next file to be transmitted.

E: Edit Text Collected   This mode enters the editor from the menu display. This will not work until X: terminal mode with text collection has been entered and a text collection file opened. Editor commands are described below.

F: Flush Text Collection Buffer to Text Collection File   This mode flushes the text collection buffer accumulated in the text collection mode. It does *not* close the file.

U: Select CP/M User Area   This mode is for users of CP/M systems that have user areas. In general, this command should be ignored.

V: Select CP/M Logical Drive   Select any of the disk drives available. The drive selected becomes the currently logged disk.

D: Print Directory for Current Drive and User Area   This mode prints the directory of files for the currently logged disk drive. The current directory may be selected using either the U (select user command) or the V (select logical drive) commands.

S: Send a File, MODEM Protocol   This mode prompts for the name of a file to send, then waits for the receiving station to synchronize. It returns to menu after completion whether successful or not. (*Note:* The receiving system *must* be using this program or one which uses the same MODEM protocol.)

R: Receive a File, MODEM Protocol   This mode prompts for the name of a file to be received, then waits for the sender to begin transmission. (*Note:* The sender *must* be using teledit or a program that employs the same MODEM protocol.)

Q: Quit   This mode quits and returns to command level. If a text file has been accumulated in X mode, the user is asked whether or not he wants it saved.

SPECIAL   This mode sends the SPECIAL character to the communication line, should that ever be necessary. The SPECIAL character is defined at compilation time by a #define statement at the beginning of the teled.c program source file.

SCREEN EDITOR COMMANDS

The editor prompts with an asterisk, "*", when entered. The current line appears directly below the prompt. The editor commands are:

A (Append)	Append a file and insert before the current line.
B (Beginning)	Go to the beginning of the file and display a page. The current line becomes the first line of the text file.

F <patt> (Find)	Find line that contains the pattern (<patt>) following the "F." If found, it becomes the current line. Search starts forward and wraps around the file.
I (Insert)	Enter insert mode. To leave insert mode, <ctrl>-Z is struck, followed by a <cr>. The escape insert mode sequence should be entered only at the beginning of a line. Lines with an embedded control –Z are lost.
K (Kill)	Kill the current line.
nK (n Kill	Kill n lines, where n is a decimal number.
L <patt> (Locate)	Locate the line that begins with the pattern (<patt>) following the "L."
O (Overwrite)	Overwrite lines of text until ctrl-Z is entered. ctrl-Z should be entered *only* at the beginning of a new line.
P (Page)	Page forward in text.
–P (Minus Page)	Page backward in a text file.
Q (Quit)	Quit editor.
Sn <cr> (Set)	Sets screen size to n lines. The default is 22 lines for a 24-line display terminal. S23 should be used for 25-line consoles, such as the Televideo series of terminals.
Z (End of file)	Go to the end of the file. This command can be used, for example, to go to the end of a file and then use –P to view the last page.
n <cr> (Forward)	Move forward in the file by n line(s).
<cr>	Move forward in the file by one line.
–n <cr> (Back)	Move backward in the file by n line(s).
Space Bar	Move backward in the file by one line.
#	Print number of text lines in a file.

Utility/Tool

teledit   Telecommunications program/editor.

Usage

teledit   Initialize the communications link and place
the user in command mode.

Function

teledit provides a sophisticated communications capability including error checking and retransmission capabilities with ease of installation and modification.

Theory of Operation

The teledit.c implementation of the XMODEM protocol can be outlined in pseudocode (an English-like description of program operation) as shown below:

XMODEM-TYPE COMMUNICATIONS PSEUDOCODE

File Transmission Protocol

```
open file
initialize modem/modem port
while (there is still file to be sent)
{
    repeat
    {
        send start-of-header (SOH);
        send sector number;
        send sector number (complemented);
        send data; calculate checksum;
        send checksum;
        wait for response;
    }
    until (response is acknowledged (ACK));
}
send an end of transmission (EOT);
wait for ACK;
close file;
```

File Reception Procedure

```
create directory entry for file;
initialize modem channel;
repeat
{
wait for initial SOH, EOT, or TIMEOUT;
   if (SOH)
   {
   get sector number;
   get sector number (complemented);
   get data; compute checksum;
   get the transmitted checksum;
   if (local checksum == transmitted checksum);
      send ACK (acknowledge);
   else
      send NACK (not acknowledge);
   }
if (EOT)
   {
   close the new file;
   send ACK;
   }
}
until (the initial character == EOT);
```

C Function	Purpose/Function
hardware.h	Header file for hardware dependent #define's in C program. Includes modem specifications, port characteristics, etc.
kbhit()	Test for console character available.
getch()	Get character from console with no echo.
getchar()	Get character from console with echo. Carriage return converted into carriage return–line feed.
putchar(c)	Write character to console. Line feed converted to carriage return–line feed pair.

moready( )	Modem output ready function. Returns TRUE if ready for output.
miready( )	Modem input ready function. Returns TRUE if input is present on modem line.
send(data)	Send character to modem.
switch(in)	Function to control and dispatch menu-based option in teledit.
diodir( )	Function for user CP/M directory call.
dump(lineptr,buf)	Dump text buffer to disk.
ed(lineptr)	Editor function within teledit.
receive(seconds)	Function to receive data from modem for time specified. This is dependent upon CPU clock frequency. The CPU clock frequency is specified in the hardware.h header file.
readfile(file)	Call the receive function (above) to receive data from modem line and output to a file. Calculates checksums and will attempt retries up to ERRORMAX number of times.
sendfile(file)	Call the send function (above) to send data from a file to the modem line. Evaluates checksums and will attempt retries up to ERRORMAX number of times.
ask(s)	Generalized user query function.
find(lineptr,linect)	Find first line having the given pattern in the line buffer. Return the line count if found.
kill(lineptr,linect,nl)	Erase nl number of lines beginning at line given by linect.
lfind(lineptr,linect)	Find the given pattern at the beginning of line in the line buffer. Return the line count if found.
pat(s,t)	Pattern match function.
show(lineptr,linect,nl)	Show the current frame on the screen.
getm(line)	Get memory for line using alloc function. Store the line and return pointer to it.
terminal( )	Terminal mode, no text. "Dumb" terminal mode for teledit.
iblock(rb,ib,cl)	Insert block of text ib into rb buffer and return current new line number cl.

IMPLEMENTATION NOTES

1. Note that modem port numbers, masks, and so on are taken from bdscio.h and hardware.h and must have the correct values for your system.

2. *Installation Notes:* teledit must be compiled with the BDS C compiler with the following constants modified to fit the specific terminal environment:

```
# define HC "s"        /* where s is the string necessary to home */
                       /* the cursor on the user's console screen */
#define CLEARS "s"     /* where s is the string necessary to clear */
                       /* the screen on the user's console */
```

3. Both the bdscio.h and hardware.h header files should be properly configured for the intended computer configuration before teledit is compiled.

4. Any of the editor commands that are not needed can be deleted by removing the corresponding case statement from the editor function in the source code and then recompiling teledit.

hardware.h—Constants and Definitions for teledit.c

```
/* module name: hardware.h */
/* This header file contains hardware-dependent definitions for C programs.
*/
/* It is #included with the teledit.c program.
*/
/* Some console (video) terminal characteristics:
*/
#define TWIDTH80 /* # of columns */
#define TLENGTH 24 /* # of lines */
#define CLEARS '\033E' /* string to clear screen on console
*/
```

```
#define INTOREV '\033p' /* string to switch console into reverse video
*/
#define OUTAREV '\033q' /* string to switch console out of reverse video
*/
#define CURSOROFF '\033x5' /* string to turn cursor off
*/
#define CURSORON '\033y5' /* string to turn cursor on
*/
#define ESC '\033' /* standard ASCII "escape" character
*/
/* The following definitions provide a portable low-level interface
*/
/* for direct I/O to the console and modem devices. The values
*/
/* used here are only for example; be certain to go in and customize
*/
/* them for your system! Note that only one of the two sections
*/
/* (I/O port vs. memory mapped) will be needed for your system,
*/
/* so feel free to edit the unused section out of the file and remove
*/
/* the conditional compilation lines around the section you end up
*/
/* using.
*/
#define IO_PORTS   1          /* Change to 0 if I/O is memory-mapped. */
#if IO_PORTS                  /* this section for status-driven I/O only */
#define CON_TBE               (inp(0x00) & 0x80) /* Console: output ready? */
#define CON_RDA               (inp(0x00) & 0x40)
#define CON_TDATA(byte) (outp(0x01, byte))
#define CON_RDATA   (inp(0x01)) /* Read data. */
#define MOD_TBE               (inp(0x08) & 0x80) /* modem */
#define MOD_RDA               (inp(0x08) & 0x40)
#define MOD_TDATA(byte)(outp(0x09, byte))
#define MOD_RDATA (inp(0x09))
#else                         /* this section for memory-mapped I/O only */
#define CON_TBE               (peek(FOO) & BAR) /* console */
```

```
#define CON_RDA        (peek(FOO) & BAR)
#define CON_TDATA(byte) (poke(FOO, BAR))
#define CON_RDATA   (peek(FOO))
#define MOD_TBE        (peek(FOO) & BAR) /* modem */
#define MOD_RDA        (peek(FOO) & BAR)
#define MOD_TDATA(byte)(poke(FOO, byte))
#define MOD_RDATA   (peek(FOO))
#endif
```

/* teledit.c—Telecommunications Program */

```
/* teledit.c v1.2 */
/* Modified for BDS C v1.50 by Leor Zolman, 10/21/82 */
/* A telecommunications program using Ward Christensen's */
/* "MODEM" File Transfer Protocol. */
#include "bdscio.h"
#include "hardware.h"
/* The following three defines must be customized by the user: */
#define HC "\33H*" /* Home cursor and print a "*". */
#define SPECIAL '^'-0x40 /* Gets out of terminal mode. */
#define CPUCLK 4 /* CPU clock rate, in MHz */
/* The rest of the defines need not be modified. */
#define SOH 1
#define EOT 4
#define ACK 6
#define ERRORMAX 10
#define RETRYMAX 10
#define LF 10
#define CR 13
#define SPS 1500 /* loops per second */
#define NAK 21
#define TIMEOUT -1
#define TBFSIZ NSECTS*SECSIZ
```

```
#define ML 1000 /* maximum source lines */
#define SEARCH_FIRST 17 /* BDOS calls */
#define SEARCH_NEXT 18
char linebuf[MAXLINE]; /* string buffer */
char fnambuf[50]; /* name of file for text collection */
int nlines, nl; /* number of lines */
int linect; /* current line */
char fflg; /* text collection file flag */
char echoflg; /* whether to echo */
char sflg; /* transmit flag */
int kbhit() /* Test for console character available. */
{
    return bios(2);
}
int getch() /* Get char from console raw, no echo. */
{
    while (!kbhit());
    return bios(3) & 0x7f;
}
int getchar() /* Get char from console with echo, expand CR to CRLF. */
{
    char c;
    if ((c = getch()) == '\r') c = '\n';
    putchar(c);
    return c;
}
putchar(c) /* Write char to console, expand LF to CRLF. */
{
    if (c == '\n') putchar('\r');
    bios(4,c);
}
int moready() /* Return TRUE if the modem is ready for output. */
{
    return MOD_TBE;
}
int miready() /* Return TRUE if input is present on the modem. */
{
    return MOD_RDA;
```

```
}
send(data) /* Send char to modem. */
char data;
{
   while(!moready())
   ;
   MOD_TDATA(data);
}
main(argc,argv)
char **argv;
{
   int i, j, k, l;          /* Scratch integers. */
   char *lineptr[ML];       /* Allow ML source lines. */
   char *inl[ML];           /* Inserted line pointers */
   char *p;                 /* Scratch pointer. */
   char buf[BUFSIZ];        /* I/O buffer */
   int in;                  /* Collect characters at in. */
   char *alloc();           /* storage allocator */
   char *getm();            /* memory procuror */
   _allocp = NULL;          /* Initialize. */
   linect = nlines = i = 0;
   fflg = echoflg = FALSE;
   lineptr[i] = NULL;
while(1)
{
   puts(CLEARS);
   printf("Teledit ver 1.1\n\n");
   printf("T: Terminal mode - no text collection\n");
   printf("X: terminal mode with teXt collection\n");
   printf("   In terminal mode:\n");
   printf("   SPECIAL (control-^): return to menu\n");
   printf("   control-E: enter editor\n");
   printf("G: toGgle echo mode (currently set to: %secho)\n",
        echoflg ? "" : "no ");
   printf("E: Edit collected text\n");
   printf("F: Flush text buffer to text collection file\n");
   printf("U: select cp/m User area\n");
   printf("V: select cp/m driVe\n");
```

```
     printf("D: print Directory for current drive and user area\n");
     printf("S: Send a file, MODEM protocol\n");
     printf("R: Receive a file, MODEM protocol\n");
     printf("Q: quit\n");
     printf("SPECIAL: send SPECIAL char to modem\n");
     printf("\nCommand: ");
     in = toupper(getchar());
     putchar('\n');
   switch(in)
   {
      case 'U':
          printf("Switch to user area: ");
          bdos(32,atoi(gets(linebuf)));
          break;
      case 'V':
          printf("Switch to drive: ");
          bdos(14,toupper(getchar()) - 'A');
          break;
      case 'D':
          dodir();
          break;
      case SPECIAL:
          send(SPECIAL);
          break;
      case 'T':
        terminal();
        break;
      case 'X':
    if (fflg)
       printf("Text collection already in effect (filename '%s')\n",
fnambuf);
    else
    {
      puts("Collection text filename = ");
      gets(fnambuf);
      puts("Wait ... ");
      if(fopen(fnambuf,buf) != ERROR)
      { printf("\nFile already exists; do you want to ");
```

```
        if(!ask("overwrite it"))
          break;
      }
      if(fcreat(fnambuf, buf) == ERROR)
      { printf("\nCan't create %s", fnambuf);
        break;
      }
      fflg = TRUE;
  }
      printf("\nReady\n");
      while(1)
      { if(miready())
        { putchar (in = MOD_RDATA);
          if(in >= ' ')
            linebuf[i++] = in;
          else
          { if(in == '\n') continue;
            if(in == CR)
            { linebuf[i++] = '\n';
              linebuf[i] = NULL;
              p = getm(linebuf);
              if(p == NULL) continue;
              lineptr[nlines++] = p;
              lineptr[nlines] = NULL;
              if(nlines > 500) putchar('\7');
                i = 0;
            }
          else if(in == '\t' || in == '\f')
                linebuf[i++] = in;
          else
                continue;
          }
        }
        if(kbhit())
        {
          if(echoflg)
            in = getchar();
          else
```

```
            in = getch();
         if(in == SPECIAL)
            break;
         else if(in == ('E' & 037))
            {
            ed(lineptr);
            printf("Terminal mode:\n\n");
            }
          else
            send(in);
          }
       }
     break;
case 'S':
case 'R':
   printf("File to %s = ", (in == 'S') ? "send" : "receive");
   gets(linebuf);
   if(in == 'R')
     readfile(linebuf);
   else
   {
     if(fopen(linebuf, buf) == ERROR)
     {  printf("\7Teledit: can't open %s\n", linebuf);
        sleep(15);
        break;
     }
     sendfile(linebuf);
   }
   putchar(7);      /* Beep when done. */
   break;
case 'E':
   ed(lineptr);
   break;
case 'D':
   dump(lineptr, buf);
   break;
case 'G':
   echoflg = !echoflg;
```

```
        break;
    case 'Q':
      if (fflg) {
          printf("\nSave file \"%s\" to ",fnambuf);
          if (ask("disk"))
              { dump(lineptr, buf);
                putc(CPMEOF, buf);
                fflush(buf);
                fclose(buf);
              }
          }
      exit(0);
      }
    }
}
dodir()
{
    char dmapos;                    /* Value returned by search calls */
    char first_time;               /* used in search routine. */
    char tmpfn[20];                /* temp filename buffer */
    char fcb[36];
    int colno;                     /* column count */
    int i;
    char name[15];
    int drive;
    bdos(26,BASE+0x80);            /* Ensure default DMA after read/write */
    printf("\nFiles = ");
    if (getline(name,15) < 2)
      setfcb(fcb,"*.*");
    else
      setfcb(fcb,name);
    drive= (fcb[0]==0 ? bdos(25) : fcb[0]-1 ) ;
    puts(CLEARS);
    printf("Directory for Drive %c, user area %d:\n\n",
        drive+'A', bdos(32,0xff));
    colno = 1;
    first_time = TRUE;
    while (1) {
```

```
      dmapos = bdos(first_time ? SEARCH_FIRST : SEARCH_NEXT,fcb);
      if (dmapos == 255) break;
      first_time = FALSE;
      hackname(tmpfn,(BASE + 0x80 + dmapos * 32));
      puts(tmpfn);
      for (i = strlen(tmpfn); i < 15; i++) putchar (' ');
      if ((colno += 15) > 65)
         {
         putchar('\n');
         colno =1;
         }
      }
   puts("\n\nHit any key to return to menu: ");
   getchar();
}
hackname(dest,source)
char *dest, *source;
{
   int i,j;
   j = 0;
   for (i = 1; i < 9; i++)
   {
      if (source[i] == ' ') break;
      dest[j++] = source[i];
   }
   if (source[9] != ' ')
      dest[j++] = '.';
   for (i = 9; i < 12; i++)
   {
      if (source[i] == ' ') break;
      dest[j++] = source[i];
   }
   dest[j] = '\0';
   return dest;
}
dump(lineptr, buf) /* dump text buffer */
char **lineptr, *buf;
{
```

```
        int i;
        for(i = 0; lineptr[i] != NULL; i++)
           if(fputs(lineptr[i], buf) == ERROR)
              printf("\n\7Error writing txt, disk full?\n");
        lineptr[0] = linect = nlines = _allocp = 0;
     }
  ed(lineptr) /* editor */
  char **lineptr;
{
  char in, *inl[ML], *p, buf[BUFSIZ];
  int i, j, k, l;
  char *getm(), *alloc();
  if(!fflg)
  {  printf("\n\7No text buffer to edit.\n");
     return;
  }
  printf("\nedit\n*");
  nl = 22;
  while (in = getchar())
     switch (tolower(in)) {
        case 'a':
           puts("Filename to yank = ");
           gets(linebuf);
           if(fopen(linebuf, buf) == ERROR) {
              printf ("\r Cannot open %s.\r*", linebuf);
              continue;
           }
           for(i = 0; fgets(linebuf, buf); i++) {
              inl[i] = getm(linebuf);
              if(inl[i] == NULL) break;
           }
           inl[i] = NULL;
           iblock(lineptr, inl, linect);
           show (lineptr, linect, nl);
           continue;
        case 'b':
           linect = 0;
           show (lineptr, linect, nl);
```

```
        continue;
case 'q':
    printf(CLEARS);
    return;
case 'f':
    gets(linebuf);
    if((i = find(lineptr, linect)) >= 0) {
        linect = i;
        show (lineptr, linect, nl);
    }
    else if((i = find(lineptr, 0)) >= 0) {
        linect = i;
        show (lineptr, linect, nl);
    }
    else
    {
        printf(HC);
        printf(" not found\r*");
    }
    continue;
case 'i':
    j = min(linect, 5);
    if(j == 0)
        printf(CLEARS);
    else {
        show(lineptr, (linect - j), j);
        j++;
        printf("\b ");
        for(; j; j--)
            putchar('\n');
    }
    while(1) {
        gets(linebuf);
        for(i = 0; linebuf[i]; i++)
            if(linebuf[i] == CPMEOF)
                break;
        if(linebuf[i] == CPMEOF) break;
        linebuf[i++] = '\n';
```

```
                 linebuf[i] = NULL;
                 inl[j++] = getm(linebuf);
             }
             inl[j] = NULL;
             iblock(lineptr, inl, linect);
             show (lineptr, linect, nl);
             continue;
case 'k':
    putchar('\n');
    showl(lineptr, linect);
    kill(lineptr, linect, 1);
    continue;
case 'l':
    gets(linebuf);
    if((i = lfind(lineptr, linect)) >= 0) {
        linect = i;
        show(lineptr, linect, nl);
    }
    else if((i = lfind(lineptr, 0)) >= 0) {
        linect = i;
        show(lineptr, linect, nl);
    }
    else {
        printf(HC);
        printf(" not found\r*");
    }
    continue;
case 'o':
    putchar('\n');
    i = linect;
    while(gets(linebuf)) {
        for(j = 0; linebuf[j]; j++)
            if(linebuf[j] == CPMEOF) break;
        if(linebuf[j] == CPMEOF) break;
        linebuf[j++] = '\n';
        linebuf[j] = NULL;
        if(lineptr[i])
            free(lineptr[i]);
```

```
        lineptr[i++] = getm(linebuf);
        if(i > nlines) lineptr[++nlines] = NULL;
      }
      show (lineptr, linect, nl);
      continue;
    case 'p':
      linect = min((linect + nl), nlines);
      show (lineptr, linect, nl);
      continue;
    case 's':
      gets(linebuf);
      nl = max((atoi(linebuf)), 1);
      show (lineptr, linect, nl);
      continue;
    case 'z':
      linect = nlines;
      show(lineptr, linect, nl);
      continue;
    case '1': case '2': case '3': case '4': case '5':
    case '6': case '7': case '8': case '9': case '-':
      linebuf[0] = in;
      for (i = 1; (isdigit(in = getchar())); i++)
        linebuf[i] = in;
      linebuf[i] = NULL;
      i =atoi(linebuf);
      if (i < 0)
        j = max((linect + i), 0);
      else
        j = min((linect + i), nlines);
      in = tolower(in);
      if(j > linect && in == 'k')
        kill(lineptr, linect, (j - linect));
      else
        linect = j;
      if (in == 'p') linect = max((linect-nl), 0);
      show (lineptr, linect, nl);
      continue;
    case '#':
```

```
          printf (" of lines: %d\r*", nlines);
          continue;
      case '\n':
        if(lineptr[linect] != NULL) {
          showl(lineptr, linect);
          linect++;
        }
        else
          printf (HC);
        continue;
      case ' ':
        if(linect)
          linect--;
        show(lineptr, linect, nl);
        continue;
      case ('E'&037):
        send(in);
        printf("\n^E sent\n");
        return;
      default:
        printf(" ?\r*");
      }
}
shocrt(sec,try,tot)
int sec,try,tot;
{
    if(sflg)
      printf("Sending #%d (Try=%d Errs=%d) \r", sec, try, tot);
    else
      printf("Awaiting #%d (Try=%d, Errs=%d) \r", sec, try, tot);
    if(try && tot) putchar ('\n');
}
receive(seconds)
int seconds;
{ char data;
  int lpc,seccnt;
  for (lpc = 0; lpc < CPUCLK; lpc++)
    { seccnt = seconds * SPS;
```

```
    while (!miready() && seccnt--);
    if(seccnt >= 0)
      { data = MOD_RDATA;
        return(data);
      }
    }
  return(TIMEOUT);
}
purgeline()
{ while (miready())
  MOD_RDATA;    /* Purge the receive register. */
}
readfile(file)
char *file;
{ int j, firstchar, sectnum, sectcurr, sectcomp, errors;
  int toterr,checksum;
  int errorflag, fd;
  int bufctr;
  char buffer[BUFSIZ];
  sflg = FALSE;
  fd = creat(file);
  if(fd == -1)
  { printf("Teledit: cannot create %s\n", file);
    exit(1);
  }
  printf("\nReady to receive %s\n", file);
  sectnum = 0;
  errors = 0;
  toterr = 0;
  bufctr = 0;
  purgeline();
  shocrt(0,0,0);
  do
    { errorflag = FALSE;
      do
       firstchar = receive (10);
      while(firstchar != SOH && firstchar != EOT && firstchar !=
TIMEOUT);
```

```
if(firstchar == TIMEOUT)
 errorflag = TRUE;
if(firstchar == SOH)
 { sectcurr = receive (1);
   sectcomp = receive (1);
   if((sectcurr + sectcomp) == 255)
    { if(sectcurr == ((sectnum + 1) & 0xFF))
       { checksum = 0;
         for(j = bufctr;j < (bufctr + SECSIZ);j++)
         { buffer[j] = receive (1);
           checksum = (checksum + buffer[j]) & 0xff;
         }
         if(checksum == receive (1))
         { errors = 0;
           sectnum = sectcurr;
           bufctr = bufctr + SECSIZ;
           if(bufctr == TBFSIZ)
            { bufctr = 0;
              write(fd, buffer, NSECTS);
            }
           shocrt(sectnum,errors,toterr);
           send(ACK);
         }
       else
         errorflag = TRUE;
       }
     else
       if(sectcurr == sectnum)
         { do;
          while(receive (1) != TIMEOUT)
           ;
          send(ACK);
          }
       else
          errorflag = TRUE;
    }
else
   errorflag = TRUE;
```

```
        }
    if(errorflag == TRUE)
        { errors++;
          if(sectnum)
           toterr++;
          while(receive (1) != TIMEOUT);
          shocrt(sectnum,errors,toterr);
        send(NAK);
        }
    }
  while(firstchar != EOT && errors != ERRORMAX);
  if((firstchar == EOT) && (errors < ERRORMAX))
    { send(ACK);
    bufctr = (bufctr + SECSIZ - 1) / SECSIZ;
    write(fd, buffer, bufctr);
    close(fd);
    printf("\nDone — returning to menu:\n");
    }
  else
    printf("\n\7Aborting\n\n");
}
sendfile(file)
char *file;
{ char *npnt;
  int j, sectnum, sectors, attempts;
  int toterr,checksum;
  int bufctr, fd;
  char buffer[BUFSIZ];
  sflg = TRUE;
  fd = open(file,0);
  if(fd == -1)
    { printf("\nTeledit: %s not found\n", file);
    return;
    }
  else
    printf("\nFile is %d sectors long.\n",cfsize(fd));
  purgeline();
  attempts=0;
```

```
     toterr = 0;
shocrt(0,0,0);
while((receive (10) != NAK) && (attempts != 8))
  { attempts++;
    shocrt(0,attempts,0);
  }
if (attempts == 8)
  { printf("\nTimed out awaiting initial NAK\n");
    exit();
  }
attempts = 0;
sectnum = 1;
while((sectors = read(fd, buffer, NSECTS)) && (attempts != RETRYMAX))
  { if(sectors == -1)
    { printf("\nFile read error.\n");
      break;
    }
    else
    { bufctr = 0;
      do
       { attempts = 0;
         do
          { shocrt(sectnum,attempts,toterr);
           send(SOH);
           send(sectnum);
           send(-sectnum-1);
            checksum = 0;
            for(j = bufctr; j < (bufctr + SECSIZ);j++)
            { send(buffer[j]);
              checksum = (checksum + buffer[j]) & 0xff;
            }
           send(checksum);
            purgeline();
            attempts++;
            toterr++;
          }
         while((receive (10) != ACK) && (attempts != RETRYMAX));
         bufctr = bufctr + SECSIZ;
```

```
                sectnum++;
                sectors--;
                toterr--;
                 }
              while((sectors != 0) && (attempts != RETRYMAX));
             }
    }
      if(attempts == RETRYMAX)
         printf("\nNo ACK on sector, aborting\n");
      else
         { attempts = 0;
           do
           { send(EOT);
             purgeline();
             attempts++;
           }
         while((receive (10) != ACK) && (attempts != RETRYMAX));
         if(attempts == RETRYMAX)
           printf("\nNo ACK on EOT, aborting\n");
         }
    close(fd);
printf("\nDone — Returning to menu:\n");
}
ask(s)
char *s;
{
      char c;
again: printf("%s (y/n)? ", s);
      c = tolower(getchar());
      if(c == 'y') {
        puts("es\n");
        return 1;
      }
      else if(c == 'n')
        puts("o\n");
      else
      {
        printf(" \7Yes or no, please ... \n");
```

```
        goto again;
    }
    return 0;
}
find(lineptr, linect) /* Find a line having the pattern in linebuf. */
char *lineptr[];
int linect;
{
    int i;
    for(i = linect; lineptr[i] != NULL; i++)
      if(pat(lineptr[i], linebuf) >= 0)
         return(i);
    return(-1);
}
kill(lineptr, linect, nl) /* Erase lines. */
char *lineptr[];
int linect, nl;
{
    int i,j;
    for (i = linect; lineptr[i] != NULL && nl > 0; i++, nl --) {
      free(lineptr[i]);
      nlines--;
    }
    lineptr[linect] = NULL;
    if(lineptr[i] != NULL) {
      j = (nlines - linect) * 2;
      movmem(&lineptr[i], &lineptr[linect], j + 2);
    }

}
lfind(lineptr, linect)    /* Find pattern at beginning of a line. */
char *lineptr[];
int linect;
{
    int i,j;
    char line[MAXLINE];
    j = strlen(linebuf);
    for (i = linect; lineptr[i] != NULL; i++) {
      strcpy(line, lineptr[i]);
```

```
        line[j] = NULL;
        if( strcmp(line, linebuf) == 0)
            return i;
    }
    return -1;
}
pat(s, t)    /* pattern match */
char s[ ], t[ ];
{
    int i, j, k;
    for(i = 0; s[i] != '\0'; i++)
      {
        for(j = i, k=0; t[k] != '\0' && s[j] == t[k]; j++, k++)
          ;
        if(t[k] == '\0')
            return(i);
      }
    return(-1);
}
show (lineptr, linect, nl) /* Screen current frame. */
char *lineptr[ ];
int linect, nl;
{
   int i;
   printf (CLEARS);
   putchar('\n');
   for (i = linect; i < (linect+nl) && lineptr[i] != NULL; i++)
      printf("%s", lineptr[i]);
   printf (HC);
   return(i);
}
show1(lineptr, linect)
char **lineptr;
int linect;
{
   int i;
   for(i = 0; i < nl; i++)
      putchar('\n');
   if((linect + nl) >= nlines)
```

```
        putchar('\n');
      else
        printf("%s", lineptr[linect+nl]);
      printf(HC);
      for(i = 0; i < 78; i++)
        putchar(' ');
      printf("\r*");
}
terminal() /* terminal mode, no text */
{
  int in;
    while(1)
      {
        if(miready())
          putchar(MOD_RDATA);
        if(kbhit())
          {
            if(echoflg)
              in = getchar();
            else
              in = getch();
            if(in == SPECIAL)
              return;
            else
              send(in);
          }
      }
}
char *getm(line)   /* Get memory for line, store it, return pointer. */
char line[];
{
  char *p, *alloc();
  if ((p = alloc(strlen(line) + 1)) != NULL)
      strcpy(p, line);
  return(p);
}
iblock(rb, ib, cl)   /* Insert block ib into rb at cl. */
char *rb[], *ib[];
```

```
int cl;
{
   int i, j;
   j = 0;
   if (rb[cl]) {
      for (i = 0; ib[i]; i++)
         ;
      j = (nlines - cl) * 2;
      movmem (&rb[cl], &rb[cl+i], j + 2);
   }
   for (i = 0; ib[i]; i++, cl++)
      rb[cl] = ib[i];
   if(!j) rb[cl] = NULL;
   nlines += i;
   return cl;   /* Return new current line. */
}
```

9

Sorting

A commonly needed set of programs are those that sort a set of entries (numbers, lines, words) into a given order. For example, game playing programs need some way to sort the possible outcomes so that an "intelligent" choice can be made. Obviously any data base system or mailing label program can make good use of sorting techniques. This chapter will present four tools for sorting.

Sorts may be classified in a two-by-two matrix of complexity versus efficiency. As the table below indicates, you trade complexity for efficiency. Highly efficient sorting algorithms are also highly complex to program.

SORTING METHODS: COMPLEXITY VS. EFFICIENCY (SPEED)

Efficiency	Complexity of Algorithm		
	Low	Medium	High
Low	shuttle bubble modified bubble		
Medium	Shell sort	Quicksort Tree sort	
High			Linear-time

Sorts can also be classified on the basis of where the sorting is accomplished. Internal sorts, which operate wholly within memory, are very fast (relative to external sorts) but are constrained by the memory limitations of the computer. External sorts operate with the use of external buffer or temporary files and are limited only by the disk storage capacity of the computer.

This chapter first presents two sort programs to illustrate the evaluation of sort algorithms and to provide a basis for experimentation on sorting algorithms. bubble.c is a simple (and slow) bubble sort program for an array of numbers. In a similar manner, Shell.c is a sample program using the Shell sort. These two internal sorts are designed to show how sorts can be incorporated into programs in a modular fashion.

The major portion of this chapter is taken up by two fully functioning software tools. alph.c is an internal sort that uses the BDS C library sort function (a Shell sort incidentally) to be the basis for a file sorting program. sort.c is a much more complex implementation of the quicksort algorithm in an external memory sort. This very rapid algorithm can operate on any size file (constrained only by disk storage limitations).

Utility/Tool

bubble.c   internal bubble sort

Usage

bubble

Function

This tool internally generates an array of random numbers and then sorts them with a bubble sort.

Example

Arrays of the following sizes are sorted in the time indicated: (the data was run on an Osborne I machine; 4MHz clock rate, Z80-A microprocessor)

Array Size # elements	Time seconds
128	2
256	13
512	53
1024	226
2048	887
4096	—

The behavior of the sort is essentially quadratic. A file of size 2n (e.g., 1024 elements at 53 seconds) takes approximately 4n the length of the original n element file (512 elements in 13 seconds).

IMPLEMENTATION NOTES

1. Conceptually the bubble sort is quite simple. In fact, it is often used in introductory programming computer language courses as an assignment. The sort rearranges elements that are out of order on each pass of the inner loop. By the end of the loop, the largest element has bubbled to the top (i.e., to the highest numbered array element). The outer loop repeats this process while decreasing the array limit by one. Variations on the basic bubble sort are possible that improve its performance somewhat. Two such modifications are noted in Appendix D.

2. The bubble program uses the internal BDS C functions srand, rand, and kbhit. srand initializes the random number generator so that the numbers generated will have a known distribution. By using this same seed and by varying the sorting algorithm, we can investigate the behavior of sort programs as a function of array size. rand is a pseudorandom number generator function supplied with BDS C. kbhit simply queries the keyboard for any character. It is useful in its application of controlled pauses in programs, as here.

3. Rarely would the bubble sort be used in a program. While simple, it is quite slow and the Shell sort of Shell.c is nearly as simple with vastly improved performance.

/* bubble.c—Simple Bubble Sort */

```
#include "bdscio.h"
#define ARRAY_SIZE   8192
#define SEED   2356
/* SEED is used to guarantee that the array always */
/* has the same amount of "disorder" */
/* when we compare the speed of various sorting */
/* algorithms. */
main()
{
```

```
    int array[ARRAY_SIZE];
    int index,elements;
srand(SEED); /* Initialize random generator. */
for (index = 0; index < ARRAY_SIZE; ++index)
    array[index] = rand();
printf("Ready to sort, hit return to begin\n");
while (!kbhit())
    ;
bsort(array,index);
printf (BELL);
printf ("The array is now sorted\n");
}
/* bubble sort function */
bsort(a,n)
    int a[];
    int n;
{
int i, j, temp;
for (i = 0; i < n -1; ++i)
    for (j = i+1; j < n; ++j)
        if (a[i] > a[j])
        {
        temp = a[i];
        a[i] = a[j];
        a[j] = temp;
        }
}
```

Utility/Tool

Shell.c   internal Shell sort

Usage

Shell

Function

Internally generates an array of random numbers and then sorts them with a Shell sort.

Example

Shell sorts arrays of the following sizes are sorted in the time indicated: (The data was run on an Osborne I machine; 4MHz clock rate, Z80-A microprocessor.)

Array Size # elements	Time seconds
128	<1 (negligible)
256	2
512	7
1024	19
2048	58
4096	152
8192	393
16384	902

The speed of this sort algorithm is much improved over that of the simple bubble sort. Here we can sort approximately eight times the elements (16384) in the time bubble can sort only 2048 elements. In mathematical terms, the complexity of the Shell sort is $n\hat{\ }1.5$. (This is an improvement over the bubble sort's quadratic $n\hat{\ }2$ behavior.)

IMPLEMENTATION NOTES

1. Conceptually the Shell sort is fairly simple; in fact, its improved performance more than justifies the slightly greater complexity of its programming. (Incidentally, the Shell sort is always capitalized in honor of its originator, D. A. Shell.) The fact that it operates by dividing the initial array into smaller shells is simply an interesting coincidence. The Shell sort divides the input array into a large number of small partitions. These smaller subsets are then sorted and merged into a final, fully sorted array. Since we are always dealing with a small number of elements in the partitioned subsets, the Shell sort is not as slow for large n as is the bubble sort. A variation on the basic Shell sort is the Shell-Metzner sort (see Appendix D).

2. The Shell program uses the internal BDS C functions srand, rand, and kbhit. srand

initializes the random number generator so that the numbers generated will have a known distribution. By using this same seed and by varying the sorting algorithm, we can investigate the behavior of sort programs as a function of array size. rand is a pseudorandom number generator function supplied with BDS C. Finally, kbhit simply queries the keyboard for any character. It is useful in its application of controlled pauses in programs, as here.

3. The Shell sort is suitable for virtually all microcomputer sized internal sorts. In fact, the BDS C routine qsort which is used in our full internal sort program alph.c is a Shell sort. Large, massive files that require an external sort are best handled with a quicksort algorithm. This is done in our utility sort.c.

/* Shell.c—Internal Shell Sort */

```
#include "bdscio.h"
#define ARRAY SIZE    8192
#define SEED    2356
/* SEED is used to guarantee that the array always */
/* has the same amount of "disorder." */
main()
{
    int array[ARRAY_SIZE];
    int index,elements;
srand(SEED); /* Initialize random generator. */
for (index = 0; index < ARRAY_SIZE; ++index)
    array[index] = rand();
printf("Ready to sort, hit return to begin\n");
while (!kbhit())
    ;
shell(array,index);
printf (BELL);
printf ("The array is now sorted\n");
}
/* shell sort function */
shell(a,n)
    int a[];
```

```
  int n;
{
int gap, i, j, temp;
for (gap = n/2; gap > 0; gap /= 2)
for (i = gap; i < n; i++)
   for (j = i-gap; j >=0 && a[j]>a[j+gap]; j -= gap)
   {
   temp = a[j];
   a[j] = a[j+gap];
   a[j+gap] = temp;
   }
}
```

Utility/Tool

alph.c   internal sort for small text files

Usage

alph <input-filename> <output-filename>

Function

alph takes the input-file and produces the sorted output file. An internal sort is performed.

Example

To sort the file small.in and produce the sorted output small.out, the following command would be used:

alph small.in small.out

IMPLEMENTATION NOTES

1. alph uses the intrinsic BDS C function qsort as its main sorting routine. If you are using a different C language compiler, there are several possible routes you might

take. Firstly, qsort may be written in your dialect of C and then be added to your system library. Secondly, many C compilers (particularly on mainframe computers) allow access to FORTRAN or system libraries of functions. If your compiler allows this, it is a simple matter to modify alph to call your particular local sorting procedure.

2. The current maximum lines is set at 500. This is defined at the beginning of alph to allow easy modification.

3. alph should be used whenever the file to be sorted can fit within the microcomputer memory constraints. By operating solely in memory, it is significantly faster and simpler than sort for small files.

4. alph may also be used to test various sort algorithms. Since the sorting, per se, is isolated within qsort, it is possible to test various sorting procedures within the framework provided in alph.

/* alph.c—Internal Sort */

```c
#include "bdscio.h"
#define MAXLINES  500   /* max number of lines */
int strcmp();
char iobuf[BUFSIZ];
char *ltab[MAXLINES];
int lcount;
char *allocp;
main(argc,argv)
char **argv;
{
  int i;
  char linbuf[5000];
  if (argc != 3) exit(puts("Usage: alph <infile> <outfile>\n"));
  if (fopen(argv[1],iobuf) == ERROR)
    exit(puts("Can't open input file\n"));
  lcount = 0;
  for (i = 0; i < MAXLINES; i++)
  {
```

```
      if (!fgets(linbuf,iobuf)) break;
      if ((allocp = sbrk(strlen(linebuf) + 1)) == ERROR)
        exit(puts("Out of allocation space\n"));
      ltab[lcount++] = allocp;
      strcpy(allocp,linbuf);
    }
  fclose(iobuf);
  if (i == MAXLINES) exit(puts("Too many lines. Change MAXLINES\n"));
/* qsort does the actual sorting. */
  qsort(ltab,lcount,2,&strcmp);
  if (fcreat(argv[2],iobuf) == ERROR)
    exit(puts("Can't creat output file\n"));
  for (i = 0; i < lcount; i++)
    fputs(ltab[i],iobuf);
  putc(CPMEOF,iobuf);
  fflush(iobuf);
  fclose(iobuf);
  puts("All done.\n");
}
int strcmp(s,t)
char **s, **t;
{
  char *sl, *tl;
  sl = *s;
  tl = *t;
  int i;
  i = 0;
  while (sl[i] == tl[i])
    if (sl[i++] == '\0')
      return 0;
  return sl[i] - tl[i];
}
```

Utility/Tool

sort.c   external sort for text files

Usage

sort <input–filename> <output–filename>

Function

This tool takes the given input file (which may be of any size, limited only by disk storage capacity) and performs an external sort on it. The resulting output file is in sorted order.

Example

To sort a data file called data.in with the output to be placed in a file called sort.out:

```
sort data.in sort.out
```

Theory of Operation

The sort utility sort.c can be outlined in pseudocode (an English-like description of program operation) as shown below:

```
initialize
initial division of input file into temporary smaller files
free initial input file
open temporary files
merge files using heap structure
close files
write sorted output file
remove temporary files
```

C Function	Purpose/Function
fclout(obuf)	Generalized output file close routine.
quick(nlines)	Quicksort for character lines.
compar(lp1,lp2)	Compare function. Returns zero (0) if strings lp1 and lp2 are equal. Returns –1 if lp1 is lexically smaller. Returns 1 if lp1 is larger.

ptext(outfil)	Output text lines from line buffer linbuf onto the buffered output file outbuf.
gtext(infile)	Get text line from the buffered input file provided and place line into the line buffer linbuf.
makfil(n,obuf)	Make a temporary file with suffix number "n" and open it for output via the specified output buffer obuf.
gname(n,name)	Create temporary filename having suffix number "n". Subsidiary function used by the makfil function above.
itoa(strptr,n)	Convert integer value n to ASCII representation at string pointer strptr and return a pointer to it.
gopen(low,lim)	Open a group of temporary files with suffix "n" from low to lim.
gremov(low,lim)	Remove a group of temporary files with suffix "n" from low to lim.
fputs(s,iobuf)	Special version of the standard C function puts. fputs aborts on output error.
merge(nfiles,outfil)	Merge function for merging the temporary files infil[1] to infil[nfiles] onto the output file specified by outfil. Uses the reheap function below.
reheap(nf)	Place the linbuf[linptr[1]] in the proper place on the heap.

IMPLEMENTATION NOTES

1. The constants used by the program are defined at the beginning. Special note should be made of MAXPTR and LOGPTR. The two values are related and should be changed in unison with each other.

2. Sort is based on the RATFOR version of SORT in Kernighan and Plauger's *Software Tools* (KERN76, Appendix D). Details of its operation may be found there.

3. The maximum file that may be sorted is limited by the disk capacity, not the memory capacity of the machine. In general, sort requires approximately three

times the disk storage of the given input file. This extra disk space is required for the temporary work files created by the program. Thus, on a 64k microcomputer with 300k disk drives, the largest file that can be sorted is approximately 100k (1/3 of disk capacity).

/* sort.c—External Sort Program */

```c
/* Main variables have been made external; this is pretty much in */
/* line with the RATFOR call-by-name convention anyway. */
/* A lot of disk space is required, up to around three times the length */
/* of the file being sorted. This program is intended for files */
/* bigger than memory; simpler, faster sorts can be implemented for */
/* really short files (like alph.c) */
/* Compile and link: */
/   A>cc sort.c -e2800 -o */
/   A>12 sort */
/   (or ...) */
/   A>cc sort.c -e2B00 -o */
/   A>clink sort */
#include "bdscio.h"
#define VERBOSE 1                       /* Give running account of file activity. */
#define MAXLINE 200                     /* Longest line we want to deal with. */
#define NBUFS 7                         /* max number of open buffered files */
#define MAXPTR 5000                     /* max number of lines (set for dict) */
#define  MERGEORDER  (NBUFS-1) /* max number of intermediate files
                                   to merge */
#define NAMESIZE 20                     /* max filename size */
#define LOGPTR 14                /* smallest value >= log (base 2) of MAXPTR */
#define EOS '\0'                        /* string termination character */
#define FILE struct _buf
#define stderr 4
#define fputc putc
char name[NAMESIZE], name2[NAMESIZE + 10];
FILE buffers[NBUFS + 1];   /* up to NBUFS general-purpose buffered files */
FILE *infil[MERGEORDER + 1]; /* tmp file ptrs for sort operation */
unsigned linptr[MAXPTR + 1], nlines;
int temp;
```

```
unsigned maxtext;   /* max number of chars in main text buffer */
char *linbuf;        /* text area starts after this variable */
main(argc,argv)
char **argv;
{
   FILE *infile, *outfile; /* main input and output streams */
   FILE *tmpfile;
   int makfil( ), min( ), gopen( ), gremov( );
   int gtext( );
   unsigned high, lim, low, t;
   linbuf = endext( );   /* start of text buffer area */
   maxtext = topofmem( ) - endext( ) - 500;
   tmpfile = buffers[0];
   if (argc != 3)
      exit(puts("Usage: sort <infile> <outfile>\n"));
   infile = buffers[1];
   if (fopen(argv[1], infile) == ERROR)
   {
      puts("Can't open"); puts(argv[1]; exit(-1);
   }
#if VERBOSE
   fputs("Beginning initial formation run\n",stderr);
#endif
   high = 0;   /* initial formation of runs */
   do {
      t = gtext(infile);
      quick(nlines);
      high++;
      makfil(high,tmpfile);
      ptext(tmpfile);
      fclout(tmpfile);
   } while (t != NULL);
   fclose(infile);   /* Free up the input file buffer. */
#if VERBOSE
   fputs("Beginning merge operation\n",stderr);
#endif
   for (low = 1; low < high; low += MERGEORDER)   /* Merge. */
   {
```

```
      lim = min(low + MERGEORDER - 1, high);
      gopen(low, lim);   /* Open files. */
      high++;
      makfil(high, tmpfile);
      merge(lim - low + 1, tmpfile);
      fclout(tmpfile);   /* Terminate, flush, and close file. */
      gremov(low, lim);
   }
      /* Now write the sorted output file: */
   fputs("Merge complete.\n",stderr);
   gname(high, name);   /* Create name of result file. */
   infile = buffers[0];
   unlink(argv[2]);   /* Remove any old copy of result file. */
   if (rename(name,argv[2]) == ERROR)
   {
      puts("An error occurred in renaming the output file from ");
      puts(name; puts(" to "); puts(argv[2]);
   }
}
fclout(obuf)
FILE *obuf;
{
   putc(CPMEOF,obuf);
   fflush(obuf);
   fclose(obuf);
}
/* Quick: Quicksort for character lines */
quick(nlines)
unsigned nlines;
{
   unsigned i,j, lv[LOGPTR + 1], p, pivlin, uv[LOGPTR + 1];
   int compar();
   lv[1] = 1;
   uv[1] = nlines;
   p = 1;
   while (p > 0)
      if (lv[p] >= uv[p]) /* only one element in this subset */
         p--;   /* Pop stack. */
```

```
else
{
  i = lv[p] - 1;
  j = uv[p];
  pivlin = linptr[j];   /* pivot line */
  while (i < j)
  {
    for (i++; compar(linptr[i],pivlin) < 0; i++)
      ;
    for (j--; j > i; j--)
      if (compar(linptr[j], pivlin) <= 0)
        break;
    if (i < j) /* out of order pair */
    {
      temp = linptr[i];
      linptr[i] = linptr[j];
      linptr[j] = temp;
    }
  }
j = uv[p];   /* move pivot to position 1 */
temp = linptr[i];
linptr[i] = linptr[j];
linptr[j] = temp;
if ( ((i - lv[p]) < (uv[p] - i))
  {
    lv[p + 1] = lv[p];
    uv[p + 1] = i - 1;
    lv[p] = i + 1;
  }
  else
  {
    lv[p + 1] = i + 1;
    uv[p + 1] = uv[p];
    uv[p] = i - 1;
  }
  p++;
}
return;
```

```
}
/* Compar: Compare two strings; return 0 if equal, -1 if first */
/* is lexically smaller, or 1 if first is bigger. */
int compar(lp1, lp2)
unsigned lp1, lp2;
{
    unsigned i, j;
    for (i = lp1, j = lp2; linbuf[i] == linbuf[j]; i++, j++)
    {
      if (linbuf[i] == EOS)
        return 0;
    }
   return (linbuf[i] < linbuf[j]) ? -1 : 1;
}
/* Ptext: */
/* Output text lines from linbuf onto the buffered */
/* output file given. */
ptext(outfil)
FILE *outfil;
{
   int i;
   for (i = 1; i <= nlines; i++) {
     if (fputs(&linbuf[linptr[i]], outfil) == ERROR) {
       fputs("Error writing output file..disk full?\n",
          stderr);
       exit(-1);
     }
   }
   return 0;
}
/* Gtext: Get text lines from the buffered input file provided, and */
/* place them into linbuf. */
int gtext(infile)
FILE *infile;
{
   unsigned lbp, len;
   nlines = 0;
   lbp = 1;
```

```
  do {
    if ( (len = fgets(&linbuf[lbp], infile)) == NULL)
      break;
    len = strlen(&linbuf[lbp]);
    nlines++;
    linptr[nlines] = lbp;
    lbp += len + 1;
  } while ( lbp < (maxtext - MAXLINE) && nlines < MAXPTR);
  return len;   /* Return 0 if done with file. */
}
/* Makfil: Make a temporary file having suffix "n" and open it for */
/* output via the supplied buffer */
FILE *makfil(n,obuf) /* make temp file having suffix 'n' */
int n;
FILE *obuf;
{
  FILE *fp;
  char name[20];
  gname(n,name);
  if (fcreat(name,obuf) == ERROR) {
    puts("Can't create "); puts(name); exit(-1);
  }
  return 0;
}
/* Gname: Make temporary filename having suffix "n." */
char *gname(n,name)
char *name;
int n;
{
  char tmptext[10];
  strcpy(name,"TEMP");   /* Create "TEMPn.$$$." */
  strcat(name,itoa(temptext,n));
  strcat(name,".$$$");
  return name;   /* Return a pointer to it. */
}
/* Itoa: Convert integer value n into ASCII representation at strptr */
/* and return a pointer to it. */
char *itoa(strptr,n)
```

```
char *strptr;
int n;
{
    int length;
    if (n < 0)
    {
        *strptr++ = '-';
        strptr++;
        n = -n;
    }
    if (n < 10)
    {
        *strptr++ = (n + '0');
        *strptr = '\0';
        return strptr -1;
    }
    else
    {
        length = strlen(itoa(strptr, n/10));
        itoa(&strptr[length], n % 10);
        return strptr;
    }
}
/* Gopen: Open group of files low...lim. */
gopen(low, lim)
int lim, low;
{
    int i;
#if VERBOSE
    fprintf(stderr,"Opening temp files %d-%d\n",low,lim);
#endif
    for (i = 1; i <= (lim - low + 1); i ++)
    {
        gname(low + i - 1, name);
        if (fopen(name, buffers[i]) == ERROR)
        {
            puts("Can't open: "); puts(name); exit(-1);;
        }
```

```
      infil[i] = &buffers[i];
   }
}
/* Remove group of files low...lim. */
/* (Should use "close" instead of "fabort" for MP/M II.) */
gremov(low, lim)
int lim, low;
{
   int i;
#if VERBOSE
   fprintf(stderr,"Removing temp files %d-%d\n",low,lim);
#endif
   for (i = 1; i <= (lim - low + 1); i++)
   {
      fabort(infil[i]->_fd);        /* Forget about the file */
      gname(low + i - 1, name);
      unlink(name);                 /* and physically remove it. */
   }
}
/* Fputs: special version that aborts on output error: */
fputs(s,iobuf)
char *s;
FILE *iobuf;
{
   char c;
   while (c = *s++)
   {
      if (c == '\n') putc('\r',iobuf);
      if (putc(c,iobuf) == ERROR)
      {
         fputs("Error on file output\n",stderr);
         exit(ERROR);
      }
   }
   return OK;
}
/* Merge: Merge infil[1]...infil[nfiles] onto outfil. */
merge(nfiles, outfil)
```

```
FILE *outfil;
{
    char *fgets();
    int i, inf, lbp, lp1, nf;
    lbp = 1;
    nf = 0;
    for (i = 1; i <= nfiles; i++) /* Get one line from each file. */
        if (fgets(&linbuf[lbp], infil[i] != NULL)
        {
            nf++;
            linptr[nf] = lbp;
            lbp += MAXLINE: /* Leave room for largest line. */
        }
    quick(nf);          /* Make initial heap. */
    while (nf > 0) {
        lp1 = linptr[1];
        fputs(&linbuf[lp1], outfil);
        inf = lp1 / MAXLINE + 1; /* Compute file index. */
        if (fgets(&linbuf[lp1],infil[inf]) == NULL)
        {
            linptr[1] = linptr[nf];
            nf--;
        }
        reheap(nf);
    }
    return;
}
/* Reheap: Propagate linbuf[linptr[1]] to proper place in heap. */
reheap(nf)
unsigned nf;
{
    unsigned i,j;
    for (i = 1; (i + i) <= nf; i = j)
    {
        j = i + i;
        if (j < nf && compar(linptr[j], linptr[j + 1]) > 0)
            j++;
        if (compar(linptr[i], linptr[j]) <= 0)
```

```
        break;
    temp = linptr[i];
    linptr[i] = linptr[j];
    linptr[j] = temp;
  }
  return;
}
```

10
OTHELLO: A Game Program

All work and no play makes Jack and Jane dull!

This final chapter of the book is unabashedly fun. It presents a game program to play Othello. It needs no other justification. Technically, this program is a good example of:

1. structured, hierarchical function organization
2. arrays as formal parameters
3. use of the qsort library function

The object of the game is for two players to alternate placing their marker somewhere on an 8 × 8 grid, so that at least one of the opponent's pieces becomes surrounded by the moving player's pieces, causing the flanked pieces to flip color and belong to the moving player. After 60 moves have been played (or if no player has a legal move left), the player with the most of his own pieces on the board wins.

The playing pieces are "*" and "@". You may choose to play either "*" or "@" for the first game; thereafter, you and the computer will alternate going first for each game. Whoever goes first always plays "*".

You enter a move as a two-digit number, each digit being from 1 to 8, first digit representing row and second representing column. For example: if playing "*", your first move might be 46, meaning the 4th row down, 6th position across.

As an alternative to entering a move, one of the following commands may be typed:

g	Causes computer to play both sides until game is over.
a	Causes computer to print out an analysis of each of your possible moves. A letter from A to Z will appear at each of your legal move positions, where A is the machine's opinion of an excellent move and Z is not.
hn	Sets handicap. n is 1,2,3, or 4. If n is positive, gives n free pieces to the computer. If n is negative, gives *you* the free pieces.
f	Forfeit the current move. This happens automatically if you have no legal moves.
q	Quit the current game.
b	Prints out board again.
s	Prints out the score, and tells who is winning.

Utility/Tool

othello	A program to play the game of Othello.

Usage

othello	Clears the screen and draws a representation of the game board.

Function

Othello is a fun game to play and provides an excellent antidote to the very complex and serious programs of previous chapters.

Theory of Operation

The program for playing the game of Othello can be outlined in pseudocode (an English-like description of program operation) as shown below:

```
initialize
clear board
```

```
print board
play game until done
check for command
B:   print board
S:   print score
Q:   quit
H:   set handicap level
A:   Analyze position
G:   solitaire version for computer
M:   enter move
F:   forfeit
```

C Function	Purpose/Function
game(b,n)	Heart of the program; plays the game.
prtscr(b)	Print current score.
getmov(i,j)	Get move or command option.
ask(s)	Generalized user query function.
skipbl( )	Skip blanks.
chkmvs(b,p)	Check for valid moves. Uses the functions chkmov and chkmov1.
notake(b,p,o,e,x,y)	Returns value depending on the status of the move for taking opposing pieces.
putmov(b,p,i,j)	Put move onto board.
my_mov(b,p,o,e,m,n)	Calculate options for computer move.
analyze(b,p,o,e)	Analyze options. Fill board with value of each possible square. An A signals an especially strong move while a Z indicates a particularly poor option.
s_move(b,p,o,e,i,j)	Analyze edges (sides) of the board.
cmpmov(a,b)	Compare two possible moves and return better move.
clrbrd(b)	Clear board and initialize display.
prtboard(b)	Print board.
cpybrd(a,b)	Copy board a to board b.
cntbrd(b,p)	Count board.

/* othello—Game Program to Play Othello */

```c
#include "bdscio.h"
#define BLACK '*'
#define WHITE '@'
#define EMPTY '_'
int handicap;
char selfplay;    /* true if computer playing with itself */
int h[4][2];      /* handicap position table */
char mine, his;   /* who has black (*) and white (@) in current game */
char mefirst;      /* true if computer goes first in current game */
main(argc,argv)
int argc;
char **argv;
{
  char b[8][8];
  int i;
  h[0][0] = h[0][1] = h[2][0] = h[3][1] = 0;
  h[1][0] = h[1][1] = h[2][1] = h[3][0] = 7;
  printf("\nWelcome to the BDS C OTHELLO program!\n");
  printf("\nNOTE: '*' always goes first...Good luck!!!\n\n");
  srand1("Do you want to go first?");
  if (toupper(getchar()) == 'Y')
    mefirst = 0;
  else
    mefirst = 1;
  printf("\n\n");
do {
  clrbrd(b);
  prtbrd(b);
  i = game(b,4);
  mefirst = !mefirst;
  if (i==4) break;
  if (i=='Q') continue;
  printf("\n");
  i = prtscr(b);
  if (i>0) printf(" You won by %d\n",i);
```

```
     else if (i<0) printf(" You lost by %d\n",-i);
     else printf(" A draw\n");
     } while (ask("Another game? ")=='Y');
}
game(b,n)
char b[8][8];
int n;
{
   char c;
   int ff;
   int i,j;
   handicap = 0;
   selfplay = ' ';
   ff=0;
   if (mefirst) {
      mine = BLACK; his = WHITE;
      printf("\nI go first:\n\n");
}
else {
   mine = WHITE; his = BLACK;
   printf("\nYou go first:\n\n");
}
while(1) {
   if (cntbrd(b,EMPTY)==0) return 'D';
   if (cntbrd(b,EMPTY)==60 && mine == BLACK) goto Istart;
   if (chkmvs(b,his)==0) {
      printf(!mefirst ? "Forfeit" : " ...Forfeit\n");
      ff |= 1;
      }
   else switch (c = getmov(&i,&j)) {
   case 'B': prtbrd(b); continue;
   case 'S': i= prtscr(b);
      if (i>0) printf(" You're winning\n");
      else if (i<0)printf(" You're losing!\n");
      else putchar('\n');
      continue;
   case 'Q': case 4: return c;
   case 'H': if (n>abs(handicap)+4)
```

```
         printf("Illegal!\n");
      else for (j=0; i!=0; j++) {
      b[h[j][0]][h[j][1]]= i>0?BLACK:WHITE;
      handicap += i>0 ? 1 : -1;
      ++n;
      i += i>0 ? -1 : 1;
      }
      prtbrd(b); continue;
   case 'A': analyze(b,his,mine,EMPTY);
      continue;
   case 'G': my_mov(b,his,mine,EMPTY),&i,&j);
   case 'M': if (chkmov(b,his,i,j)>0) {
      printf(!mefirst ? "%ld-%ld" : " ...%ld-%ld\n",
         i+1,j+1);
      putmov(b,his,i,j);
      }
      else {
         printf("Illegal!\n");
         continue;
         }
      break;
   case 'F': if (n>abs(handicap)+4) {
      printf ("Illegal!\n");
      continue;
      }
      else printf(!mefirst ? "Forfeit" :
         " ...Forfeit\n");
      }

Istart: if (cntbrd(b,EMPTY) == 0) return 'D';
   if (chkmvs(b,mine)==0) {
   printf(!mefirst ? "...Forfeit\n": "Forfeit...\n");
   ff|=2;
   }
   else {
   my_mov(b,mine,his,EMPTY,&i,&j);
   printf(!mefirst ? "...%ld-%ld\n" : "%ld-%ld...\n",
      i+1,j+1);
   putmov(b,mine,i,j);
```

OTHELLO: A Game Program   281

```
      ++n;
       }
    if (ff==3 || n>64) return 'D';
    if (!(ff & 1)) prtbrd(b);
    ff = 0;
    }
}
prtscr(b)
char *b;
{
  int i,j;
  printf("%1d-%1d",i = cntbrd(b,his),j=cntbrd(b,mine));
  return i-j;
}
char getmov(i,j)
int *i, *j;
{
  char a,c;
  int n;
  char *p;
  char skipbl();
  if (selfplay == 'G') {
    if (!kbhit()) return 'G';
    selfplay = ' ';
    getchar();
  }
  printf("Move: ");
  while(1) switch (c=skipbl()) {
    case '\n': printf("Move? "); continue;
    case 'G': if ((c = skipbl()) != '\n')
        goto flush;
      selfplay='G';
      return 'G';
    case 'B': case 'S': case 'Q':
    case 'F': case 'A':
      a=c;
      if (( c = skipbl()) != '\n') goto flush;
      return a;
    case 'H': if ((a=c=skipbl()) == EMPTY)
```

```
          c=getchar();
        if (c<'1' || c >'4' || skipbl() !='\n')
          goto flush;
        *i = a== EMPTY? -(c-'0') : (c-'0');
        return 'H';
    case 4: return c;
    default: if (c<'1' || c>'8') goto flush;
        *i = c-'1';
        c = skipbl();
        if (c<'1' || c>'8') goto flush;
        *j = c- '1';
        if ((c=skipbl()) == '\n') return 'M';
    flush:while (c != '\n' && c != 4)
          c=getchar();
        if (c==4) return c;
        printf ("Huh?? ");
    }
}
char ask(s)
char *s;
{
    char a,c;
    printf ("%s ",s);
    a=skipbl();
    while (c != '\n' && c != 4) c= getchar();
    return a;
}
char skipbl()
{
    char c;
    while ((c = toupper(getchar())) == ' ' || c=='\t');
    return c;
}
chkmvs(b,p)
char b[8][8];
char p;
{
int i,j,k;
```

```
k=0;
for (i=0; i<8; i++) for (j=0; j<8; j++)
k += chkmov(b,p,i,j);
return k;
}
chkmov(b,p,x,y)
char b[8][8],p;
int x,y;
{
  if (b[x][y] != EMPTY) return 0;
  returnchkmv1(b,p,x,y,0,1) + chkmv1(b,p,x,y,1,0) +
   chkmv1(b,p,x,y,0,-1)+ chkmv1(b,p,x,y,-1,0)+
   chkmv1(b,p,x,y,1,1) + chkmv1(b,p,x,y,1,-1)+
   chkmv1(b,p,x,y,-1,1)+ chkmv1(b,p,x,y,-1,-1);
}
chkmv1(b,p,x,y,m,n)
char b[8][8],p;
int x,y,m,n;
{
  int k;
  k=0;
  while ((x += m) >= 0 && x < 8 && (y += n) >= 0 && y<8)
  {
   if (b[x][y]==EMPTY) return 0;
   if (b[x][y]== p ) return k;
   if (x==0 || x==7 || y==0 || y==7)
      k += 10;
    else k++;
  }
  return 0;
}
notake(b,p,o,e,x,y)
char b[8][8];
char p,o,e;
int x,y;
{
  return notak1(b,p,o,e,x,y,0,1)&&
    notak1(b,p,o,e,x,y,1,1)&&
```

```
        notak1(b,p,o,e,x,y,1,0)&&
        notak1(b,p,o,e,x,y,1,-1);
}
notak1(b,p,o,e,x,y,m,n)
char b[8][8],p,o,e;
int x,y,m,n;
{
    int c1,c2;
    c1 = notak2(b,p,o,e,x,y,m,n);
    c2 = notak2(b,p,o,e,x,y,-m,-n);
    return !(c1==o && c2==e || c1==e && c2==o);
}
notak2(b,p,o,e,x,y,m,n)
char b[8][8],p,o,e;
int x,y,m,n;
{
    x += m; y +=n;
    if (x>=0 && x<=7 && y>=0 && y<=7)
        while(b[x][y] == 0) {
        x += m; y += n;
        if (x<0 || x>7 || y<0 || y>7 || b[x][y]==e)
            return o;
        }
    while (x>=0 && x<=7 && y>=0 && y<=7 && b[x][y]==p)
        { x +=m; y+=n; }
    if (x<0 || x>7 || y<0 || y>7) return p;
    return b[x][y];
}
putmov(b,p,x,y)
char b[8][8];
char p;
int x,y;
{
    int i,j;
    b[x][y] = p;
    for (i= -1; i<=1; i++) for (j= -1; j<=1; j++) {
        if ((i != 0 || j!=0)&&chkmv1(b,p,x,y,i,j)>0)
            putmv1(b,p,x,y,i,j);
```

```
      }
}
putmvl(b,p,x,y,m,n)
char b[8][8];
char p;
int x,y,m,n;
{
    while ((x += m) >= 0 && x<8 && (y += n)>= 0 && y<8) {
        if (b[x][y] == EMPTY || b[x][y] == p) return;
        b[x][y] = p;
    }
}
struct mt {
        int x;
        int y;
        int c;
        int s;
    };
my_mov(b,p,o,e,m,n)
char b[8][8],p;
int *m, *n;
{
    struct mt t[64];
    int i,k;
    int cmpmov();
    k = fillmt(b,p,o,e,t);
    if (!k) return 0;
    qsort (&t, k, 8, &cmpmov);
    for (i=1; i<k; i++)
        if (t[i].s != t[0].s || t[i].c != t[0].c)
            break;
    k = rand() %i;
    *m = t[k].x;
    *n = t[k].y;
    return 1;
}
analyze(b,p,o,e)
char b[8][8], p,o,e;
```

```
{
    struct mt t[64];
    char a[8][8];
    int i,k,c;
    k = fillmt(b,p,o,e,t);
    cpybrd(a,b);
    for (i=0; i<k; i++)
        a[t[i].x][t[i].y] = ((c = 'F' - t[i].s) <= 'Z')?c:'Z';
    prtbrd(a);
}
fillmt(b,p,o,e,t)
char b[8][8],p,o,e;
struct mt t[64];
{
    int i,j,k;
    k = 0;
    for (i=0; i<8; i++) for (j=0; j<8; j++)
        if (t[k].c = chkmov(b,p,i,j)) {
            t[k].x =i;
            t[k].y =j;
            t[k].s = s_move(b,p,o,e,i,j);
            ++k;
        }
    return k;
}
s_move(b,p,o,e,i,j)
char b[8][8], p, o, e;
int i,j;
{
    char a[8][8];
    int ok,s,k,l,side,oside;
    int c,dkl;
    cpybrd(a,b);
    putmov(a,p,i,j);
    side = 0;
    if (i==0 || i==7) side++;
    if (j==0 || j==7) side ++;
    s = 0;
    ok = 0;
```

```
        if (side==2 || notake(b,p,o,e,i,j)) ok++;
        oside = 0;
        for (k=0; k<8; k++) for (l=0; l<8; l++)
        {
            c=chkmov(a,o,k,l);
            if (c==0) continue;
            dkl = 1;
            if (k==0 || k==7) { dkl+=2; oside|=4;}
            if (l==0 || l==7) {dkl+=2; oside|=4; }
            if (dkl==5) {dkl = 10; oside |= 16; }
                else if (!notake(a,o,p,e,k,l))
                    continue;
            oside |= 1;
            s -= dkl;
            if (c>=10) { s -= 4; oside |= 8; }
            }
        if (s< -oside) s= -oside;
        if (side>0) return s+side-7+10*ok;
        if (i==1 || i==6) {s--; side++;}
        if (j==1 || j==6) {s--; side++;}
        if (side>0) return s;
        if (i==2 || i==5) s++;
        if (j==2 || j==5) s++;
        return s;
}
cmpmov(a,b)
struct mt *a, *b;
{
    if((*a).s > (*b).s) return -1;
    if((*a).s < (*b).s) return 1;
    if((*a).c > (*b).c) return -1;
    if((*a).c < (*b).c) return 1;
    return 0;
}
clrbrd(b)
char b[8][8];
{
    int i,j;
    for (i=0; i<8; i++)
```

```
    for (j=0; j<8; j++)
        b[i][j]= EMPTY;
   b[3][3] = b[4][4] = BLACK;
   b[3][4] = b[4][3] = WHITE;
}
prtbrd(b)
char b[8][8];
{
   int i,j;
   printf(" 1 2 3 4 5 6 7 8\n");
   for (i=0; i<8; i++) {
     printf("%2d",i+1);
     for (j=0; j<8; j++) {
       putchar (' ');
       putchar(b[i][j]);
     }
     putchar('\n');
   }
   putchar('\n');
}
cpybrd(a,b)
char *a, *b;
{
int i;
i=64;
while (i--)
*a++ = *b++;
}
cntbrd(b,p)
char *b, p;
{
   int i,j;
   i= 64; j=0;
   while (i--)
     if (*b++ == p) ++j;
   return (j);
}
```

Appendix A
C Sources

Books, periodicals, and newsletters are all sources of material on C. These are listed below along with sources of public domain software. Periodical articles are cross indexed by author and by subject.

Books

The books listed below are all valuable to the C programmer. The works by Plum concerning standards and the Bell Laboratory materials are perhaps the most specialized. With the increasing popularity of C, the majority of these books are available in bookstores that carry computer-related books and magazines.

BELL83 Bell Laboratories. *Unix Programmer's Manual.* 2 volumes. (New York: Holt, Rinehart and Winston, 1983).

CHIR84 Chirlian, Paul M. *Introduction to C.* (Beaverton, OR: Matrix Publishers, Inc., 1984).

FEUE82 Feuer, Alan R. *The C Puzzle Book.* (Englewood Cliffs, NJ: Prentice-Hall, 1982).

HANC82 Hancock, Les, and Morris Krieger. *The C Primer.* (New York: Byte/McGraw-Hill, 1982).

HEND84 Hendrix, James E. *The Small-C Handbook.* (Reston, VA: Reston Publishing Company, 1984).

HUNT84 Hunter, Bruce. *Understanding C.* (Berkeley, CA: Sybex, 1984).

KERN78 Kernighan, Brian W., and Dennis M. Ritchie. *The C Programming Language.* (Englewood Cliffs, NJ: Prentice-Hall, 1978).

Alpha Omega Computer Systems P.O. Box U Corvallis, OR 97339	CP/M	small-C derivative
BD Software P.O. Box 2368 Brighton, MA 02135	CP/M	subset with extensive source included with compiler
Caprock Systems P.O. Box 13814 Arlington, TX 76013	IBM PC	small-C derivative
Carousel Microtools 609 Kearney Street El Cerrito, CA 94530	CP/M, MSDOS, IBM PC	software tools for microcomputers
The Code Works 5266 Hollister #224 Santa Barbara, CA 93110	CP/M	Q/C: Unix/C subset; includes complete source code
Computer Innovations 980 Shrewsbury Avenue Tinton Falls, NJ 07724	MSDOS, CP/M-86, IBM PC	full C for 16-bit environment
Control-C Software 6441 S.W. Canyon Court Portland, OR 97221	CP/M-86, IBM PC	full C for CP/M-86
Creative Solutions 21 Elm Avenue Box D4 Richford, VT 05476	IBM PC	screen management tools for the PC; windows, etc.
c-Systems P.O. Box 3253 Fullerton, CA 92634	IBM PC	full compiler; excellent c-Window debugger

C Ware P.O. Box 710097 San Jose, CA 95171	IBM PC	DeSmet C—full C; includes screen editor
Datalight 11557 8th Avenue, N.E. Seattle, WA 94620	IBM PC	Small-C and CBUG debugger for small-C
Digital Research P.O. Box 579 Pacific Grove, CA 93950	CP/M-86	full C; includes "lint"-like facility
Ecosoft 6413 N. College Avenue Indianapolis, IN 46220	CP/M, CP/M-86	full C compiler
Elfin Systems 265 Nogal Drive Santa Barbara, CA 93110	CP/M	subset (no floating point) with C toolset
Greenleaf Software 2101 Hickory Road Carrollton, TX 75006	IBM PC	extensive (200 function) library for IBM PC C compilers
InfoSoft 25 Sylvan Road South Westport, CT 06880	CDOS, special O/S	subset C with C toolset included
Intermetrics Inc. Software Products Division 733 Concord Avenue Cambridge, MA 02138	VAX or VMS	IntraC VAX based cross-compiler for 8086 or 68000
Introl Corp. 647 W. Virginia St. Milwaukee, WI 53204	6809 systems	C/6809 subset C
ISE-USA 85 W. Algonquin Rd., Suite 400 Arlington Heights, IL 60005	CP/M, PCDOS, TRSDOS,MSDOS	subset C for wide variety of machines

J. E. Hendrix Box 8378 University, MS 38677-8378	CP/M, NorthStar	small-C (v. 2), small-tools; small-VOS
JMI Software Consultants 1422 Easton Road Roslyn, PA 19001	numerous	Portable C library; C Executive (multi- tasking); Basic-to-C translator
Kadak Products Ltd. 206-1847 W. Broadway Ave. Vancouver, B.C. Canada V6J 1Y5	CP/M	real-time C library for Whitesmith
Knowology P.O. Box 283 Wilsonville, OR 97070	CP/M	Unica—software shell
LanTech Systems 9635 Wendell Road Dallas, TX 75243	IBM PC	uNETix—UNIX for the PC
Lifeboat Associates 1651 Third Avenue New York, NY 10028	MSDOS, CP/M-86	Lattice C; toolsets and utilities for 16-bit environment
LSI Japan Co. Ltd. 2-24-9 Yoyogi Shibuya-Ku Tokyo (151) Japan	CP/M	subset C from Japan
Manx Software Box 55 Shrewsbury, NJ 07701	Apple Dos, CP/M,CP/M-86, HDOS, IBM PC	complete C for a wide variety of machines
Mark Williams Co. 1430 W. Wrightwood Ave. Chicago, IL 60614	IBM PC	full C and Unix-like Coherent O/S
Microsoft Corp. 10700 Northrup Way Bellevue, WA 98004	MSDOS	full C for IBM PC

New Generation Systems 1800 Michael Faraday Dr. Suite 206 Reston, VA 22090	CP/M	MicroTools for CP/M; MicroShell
Novum Organum 29 Egerton Road Arlington, MA 02174	IMB PC	C Building Blocks (function library)
Programmer's Shop 128-M Rockland Street Hanover, MA 02339		dealer for virtually all C compilers
Rational Systems P.O. Box 480 Natick, MA 01760	numerous	integrated C com- piler environment for CPM-86, PCDOS, or MSDOS
Software Kinetics, Ltd. 3 Amberwood Crescent Nepean, Ontario K2E 7L1 Canada	Dec Pro 350, IBM PC	UNIX for big micros
Software Toolworks 15233 Ventura Blvd. Suite 1118 Sherman Oaks, CA 91403	CP/M HDOS	best price/perform- ance C available; MATHPAK available
Standard DataCom Inc. 1550 San Francisco Street Suite 6195 San Francisco, CA 94109	MSDOS PCDOS	X-Shell software tools
Supersoft P.O. Box 1628 Champaign, IL 61820	CP/M, CP/M-86 MSDOS PCDOS	full C
Sure-Wing Systems P.O. Box 20008 Oakland, CA 94620	IBM PC	full C for IBM PC

Telecon Systems 1155 Meridian Ave., Suite 218 San Jose, CA 95125	CP/M,CP/M-86, RT-11, RSX-11, PCDOS,MSODS	full C for virtually any system
tiny-C Associates P.O. Box 269 Holmdel, NJ 07733	8080, PDP-11, HDOS, 6809, TRSDOS	unique tiny-C inter- active C-like product; excellent documen- tation
Unipress Software 2025 Lincoln Highway Suite 312 Edison, NJ 08817	Apple LISA	full C for Lisa
Unisource Software 71 Bent Street Cambridge, MA 02141	IBM PC	Unix/C for IBM PC
Vandata 17544 Midvale Ave. North Suite 107 Seattle, WA 98133	VAX, RSX-11	C cross compiler
Western Wares Box C Norwood, CO 81423	CP/M	C screen editor and other utilities (with source code)
Whitesmith's Ltd. 97 Lowell Road Concord, MA 01742	CP/M UNIX,VAX,etc.	full C and Idris, writing tools, etc.
XOR Corporation 5421 Opportunity Court Minnetonka, MN 55343	IBM PC	C Tools for C86 on IBM

C Software (Source Code Included)

The firms listed below provide (generally for very nominal fees) C programs and utilities that include source code. This allows modification of programs and provides an excellent means of learning C programming techniques and skills.

Algorithmic Technology, Inc.
P.O. Box 278
Exton, PA 19341-0278

Blaise Computing
2034 Blake Street
Berkeley, CA 94704

C Source
12801 Frost Road
Kansas City, MO 64138

C Users Group
415 E. Euclid
McPherson, KS 67460

Dedicated Micro Systems
Box 287
Yates Center, KS 66783

Dr. Dobb's Journal
M&T Publishing Company
2464 Embarcadero Way
Palo Alto, CA 94303

Greenleaf Software
2101 Hickory Road
Carrollton, TX 75006

J. E. Hendrix
Box 8378
University, MS 38677-8378

JMI Software Consultants
1422 Easton Road
Roslyn, PA 19001

Programmer's Shop
128-M Rockland Street
Hanover, MA 02339

Que Corporation
7960 Castleway Drive
Indianapolis, IN 46250

Ed Ream
1850 Summit Avenue
Madison, WI 53705

Software Toolworks
15233 Ventura Blvd., Suite 1118
Sherman Oaks, CA 91403

Western Wares Software
Box C
Norwood, CO 81423

XOR Corporation
5421 Opportunity Court
Minnetonka, MN 55343

C Articles

Listed below are articles about C programming, software tools and utilities written in C. The topical index following the article list provides a guide to the subjects of the articles. More details concerning the articles themselves may be obtained from my previous annotated bibliographic articles:

WARD83 Ward, Terry A. "An Annotated Bibliography on C." *Byte* 8(8) (August 1983).

WARD84 "A Guide to Resources for the C Programmer," *Dr. Dobb's Journal* (forthcoming, November 1984).

ALLI80A Allison, Dennis. "A Monthly Algorithm Column," *Dr. Dobb's Journal* 44:44-45 (January 1980).

ALLI80B Allison, Dennis. "A Monthly Algorithm Column," *Dr. Dobb's Journal* 46:47-48 (August 1980).

ALLI80C Allison, Dennis. "A Monthly Algorithm Column," *Dr. Dobb's Journal* 48:44-45 (August 1980).

ANDE80B Anderson, Bruce. "Type Syntax in the Language C: An Object Lesson in Syntactic Innovation," *ACM SIGPLAN Notices* 15(3):21–27 (March 1980).

ANDE84 Anderson, Bruce. "Type Syntax in the Language C: An Object Lesson in Syntactic Innovation." In Feuer, Alan, and Narain Gehani (eds.). *Comparing and Assessing Programming Languages: Ada, C, and Pascal.* (Englewood Cliffs, NJ: Prentice-Hall, 1984, pp. 187–193).

ANDE82B Anderson, Gordon E., and Kenneth C. Shumate. "Selecting a Programming Language, Compiler and Support Environment: Method and Example," *IEEE Computer* 13(8):29-36 (August 1982).

ANON79 Anonymous. "Review of the C Programming Language" (Kernighan and Ritchie), *Computer Languages* 4:199–200 (1979).

ANON81A Anonymous. "Bell Labs' 32 Bit C/UNIX Micro," *Pipes and Filters* 1(1):4 (June 1981).

ANON81B Anonymous. "The C Programming Language," *Mini-Micro Software* 6 (1981).

ARCH83A Archer, Rowland. "The Intersoft C Compiler," *80 Micro* 4(2):198-199 (February 1983).

ARCH83B Archer, Rowland. "A Closer Look at the Listing," *80 Micro* 4(2):200 (February 1983).

ASHC81 Ashcraft, Steven E. "Ultra Low Level Programming Using a High Level Language." In *Microcomputer Research and Applications: Proceedings of the First Conference of the HP/1000 International Users Group*. Helen K. Brown (ed.). (Elmsford, NY: Pergamon, 1981, pp. 168-184).

AZLI83 Azlin, Lawrence A. "A DEBUG Subroutine: A Technique for Making Program Debugging Simpler," *Microsystems* 4(12):100 (December 1983).

BAIL79 Bailes, P. A. C. "A Coroutine Package for C," *Australian Computer Science Communications* 1(4):306-309 (December 1979).

BAIL83 Bailey, Kirk, "Small-C: Bug-Fix Bug," *Dr. Dobb's Journal* 57:4 (July 1981).

BAIR83 Bairstow, Jeffrey. "Getting Started with a New Language," *Personal Computing* 7(12):250 December 1983).

BAKE84A Baker, Leslie, and Nat Sakowski. "New Improved Lattice C," *PC Magazine* 3:138-141 (March 20, 1984).

BAKE84B Baker, Leslie, and Nat Sakowski. "Getting Your C-Legs," *PC Magazine* 3:118-123 (March 20, 1984).

BARA82A Barach, David R., and David H. Taenzer. "A Technique for Finding Storage Allocation Errors in C Language Programs," *ACM SIGPLAN Notices* 17(5):16-23 (May 1982).

BARA82B Barach, David R., and David H. Taenzer. "A Technique for Finding Storage Allocation Errors in C Language Programs," *ACM SIGPLAN Notices* 17(7):32-38 (July 1982).

BARR84 Barry, Steve, and Randy Jacobsen. "The TRS-80 Model 16B with Xenix," *Byte* 9(1):288-320 (January 1984).

BATE82 Bates, Dan. "I Can C Forever," *Dr. Dobb's Journal* 67:6-7 (May 1982).

BERE82 Berenbaum, Alan D., Michael W. Condry, and Priscilla M. Lu. "The Operating System and Language Support Features of the BELLMAC-32 Microprocessor," *ACM SIGPLAN Notices* 17(4):30-38 (April 1982).

BELS84 Belsher, John F. "The Future of Programming Languages," *Byte* 9(1):32 (January 1984).

BERG83 Bergmann, Ernest E. "PISTOL" A FORTH-like Portably Implemented STack Oriented Language," *Dr. Dobb's Journal* 76:12-15 (February 1983).

BIRM78 Birman, H.K, L. N. Rolnitzky, and J. R. Biggee. "A Shape Oriented System for Holter ECG Analysis." In *Computers in Cardiology* (1978).

BLAC81 Black, Rodney. "Oh Say, Can I C!" *Dr. Dobb's Journal* 61:4, 51 (November 1981).

BOLS83 Bolstad, Terje. "CP/M BDOS and BIOS Calls for C," *Dr. Dobb's Journal* 80:22-27 (June 1983).

BOLT81 Bolton, Bill. "Some Useful C Time Functions," *Dr. Dobb's Journal* 6(8):16-21 (August 1981).

BOUR83 Bourne, Stephen J. "The Unix Shell," *Byte* 8:187-204 (October 1983).

BOYD83A Boyd, Stowe. "Modular C," *ACM SIGPLAN Notices* 18(4):48-54 (April 1983).

BOYD83B Boyd, Stowe. "Abstract Exceptions in Modular C," *Azrex R/D Technical Report* (1983).

BOYD84 Boyd, Stowe. "Free and Bound Generics: Two Techniques for Abstract Data Types in Modular C," *ACM SIGPLAN Notices* 19(3):12-20 (March 1984).

BROO82 Brooker, R. A. "A Database Subsystem for BCPL," *Computer Journal* 25(4):448-464 (December 1982).

BUDD82 Budd, Timothy C. "An Implementation of Generators in C," *Computer Languages* 7:68-87 (January 1982).

BURG80 Burger, John, David Brill, and Filip Machi. "Self-Reproducing Programs" *Byte* 5(8):73-74 (August 1980).

BURK77 Burkowski, F.J., W. F. Mackey, and M. H. Hamza. "Micro-C: A Universal High Level Language for Microcomputers," *Proceedings of the IEEE International Symposium on Mini and Micro Computers* (Canada/U.S.A. 1977/1978).

BYTE83 *Byte* 8(8) "The C Language," (topical language issue) (August 1983).

CAIN80A Cain, Ron. "A Small-C Compiler for the 8080's," *Dr. Dobb's Journal* 45:5-46 (May 1980).

CAIN80B Cain, Ron. "Runtime Library for the Small-C Compiler," *Dr. Dobb's Journal* 48:4-15 (September 1980).

CAIN83 Cain, Ron. "High Praise for Small-C," *Dr. Dobb's Journal* 76:10 (February 1983).

CALH81 Calhoun, Herb. "Malpractice?" *Dr. Dobb's Journal* 60:4-5 (October 1981).

CAME82A Cameron, A.G.W. "The Software Tools Computing Environment," *Microsystems* 4:58-63 (September 1983).

CAME83B Cameron, A.G.W. "The Ratfor Preprocessing Language," *Microsystems* 4:52-56 (September 1983).

CANN83 Cann, Peter. "C Source-Code Formatting," *Byte* 8:18 (December 1983).

CHER83 Cherry, Lorinda L., and Nina H. Macdonald. "The Unix Writer's Workbench Software," *Byte* 8:244-253 (October 1983).

CHRI81 Christensen, Ward. "The CP/M Users Group Volume 48: Catalogue and Abstracts," *Lifelines* 1(10):15-16 (March 1981).

CHRI82A Christensen, Ward. "Full Screen Program Editors for CP/M-80: MINCE," *Lifelines* 2(11):7-11 (April 1982).

CHRI82B Christensen, Ward. "Full Screen Program Editors for CP/M-80: Ed Ream's Editor in C," *Lifelines* 3(5):43-45 (October 1982).

CHRI82C Christensen, Ward. "MINCE Revisited" *Lifelines* 3(5):45 (October 1982).

CIAR84A Ciarcia, Steve. "Trump Card. Part 1: Hardware" *Byte* 9:40-55 (May 1984).

CIAR84B Ciarcia, Steve. "Trump Card. Part 2: Software" *Byte* 9:115-122 (June 1984).

CLAP83 Clapp, Douglas. "Microsoft C Unveiled," *PC Magazine* 2:503-508 (October 1983).

CLAR83 Clark, David D. "Lmodem: A Small Remote-Communication Program," *Byte* 8(11):410-428 (November 1983).

CLAR84 Clark, David D. "Two More Versions of C for CP/M" *Byte* 9:246-256 (May 1984).

COLL80 Colley, William C. "6800 and 1802 Cross-Assemblers for CP/M," *Dr. Dobb's Journal* 50:38-39 (December 1980).

COLS81 Colstad, Ken. "A High-Level Language for Easy X.25 Updates," *Data Communications* 10:65-77 (September 1981).

COLV81 Colvin, James L. "Small-C Compiler," *Dr. Dobb's Journal* 52:7,37 (February 1981).

CORT83 Cortesi, D. E. "Dr. Dobb's Clinic," *Dr. Dobb's Journal* 8:11-19 (November 1983).

CORT84 Cortesi, D. E. "Cortesi Replies . . . ," *Dr. Dobb's Journal* 9:9 (January 1984).

COTT81 Cotton, G. "A Master Disk Directory," *Interface Age* 6(11):104-105, 162-167 (November 1981).

CURR83 Currie, Edward H. "Form over Substance . . . ," *Lifelines* 3:10 (April 1983).

DANE83 Danliuk, Tim "LC, a C Compiler for LDOS-based Machines," *InfoWorld* 5(25):53-54 (June 6, 1984).

DARW83 Darwin, Ian F. "The Unix File," *Microsystems* 4:24-27 (September 1983).

DATA80 Datapro. "An Introduction to the "C" Language." In *Applications Software Directory* (Delran, NJ: Datapro Research, 1980).

DESS83A Dessey, Raymond (ed.). "Languages for the Laboratory, Part I," *Analytical Chemistry* 55(6):650A-662A (May 1983).

DESS83B Dessey, Raymond (ed.). "Languages for the Laboratory, Part II," *Analytical Chemistry* 55(7):754A-764A (June 1983).

DIET83 Dietz, Paul F. "Don't Knock C," *Byte* 8:576-577 (November 1983).

DITZ82 Ditzel, David R., and H. R. McLellan. "Register Allocation for Free: The C Machine Stach Cache," *ACM SIGPLAN Notices* 17(4):48-55 (April 1982).

DOBY81A Dobyns, Barry A. "MINCE: Not Just Another Editor," *Dr. Dobb's Journal* 6(4):48-52 (April 1981).

DOBY81B Dobyns, Barry A. "Mincemeat and Minced Words" *Dr. Dobb's Journal* 56:4 (June 1981).

DUNC79 Duncan, Ray. "Tiny-C Interpreter on CDOS," *Dr. Dobb's Journal* 35:37-39 (September 1979).

ELLI82 Elliott, Comal. "A Very General Problem-Oriented CAI System," *Behavior Research Methods and Instrumentation* 14(2):165-169 (April 1982).

EVAN84 Evans, Arthur. "A Comparison of Programming Languages: Ada, Pascal, and C." In Feuer, Alan, and Narain Gehani (eds.). *Comparing and Assessing Programming Languages: Ada, C, and Pascal.* (Englewood Cliffs, NJ: Prentice-Hall, 1984), pp. 66-94.

EMER83 Emerson, Sandra L. "Usenet: A Bulletin Board for Unix Users," *Byte* 8:219-236 (October 1983).

FAVI83 Favitta, Michael. "Unica and XM-80," *Dr. Dobb's Journal* 78:83-85 (April 1983).

FAWC83 Fawcett, G. S. "Letter to the Editor: RE: Supersoft C Compiler vs. Kadak Real-Time Library" *Microsystems* 4:22 (December 1983).

FEUE82 Feuer, Alan R., and Narain H. Gehani. "A Comparison of the Programming Languages C and Pascal," *ACM Computing Surveys* 14(1):73-92 (March 1982).

FEUE84A Feuer, Alan, and Narain Gehani, (eds.). *Comparing and Assessing Programming Languages: Ada, C, and Pascal.* (Englewood Cliffs, NJ: Prentice-Hall, 1984).

FEUE84B Feuer, Alan R., and Narain H. Gehani. "A Comparison of the Programming Languages C and Pascal." In Feuer, Alan, and Narain Gehani (eds.). *Comparing and Assessing Programming Languages: Ada, C, and Pascal.* (Englewood Cliffs, NJ: Prentice-Hall, 1984).

FIED82 Fiedler, David. "The BDS C Compiler." In Libes, Sol, (ed.). *Programmer's Guide to CP/M* (Morris Plains, NJ: Creative Computing Press, 1982).

FIED83A Fiedler, David. "Unix Facilities on CP/M: Microshell," *Microsystems* 4:51-53 (January 1983).

FIED83B Fiedler, David. "The Unix Tutorial: Part 1: An Introduction to Features and Facilities," *Byte* 8:186-219 (August 1983).

FIED83C Fiedler, David. "The Unix Tutorial: Part 2: Unix as an Applications-Programs Base," *Byte* 8:257-278 (September 1983).

FIED83D Fiedler, David. "The Supersoft C Compiler," *Microsystems* 4:9-12 (September 1983).

FIED83E Fiedler, David. "The Unix Tutorial: Part 3: Unix in the Microcomputer Marketplace," *Byte* 8:132-160 (October 1983).

FISH82 Fishman, Harvey. "Janus—A New Ada Compiler for Z80 Systems," *Microsystems* (6):70-81 (November/December 1982).

FITZ81 Fitzhorn, Patrick A., and Geatold R. Johnson. "C: Toward a Concise Syntactic Definition," *ACM SIGPLAN Notices* 16(12);14-21 (December 1981).

FITZ82 Fitzhorn, Patrick A., and Geatold R. Johnson. "C: Toward a Concise Syntactic Definition: Appendix," *ACM SIGPLAN Notices* 17(8):89-95 (August 1982).

FLEM84 Fleming, Jim. "Virtual Personal Computer," *Dr. Dobb's Journal* 9:32-59 (February 1984).

FOUL83 Foulk, Richard. "Standard Deviation," *Dr. Dobb's Journal* 77:11,90 (March 1983).

GARR81A Garrett, Roger C. "Structured English for the C Programmer," *Interface Age* 6(10):30-34 (October 1981).

GARR81B Garrett, Roger C. "More on C Programming," *Interface Age* 6(11):26-28, 158 (November 1981).

GARR81C Garrett, Roger C. "C.Plus (Conclusion)" *Interface Age* 6(12):34-38, 142-143 (December 1981).

GEWI81 Gewirtz, David A. "An Introduction to the C Programming Language," *Microsystems* 2(6):20-38 (November/December 1981).

GEWI82A Gewirtz, David A. "An Introduction to the C Programming Language, (Part II)" *Microsystems* 3(1):50-58 (January/February 1982).

GEWI82B Gewirtz, David A. "A Reply to Larry Hamelin," *Microsystems* 3(4):12 (July/August 1982).

GEWI82C Gewirtz, David A. "Two More C Compilers: A Comparative Review of the Aztec C II and C/80 Compiler," *Microsystems* 83-89 (November/December 1982).

GIBS80 Gibson, T. A., and S. B. Guthery. "Structured Programming, C and tiny-C," *Dr. Dobb's Journal* 5(5):30-33 (May 1980).

GILB81 Gilbreath, Jim. "A High-Level Language Benchmark," *Byte* 6(9):180-198 (September 1981).

GILB83 Gilbreath, Jim, and Gary Gilbreath. "Erasthosthenes Revisited: Once More Through the Sieve," *Byte* 8(1):283-326 (January 1983).

GORE81 Gore, Mike, and Bernie Roehl. "Small-C Bug-Fix Bug," *Dr. Dobb's Journal* no. 57:4-6,8 (July 1981).

GORM76 Gorman, Walter, and Michael Groussard. "Minicomputer Programming Languages," *ACM SIGPLAN Notices* 11(4):4-15 (April 1, 1976).

HAGL84 Hagler, David. "Supersoft Speaks Up," *Byte* 9:20 (February 1984).

HALF82 Halfant, Matthew. "Small-C for the 9900" *Dr. Dobb's Journal* 69:66-71 (July 1982).

HALF83 Halfant, Matthew. "The Unix C Compiler in a CP/M Environment," *Byte* 8:243-267 (August 1983).

HAME82 Hamelin, Larry. "Intro to the C Programming Language," *Microsystems* (4):12 (July/August 1982).

HANC79 Hancock, Les. "Growing, Pruning, and Climbing Binary Trees with tiny-C," *Dr. Dobb's Journal* 4(5):37-41, 54 (May 1979).

HANC80 Hancock, L. "Implementing a Tiny Interpreter with a CP/M flavored C," *Dr. Dobb's Journal* 5(1):20-28 (January 1980).

HANN84 Hannotte, Dean. "A Good Buy on UNIX [Mark Williams' COHERENT" *PC Magazine* 3:250-254 (June 12, 1984).

HARE83 Hare, Van Court. "Learning C Inexpensively," *Lifelines* 3:30-34 (December 1983).

HARR84 Harrell, John B. "So Much to C," *80 Micro* 5:100-106 (February 1984).

HATC83 Hatch, William E. "Letter to the Editor," *Microsystems* 4:22 (December 1983).

HEND81A Hendrix, J. E. "Small-C Compiler (Bug Fixes)," *Dr. Dobb's Journal* 56:6 (June 1981).

HEND81B Hendrix, J. E. "Small VM: Nucleus of a Portable Software Development Environment" *Dr. Dobb's Journal* 61:34-45 (November 1981).

HEND81C Hendrix, J. E. "Small-C Expression Analyzer," *Dr. Dobb's Journal* 6(12):40-43 (December 1981).

HEND82A Hendrix, J. E. "Small Shell: Part 2 of a North Star VOS" *Dr. Dobb's Journal* 63:27-35 (January 1982).

HEND82B Hendrix, J. E. "Small-C Compiler, V. 2," *Dr. Dobb's Journal* 74:16-52 (December 1982).

HEND83A Hendrix, J. E. "Small-C Compiler, V. 2 Continued," *Dr. Dobb's Journal* 75:48-64 (January 1983).

HEND83B Hendrix, J. E. "Small-C Notes, Bug Fix" *Dr. Dobb's Journal* no. 75:6, 8 (January 1983).

HEND83C Hendrix, J. E. "A Slightly Slicker Fix for Small-C," *Dr. Dobb's Journal* 77:6 (March 1983).

HEND84 Hendrix, J. E., and E. Payne. "A New Library for Small-C," *Dr. Dobb's Journal* no. 91:50-81 (May 1984).

HINS83 Hinsch, Hanno. "Five C Language Compilers," *PC Magazine* 2:210-216 (February 1983).

HOGA77 Hogan, W. L. "An Evaluation of a Raster Scan Display for Use in an Aircraft Information Handling System," (Master's thesis, Naval Postgraduate School, Monterey, CA 1977).

HOUS83 Houston, Jerry, Jim Broderick, and Les Kent. "Comparing C Compilers for CP/M-86," *Byte* 8:82-106 (August 1983).

HOUS84 Houston, Jerry. "Reply to 'Supersoft Speaks Up'" *Byte* 9:20-21 (February 1984).

HOWA83 Howard, Alan D. "Enhancing the C Screen Editor," *Dr. Dobb's Journal* 79:38-63 (May 1983).

HOWA77 Howard, J. E. "An Implementation of a Codasyl Based Data Base Management System Under the UNIX Operating System," (Master's thesis, Naval Postgraduate School, Monterey, CA 1978).

HUGH81 Hughes, Phil. "BASIC, Pascal or Tiny-C? A Simple Benchmarking Comparison," *Byte* 6(10):372-375 (October 1981).

HUNT83A Hunt, Bill. "C and the PC: Part 1," *PC Tech Journal* 1:110-130 (November/December 1983).

HUNT83B Hunt, Bill. "C and the PC: Part 2," *PC Tech Journal* 2:91-124 (January 1984).

HUNT84A Hunter, Bruce. "A Comparison of C Compilers," *Lifelines* 3(12):15-21 (May 1983).

HUNT83B Hunter, Bruce N. "A Review of Microshell—A Unix-like Utility," *Lifelines* 3(11):17-21 (April 1983).

ISAA84 Isaak, James. "Designing Systems for Real-Time Applications" *Byte* 9:127-132 (April 1984).

JACK82 Jackson, T. R. "Letter to the Editor," *Microsystems* 3(5):22–23 (September/October 1982).

JAES84A Jaeschke, Rex. "Let's C Now . . . Part 1, In the Beginning . . .," *The DEC Professional* 2:42-50 (January 1984).

JAES84B Jaeschke, Rex. "Let's C Now . . . Part 2, Looping and Testing," *The DEC Professional* 2:26-38 (March 1984).

JAES84C Jaeschke, Rex. "Let's C Now . . . Part 3, Arrays and Functions," *The DEC Professional* 2:42-55 (May 1984).

JALI83 Jalics, Paul J. and Thomas S. Heines. "Transporting a Portable Operating System: Unix to an IBM Minicomputer," *Communications of the ACM* 26(12):1066-1072 (December 1983).

JOHA82 Johannson, Jan-Henrik. "Argc and Argv for Small-C," *Dr. Dobb's Journal* 74:62-64 (December 1982).

JOHN78A Johnson, S. C. "A Portable Compiler: Theory and Practice." In *Proceedings 5th ACM Conference on Principles of Programming Languages* (Association for Computing Machinery, New York, NY 1978).

JOHN78B Johnson, S.C., and D. M. Ritchie. "Portability of C Programs and the UNIX System," *Bell System Technical Journal* 57:2021-2048 (July/August 1978).

JOHN83 Johnson, Stephen C., and Brian W. Kernighan. "The C Language and Models of Systems Programming," *Byte* 8:48-60 (August 1983).

JOLL83 Jolly, George W. "Review of BCPL—The Language and Its Compiler (Martin Richards and Colin Whitby-Strevens)," *Dr. Dobb's Journal* 79:70 (May 1983).

JOYC82 Joyce, James. "Review of The C Puzzle Book," *ACM Computing Reviews* 23:286 (June 1982).

JOYC83A Joyce, James. "A C Language Primer: Part 1: Constructs and Conventions in C," *Byte* 8:64-78 (August 1983).

JOYC83B Joyce, James. "A C Language Primer. Part 2: Tool Building in C," *Byte* 8:289-302 (September 1983).

JOYC83C Joyce, James. "A Tour Through the Unix File System," *Byte* 8:170-182 (October 1983).

KATZ83A Katzenelson, Jacob. "Introduction to Enhanced C (EC)," *Software Practice and Experience* 13(7):551-576 (July 1983).

KATZ83B Katzenelson, Jacob. "Higher Level Programming and Data Abstractions—A Case Study Using Enhanced C," *Software Practice and Experience* 13(7):577-595 (July 1983).

KERN79 Kern, Christopher. "A User's Look at tiny-C," *Byte* 4(12):196-206 (December 1979).

KERN81A Kern, Christopher. "Printf for the C Function Library," *Byte* 6(5):430-434 (May 1981).

KERN81B Kern, Christopher. "The BDS C Compiler," *Byte* 6(6):356-362 (June 1981).

KERN81C Kern, Christopher. "MINCE: A Text Editor," *Byte* 6:150-160 (September 1981).

KERN82 Kern, Christopher. "Microshell and Unica: Unix-Style Enhancements for CP/M," *Byte* 7:206-219 (December 1982).

KERN83A Kern, Christopher. "Supervyz and Organizr: Two Menu-Driven Front Ends for CP/M," *Byte* 8:446-451 (January 1983).

KERN83B Kern, Christopher. "The Scribble Text Processor," *Byte* 8:302-310 (February 1983).

KERN83C Kern, Christopher. "Five C Compilers for CP/M-80," *Byte* 8:110-130 (August 1983).

KERN83D Kern, Christopher. "More Unix-Style Software Tools for CP/M," *Byte* 8:428-434 (October 1983).

KERN84 Kern, Christopher. "Another Look at CP/M-80 C Compilers" *Byte* 9:303-319 (June 1984).

KERN81 Kernighan, B. "Why Pascal Is not my Favorite Programming Language," *Computer Science Technical Report* #100 (Bell Laboratories July 18, 1981).

KERN84 Kernighan, B. "Why Pascal Is not my Favorite Programming Language." In Feuer, Alan, and Narain Gehani (eds.). *Comparing and Assessing Programming Languages: Ada, C, and Pascal.* (Englewood Cliffs, NJ: Prentice-Hall, 1984), pp. 170-186.

KING83 King, B. "The Flexibility of C," *CP/M Review* 1(2):22-23,75 (January/February 1983).

KRIE80 Krieger, M. S., and P. J. Plauger. "C Language's Grip on Hardware Makes Sense for Small Computers," *Electronics* 53:129-133 (May 8, 1980).

KRIE83 Krieger, Mark, and Fred Pack. "Unix as an Application Environment," *Byte* 8:209-214 (October 1983).

KVAL82A Kvaleberg, Egil. "Small-C DISKDOC: A Repair and Maintenance Utility," *Dr. Dobb's Journal* 66:26-34 (April 1982).

KVAL82B Kvaleberg, Egil. "Doctoring DISKDOC," *Dr. Dobb's Journal* 67:6-7 (May 1982).

LEAS83 Leas, Dennis, and Paul Wintz. "Chisel Your Code with a Profiler," *Byte* 8:286-290 (August 1983).

LEE83 Lee, P. A. "Exception Handling in C Programs," *Software—Practice and Experience* 13:389-405 (1983).

LIBE82 Libes, Don. "Reply to T. R. Jackson," *Microsystems* 3(5):23-26 (September/October 1982).

LIBE83A Libes, Don. "Unix and CP/M," *Microsystems* 4:26-34 (January 1983).

LIBE83B Libes, Don. "Unix on Microcomputers," *Microsystems* 4:42-44 (January 1983).

LINH83 Linhart, Jason. "Managing Software Development with C," *Byte* 8:172-182 (August 1983).

MACP83 MacPherson, Andrew. "Catching Bugs in Small-C," *Dr. Dobb's Journal* 81:6-7 (July 1983).

MADD77 Madden, J. Gregory. "C: A Language for Microprocessors?" *Byte* 2(10):130-138 (October 1977).

MAGE82 Magenat-Thalmann, Nadia. "Choosing an Implementation Language for Automatic Translation," *Computer Languages* 7:161-170 (April 1982).

MANN82 Mann, Stephen. "Software Tools for CP/M Systems from Unicorn" *Infoworld* 4:30-31 (August 9, 1982).

MARK81 Mark of the Unicorn. *MINCE Text Editor Documentation.* (Mark of the Unicorn, 1981).

MATE79 Mateti, Prabhaker. "Pascal Versus C: A Subjective Comparison." In *Proceedings of the Symposium on Language Design and Programming Methodology* (Sydney, September 10-11, 1979), p. 37-69.

MATE79 Mateti, Prabhaker. "Pascal Versus C: A Subjective Comparison." In Feuer, Alan, and Narain Gehani (eds.). *Comparing and Assessing Programming Languages: Ada, C, and Pascal.* (Englewood Cliffs, NJ: Prentice-Hall, 1984); pp. 32-54.

MATT83 Matthews, M.M. "Review: The C Primer," *ACM Computing Reviews* 24(9):384 (September 1983).

MCCA83 McCall, Caddy. "Microshell and Microtools" *CP/M Review* 1:26-35 (November/December 1983).

MCCL83 McClure, Robert L. "Likes to C It Standard, Too," *Dr. Dobb's Journal* 79:7 (May 1983).

MCDE84 McDermott, Edward. "Optimizing Strings in C" *Dr. Dobb's Journal* no. 90:18-23. (April 1984).

MCKE83 McKeon, Brian. "A Small-C Operating System," *Dr. Dobb's Journal* 77:36-61 (March 1983).

MCSK78 McSkimin, J. R. "REDAS—A Relational Data Access System for Real-Time Applications." In *Proceedings of COMPSAC 1978* (Computer Software and Applications Conference 1978).

MEIS82 Meissner, Michael. "Letter to the Editor: Reply to Fitzhorn and Johnson," *ACM SIGPLAN Notices* 17(8):84-88 (August 1982).

MOHL81 Mohler, Lorin S. "A Disk Alignment Routine," *Microsystems* 2(6):70 (November/December 1981).

MURP83 Murphy, Walter V. "RECLAIM: A File Reclamation Utility for Destroyed Directories," *Dr. Dobb's Journal* 78:14-23 (April 1983).

NESS81 Ness, David and A. Krigman. "MINCE Editor from Mark of the Unicorn," *InfoWorld* 3:11-13 (May 11, 1981).

NORR82 Norris, Bill. "C-Bits (All About BDS C Version 1.45)," *Lifelines* 2(9):37-38 (February 1982).

NOWE83 Nowell, Scott. "Cross Check," *Microsystems* 4:98-102 (September 1983).

PETE80 Petersen, Holger. "Review of the BDS C Compiler," *Dr. Dobb's Journal* 47:49-50 (September 1980).

PHRA83 Phraner, Ralph A. "Nine C Compilers for the IBM PC," *Byte* 8:134-168 (August 1983).

PLAU79 Plauger, P. J. "Review of the C Programming Language," *ACM Computing Reviews* 29:2-4 (January 1979).

POUR82A Pournelle, Jerry. "User's Column . . . MINCE is Not Complete EMACS . . . ," *Byte* 7:294, 298, 300 (July 1982).

POUR82B Pournelle, Jerry. "User's Column . . . Kernighan's Lament . . . There's a New C A'Comin . . . ," *Byte* 7:226-236 (December 1982).

POUR82C Pournelle, Jerry. "User's Column . . . There's a New C A'Comin . . . ," *Byte* 7:230, 235, 236 (December 1982).

POUR83 Pournelle, Jerry. "The Debate Goes On . . . ," *Byte* 8:324 (August 1983).

POUR84 Pournelle, Jerry. "User's Column . . . BDS C," *Byte* 9:88-89 (January 1984).

PUGH80A Pugh, T. "MCALL-C: A Communications Protocol for Personal Computers," *Dr. Dobb's Journal* 5(2):16-20 (June/July 1980).

PUGH80B Pugh, T. "BDS C, A Full Compiler from Lifeboat Associates," *Infoworld* 2:6-7 (March 31, 1980).

REAM82A Ream, Edward K. "A Portable C Screen-Oriented Editor," *Dr. Dobb's Journal* 63:18-61 (January 1982).

REAM82B Ream, Edward K. "Screen-Oriented Bugs" *Dr. Dobb's Journal* 67:4-7 (May 1982).

REAM83A Ream, Edward K. "RED: A Better C Screen Editor, Part I," *Dr. Dobb's Journal* 81:34-65 (July 1983).

REAM83B Ream, Edward "RED: A Better C Screen Editor, Part II," *Dr. Dobb's Journal* 82:62-97 (August 1983).

REED82 Reed, Adam. "An Underline Filter for Matrix Printers," *Byte* 7(3):300-306 (March 1982).

REID83 Reid, Larry, and Andrew P. McKinlay, "Whitesmith's C Compiler," *Byte* 8(1):330-344 (January 1983).

REIT83 Reitz, Randy. "Small-VOS and Small-Tools," *Microsystems* 4(1):66-69 (January 1983).

RIFK83 Rifkin, Edward M., and Steve Williams. "The C Language: Key to Portability," *Computer Design* 22:143-150 (August 1983).

RITC78 Ritchie, D. M., S. C. Johnson, M. E. Lesk, and B. W. Kernighan. "The C Programming Language," *Bell System Technical Journal* 57(6):1991-2019 (July/August 1978).

RITC80 Ritchie, D. M., S. C. Johnson, M. E. Lesk, and B. W. Kernighan. "The C Programming Language," *Dr. Dobb's Journal* 5(5):20-29 (May 1980).

RITC83A Ritchie, D. M., S. C. Johnson, M. E. Lesk, and B. W. Kernighan. "The C Programming Language." Reprinted from *Bell System Technical Journal* 57(6):1991-2019 (July/August 1978). In Horowitz, Ellis (ed.). *Programming Languages: A Grand Tour* (Computer Science Press, 1983).

RITC83B Ritchie, D. M. "C Reference Manual." Reprinted from *Bell System Technical Journal* 57 no. 6:1991-2019 (July/August 1979). In Horowitz, Ellis (ed.). *Programming Languages: A Grand Tour* (Computer Science Press, 1983).

RITC84 Ritchie, D. M., S. C. Johnson, M. E. Lesk, and B. W. Kernighan. "The C Programming Language." In Feuer, Alan, and Narain Gehani (eds.). *Comparing and Assessing Programming Languages: Ada, C, and Pascal.* (Englewood Cliffs, NJ: Prentice-Hall, 1984).

ROBE83 Roberts, Bruce. "C," *Popular Computing* 7:111-119 (September 1983).

ROBE77 Robertson, M. D. "An Extended BASIC Compiler with Graphics Interface for the PDP-11/50 Computer," (Master's thesis, Naval Postgraduate College, Monterey, CA 1977).

ROTH81 Roth, Richard. "Small C Grows Up," *Dr. Dobb's Journal* 61:46-50 (November 1981).

ROTH82 Roth, Richard L. "C Language Prints Multiple Text Lines," *Electronics Design News* 27:171 (August 4, 1982).

ROTH84 Rothstein, Joseph B. "Review of *C Programming Guide* (Purdum)" *Dr. Dobb's Journal* 88:81 (February 1984).

ROVE77 Rovegno, H. D. "Using C Language for Microprocessors," *Electro/77 Conference Record* (1977).

ROVE78 Rovegno, H. D., "A Support Environment for MAC-8 Systems," *Bell Systems Technical Journal* 57(6, pt. 2):2251-2264 (July/August 1978).

RUNY82 Runyon, John. "Review of C Notes: A Guide to the C Programming Language," *DEC Professional* 8:22-26 (November 1982).

SALO78 Saloman, F. A. "Software Development for Microprocessors—A Case Study," *Proceedings of COMPSAC 1978* (Computer Software and Applications Conference 1978).

SCHE83 Scherrer, Deborah, K. Philip, H. Scherrer, Thomas H. Strong and Samuel J. Penny. "The Software Tools: Unix Capabilities on Non-Unix Systems," *Byte* 8:430-446 (November 1983).

SETH80 Sethi, Ravi. "A Case Study in Specifying the Semantics of a Programming Language." In *Proceedings of the 7th ACM Symposium on Principles of Programming Languages* (Las Vegas, NV, January 28-30 1980), pp. 117-130 (ACM, 1980).

SKJE82A Skjellum, Anthony. "Argum—A C Command Line Processor" *Dr. Dobb's Journal* no. 70:10-31 (August 1982).

SKJE82B Skjellum, Anthony. "Using C Instead of Assembly Language," *Microsystems* 3:33-36 (September/October 1982).

SKJE82C Skjellum, Anthony. "Expanding Wildcards Under UNIX," *Dr. Dobb's Journal* 73:12-16, 43 (November 1982).

SKJE83A Skjellum, Anthony. "UNICA: A UNIX-like Utility System for CP/M," *Microsystems* no. 75:59-65 (January 1983).

SKJE83B Skjellum, Anthony. "C/UNIX Programmer's Notebook," *Dr. Dobb's Journal* no. 84:16-18 (October 1983).

SKJE83C Skjellum, Anthony. "C/UNIX Programmer's Notebook," *Dr. Dobb's Journal* no. 86:14-17 (December 1983).

SKJE84A Skjellum, Anthony. "C/UNIX Programmer's Notebook," *Dr. Dobb's Journal* no. 88:94-97 (February 1984).

SKJE84B Skjellum, Anthony. "C/UNIX Programmer's Notebook," *Dr. Dobb's Journal* no. 90:94-96 (April 1984).

SPRI79 Springer, Allen. "A Comparison of Language C and Pascal," *Technical Report G320-2128* (IBM Cambridge Scientific Center, Cambridge, MA 1979).

STAL84 Stallings, S. "C Into the Future," *PC Magazine* 3:142-147 (March 20, 1984).

STAN76 Stankowski, J. B. "The Design and Implementation of a General Purpose Graphics Subroutine Library," (Master's thesis, Naval Postgraduate College, Monterey, CA 1976).

STAN83 Staneff, John. "A Small-C Help Facility," *Dr. Dobb's Journal* 9 84:40-69 (October 1983).

STRO82 Stroustrup, Bjarne. "Classes: An Abstract Data Type Facility for the C Language," *ACM SIGPLAN Notices* 7(1):42-51 (January 1982).

STRO83 Stroustrup, Bjarne. "Adding Classes to the C Language," *Software—Practice and Experience* 13:139-161 (January 1983).

SUCK84 Suckow, Harry. "We'll C You and Raise You . . . ," *Dr. Dobb's Journal* no. 87:8-9, 12-16 (January 1984).

TAYL81 Taylor, Jeff. "LIST—A Source-Listing Program for the C Language," *Byte* 6(6):234-246 (June 1981).

TAYL82 Taylor, Jeffrey L. "Cross-Reference Generator in C: A Program Conversion Aid," *Dr. Dobb's Journal* 68:50-54 (June 1982).

TAYL83 Taylor, Jeffrey L. "CREF Update," *Dr. Dobb's Journal* 79:7,9 (May 1983).

TERR82 Terry, Chris. "Mince—A New Text Editor," *Microsystems* 3:76-79 (May/June 1982).

TERR83 Terry, Chris. "Book Review: *The C Primer, Learning to Program in C*, and *C Programming Guide*," *Microsystems* 4:120 (September 1983).

THOM83 Thomas, Rebecca. "What Is a Software Tool?" *Byte* 8:222-238 (August 1983).

TILS83 Tilson, Michael. "Moving UNIX to New Machines," *Byte* 8:266-276 (October 1983).

TORK82 Torkildson, Chris L. "Micro Compiler in Brobdingnang," *Dr. Dobb's Journal* 72:6 (October 1982).

TUTH83 Tuthill, Bill. "Typesetting on the Unix System," *Byte* 8:253-262 (October 1983).

VANZ82 Van Zandt, James R. "Micro Compiler in Brobdingnang," *Dr. Dobb's Journal* 72:6, 59-60 (October 1982).

WATS83 Watson, Ron. "Learning the C Language with C-System's C Compiler," *Lifelines* 4(6):7-8 (November 1983).

WATS84 Watson, Ron. "Software Notes: C-Systems C-Window," *Lifelines* 4:26 (January 1984).

WILK83 Wilkinson, James B. "YACC is Alive and Well and Running on RSTS," *VAX/RSTS Professional* 1:56-61 (October 1983).

WILL83 Willman, Bryan M. "C Clearly with Descriptive Operators," *Dr. Dobb's Journal* 82:9 (August 1983).

WILS84 Wilson, Dale. "More on Binary Magic Numbers" *Dr. Dobb's Journal* no. 89:78-83 (March 1984).

WILS83 Wilson, W. E. "Unix to CP/M Floppy Disk File Conversion" *Dr. Dobb's Journal* no. 84:20-39 (October 1983).

WOOD81A Woods, P. L. "Small-C: An Implementor's Notes and a Bug Corrected," *Dr. Dobb's Journal* 52:20-21,32,33 (February 1981).

WOOD81B Woods, P. L. "Small-C: Current Status," *Dr. Dobb's Journal* 53:20,36-37 (March 1981).

YATE83 Yates, Jean L. "Unix and the Standardization of Small Computer Systems," *Byte* 8:160-166 (October 1983).

ZACH84A Zachmann, Mark S. "The MWC-86C Compiler," *PC Magazine* 3:124-129 (March 1984).

ZACH84B Zachmann, Mark S. "The Whitesmith's C Native Compiler," *PC Magazine* 3:130-137 (March 1984).

ZINT83 Zintz, Walter. "A Survey of Unix and C Resources," *Byte* 8:212-213 (August 1983).

TOPICAL INDEX TO C BIBLIOGRAPHY

Advanced Topics

ANDE80B, ASHC81, BAIL79, BARA82A, BARA82B, BERE82, BOYD83, BUDD82, COLS81, DITZ82, FITZ81, FITZ82, JOHN78A, JOHN78B, JOLL83, KATZ83A, KATZ83B, LEE83, MEIS82, ROVE77, ROVE78, SALO78, SETH80, STRO82, STRO83, WILK83

Algorithms

ALLI80A, ALLI80B, ALLI80C, FISH82, GILB81, GILB83, HANC79

BCPL

BROO82, JOLL83

Benchmarks

FISH82, GEWI81, GEWI82A, GEWI82B, GEWI82C, GILB81, GILB83, HUGH81

Bibliographies

WARD83, WARD84, ZINT83

Book Reviews

ANON79, ANON81B, BYTE83, JOLL83, JOYC82, MATT83, PLAU79, ROBE83, RUNY82, TERR83, WARD83, WARD84, ZINT83

C-like Languages

C.Plus

GARR81A, GARR81B, GARR81C

tiny-C

DUNC79, GIBS80, HANC79, HUGH81, KERN79

C Compiler Reviews (by environment)

CP/M

BYTE83, FIED82, FIED83D, GEWI81, GEWI82A, GEWI82B, GEWI82C, HALF83, HUNT83A, KERN79, KERN81B, KERN83C, NORR82, PETE80, PUGH80B, REID83, ROBE83

CP/M-86

BYTE83, HOUS83, HUNT83A

MSDOS (PCDOS)

BAKE84A, BAKE84B, CLAP83, HINS83, HOUS83, HUNT83, HUNT84, HUNT83A, PHRA83, WARS83, ZACH84A, ZACH84B

C Compilers

Microsoft C

CLAP83, HINS83, HOUS83, HUNT83, HUNT84, HUNT83A, PHRA83

LC (Tandy/Radio Shack)

DANE83, HARR84

Supersoft C

FIED83D, GEWI81, GEWI82A, GEWI82B, HAGL84, HOUS83, HOUS84, HUNT83A, KERN83C, PHRA83

Aztec C II

GEWI82C, HUNT83, HUNT84, KERN83C

Software Toolworks C/80

GEWI82C, HARE83, KERN83C

Intellect Associates C88

HINS83, HOUS83, HUNT83A, PHRA83

C-Systems

HINS83, HOUS83, HUNT83A, PHRA83, WATS83, WATS84

Computer Innovations Ci-C86

HINS83, HOUS83, HUNT83, HUNT84, HUNT83A, PHRA83, WATS83

Telecon

GEWI81, GEWI82A, HINS83, HUNT83A, KERN83C, PHRA83

Lattice

BAKE84A, CLAP83, HINS83, HOUS83, HUNT83, HUNT84, HUNT83A, PHRA83

DeSmet

GEWI81, GEWI82A, GEWI82B, HINS83, HOUS83, HUNT83A, KERN83C, PHRA83

Digital Research

GEWI81, GEWI82A, GEWI82B, HINS83, HOUS83, HUNT83A, KERN83C, PHRA83

Mark Williams

GEWI81, GEWI82A, GEWI82B, HINS83, HOUS83, HUNT83A, KERN83C, PHRA83, ZACH84A

B D Software C

GEWI81, GEWI82A, GEWI82B, HARE83, HINS83, HOUS83, HUNT83A, KERN83C, PHRA83, FIED82, KERN81B, NORR82, PETE80, POUR84, PUGH80B

Whitesmith's

GEWI81, GEWI82A, GEWI82B, HINS83, HOUS83, HUNT83A, KERN83C, PHRA83, REID83, ZACH84B

tiny-C

GEWI81, GEWI82A, GEWI82B, HINS83, HOUS83, HUNT83A, KERN83C, PHRA83, DUNC79, GIBS80, HANC79, HUGH81, KERN79

C vs. Pascal Comparisons

FEUE82, GORM76, HUGH81, JOHN83, KERN81, MATE79, POUR82B, SPRI79

Introductory Tutorials

BAIR83, BAKE84B, BYTE83, DATA80, GEWI81, GEWI82A, GEWI82B, GIBS80, HAME82, JAES84, JOHN83, JOYC83A, JOYC83B, KING83, MADD77, RITC80, ROBE83, STAL84, WATS83

Language Definition

BYTE83, FITZ81, FITZ82, JOHN78A, JOHN83, MEIS82, RITC78, RITC80, RITC83, SETH80

Language Extensions

ANDE80B, ANDE82B, BAIL79, BARA82A, BARA82B, BOYD83, BUDD82, BURK77, KATZ83A, KATZ83B, LEE83, STRO82, STRO83, WILK83

Language Selection Criteria

ANDE82B, BYTE83, COLS81, DESS83A, DESS83B, FEUE82, GILB81, GILB83, GORM76, HUGH81, KRIE80, MADD77, MAGE82, RIFK83, ROVE77, SALO78, SPRI79

Programming Hints

CANN83, CORT83, DIET83, FOUL83, HATC83, JACK82, LIBE82, MCCL83, POUR82A, POUR82B, POUR83, ROTH82, SKJE83B, WILL83

Programs (Including Source Code)

Command Shells

HEND81B, HEND81C, HEND82A, JOHA82, REIT83, SKJE82A, SKJE83C

CP/M Interfacing

BOLS83, FIED83A, HALF83, KERN83C, LIBES83A

Cross Assemblers

COLL80

Cross Reference Generators

NOWE83, TAYL82, TAYL83

Debuggers

AZLI83, BARA82A, BARA82B, BOYD83, LEAS83

Disk Utilities

COTT81, KVAL82A, KVAL82B, MOHL81, MURP83

Editor (Ed Ream—ED2)

CHRI82B, HOWA83, REAM82A, REAM82B

Editor (Ed ream—RED)

REAM83A, REAM83B

Filters

KERN81A, ROTH82, SKJE82C, TAYL81

FORTH-like Language

BERG83

Help Facilities

STAN83

Hardware Interfacing

ASHC81, BOLS83, BOLT81, COLS81, DESS83A, DESS83B, DITZ82, HOGA77, KRIE80, ROBE77, ROVE78, STAN76

Operating Systems

HEND81B, HEND81C, HEND82A, MCKE83, REIT83

Scientific Instrumentation

ASHC81, BOLS83, BOLT81, COLS81, DESS83A, DESS83B, DITZ82, HOGA77, KRIE80, ROBE77, ROVE78, STAN76

small-C (Cain)

BAIL83, BATE82, BLAC81, CAIN80A, CAIN80B, COLV81, DUNC79, GORE81, HALF82, HANC80, HEND81C, JOHA82, MACP83, MCCL83, ROTH81, SKJE82A, TORK82, VANZ82, WOOD81A, WOOD81B

small-C, v. 2 (Hendrix)

CAIN83, HEND82B, HEND83A, HEND83B, HEND83C

small-VOS

HEND81B, HEND82A, REIT83

Telecommunications

CLAR83, COLS81, EMER83, PUGH80A

Time/Date Functions

BOLT81

RATFOR

CAME83A, CAME83B, SCHE83

Software Design and Development

ANDE82B, BERE82, GIBS80, JOHN83, JOYC83A, JOYC83B, KRIE83, LINH83, RIFK83, SALO78

Software Portability

BERG83, JALI83, JOHN78A, JOHN78B, JOHN83, RIFK83, TILS83

Software (Noncompilers) Reviews
Command Shells

CAME83A, FAVI83, FIED83A, HUNT83B, KERN82, KERN83A, KERN83D, MCCA83, REIT83, SCHE83, SKJE83A

MINCE Text Editor

CHRI82A, CHRI82C, DOBY81A, DOBY81B, KERN81C, MARK81, NESS81, POUR82A, TERR82

SCRIBBLE Text Formatter

KERN83B

Other Software

REIT83

ED Editor

CHRI82B, HOWA83, REAM82A, REAM82B

RED Editor

REAM83A, REAM83B

Software Tools

BOUR83, CAME83A, JOYC83B, REIT83, SCHE83, THOM83

UNIX-Related

ANON81A, BARR84, BOUR83, DARW83, EMER83, FIED83B, FIED83C, FIED83E, HALF83, JALI83, JOHN78B, JOYC83C, KRIE83, LIBE83A, LIBE83B, SCHE83, SKJE82C, SKJE83B, TILS83, YATE83

Writing Tools

CHER83, TUTH83

Appendix B
Guide to Public Domain C Software

In addition to the printed material relating to the C programming language listed in Appendix A, there exists a substantial amount of high quality software written in C that is available for minimal cost. The major software products are noted and listed. Minor programs (e.g., filters, small utilities) are not explicitly noted.

In general, each disk contains approximately 256k (i.e., a standard 8-in. CP/M disk). The two firms listed at the end of the directory provide diskette conversion services from the 8-in. CP/M standard to virtually all other microcomputer disk formats. Contact them directly for prices and details of the conversion process.

All the software listed below include source code and thus are an excellent means of learning C and structured programming.

C Users Group

415 E. Euclid
McPherson, KS 67460
(316) 241-1065

Also available from
Elliam Associates
24000 Bessemer Street
Woodland Hills, CA 91367
(818) 348-4278

Disk Name	Contents
BASTOC	BASIC to C translator

Blaise Computing
2034 Blake Street
Berkeley, CA 94704

Disk Name	Contents
TOOLS	Strings, screen access, access to BIOS IBM/PC
TOOLS 2	General DOS interface IBM/PC
VIEW MGR	Screen support for IBM/PC

Greenleaf Software
2101 Hickory Drive
Carrollton, TX 75006

Disk Name	Contents
Greenleaf Fcns	200 functions for strings, graphics, etc. (IBM/PC)

Que Corporation
7960 Castleway Drive
Indianapolis, IN 46250

Disk Name	Contents
C Programmer's Library	Companion diskette to Purdum, Leslie, and Stegemoller book (see Appendix A). Recursion, linked lists, sorting algorithms, Huffman text compression, etc.

Dedicated Micro Systems
P.O. Box 481
Chanute, KS 66720
(316) 431-0018

Disk Name	Contents
NPFLF2	Extended precision floating point extensions to BDS C
NPFLA3	S-ARGUM command line parser for BDS C

J E. Hendrix
Box 8378
University, MS 38677-8378

Disk Name	*Contents*
Small-VOS	Virtual operating system for NorthStar DOS, includes small-C version 2.0 compiler.
Small-Tools	Programs for text processing: change, copy, count, format, detab, entab, sort, transliterate in small-C

Algorithmic Technology
P.O. Box 278
Exton, PA 19341-0278
(215) 363-7028

Disk Name	*Contents*
Contact Algorithmic Technology	Publishes a large directory (40+ pages) of public domain software for CP/M-80, PCDOS, MSDOS, BDS C and Software Toolworks C/80. Incredible selection of C software.

Diskette Conversion Firms

The firms listed below provide services to convert standard CP/M diskettes (8″ CP/M ss/sd) to other microcomputer disk formats at a minimal cost.

Elliam Associates
24000 Bessemer Street
Woodland Hills, CA 91367
(818) 348-4278

Fred Greeb
LogiCom, Inc.
P.O. Box 27465
Lakewood, CO 80227
(303) 986-6651

Appendix C
Notes on Converting BDS C

"Whenever I use a word, it means whatever I wish it to mean."

(Lewis Carroll, *Through the Looking Glass*)

Computer languages exist in numerous, slightly different dialects that require modification to go from one to the other. The case of BDS C vis-à-vis standard C is an example of a situation requiring translation. This appendix outlines the basic procedure for converting a BDS C program to a standard C dialect. Specifically, we will consider the program from Chapter 10, the othello game playing program. Shown below are the basic steps required for the conversion process:

Step 1. header file   Insure that the standard header file from BDS C is available on the target machine. This file "bdscio.h" is listed below. It includes the #defines and macro definitions used by most BDS C programs.

Step 2. comment lines   Change the BDS C comment format to conform to standard C usage. BDS C allows comments to be delimited by /* and */ pairs that may extend across several lines. For example, the following comment is valid in BDS C, but not in standard C:

```
/*
        This is a multiline BDS C
        comment.
*/
```

In standard C, this comment would be coded as follows:

```
/* This is a multiline C */
/* comment. */
```

This step is quite important, because C compilers have notorious difficulty in handling unmatched comment delimiters. *Note:* All the programs in this book have standard C comment lines.

Step 3. trial compilation   Attempt to compile the program at this point. If it is a relatively straightforward C program, it may compile with no errors. In this case, we can proceed with the linking operation. In general, well-written BDS C programs will compile correctly regardless of compiler. The difficulty will arise in the linking operation.

Step 4. trial linking   Attempt to link the result of the compilation above to produce the executable program. In general, this step will fail. The difficulty here arises because of the richness of the BDS C library functions. Recall that BDS C includes more than 150 library functions. In general, these are not all directly transportable to other computer systems.

Step 5. library functions   At this point, we must supply the functions that are available in BDS C but that are missing from our more standard C compiler. As an example, the othello program of Chapter 10 calls the following BDS C library functions that are not present on our mainframe C compiler:
        kbhit
        abs
        rand, srand1
        qsort
At this point we have two options:

(a) We can see if our target compiler has comparable functions to those missing. In our example, our mainframe C compiler can access a rather extensive FORTRAN library of functions that includes analogous functions to kbhit (wait for keyboard input), rand (initialize a random number generator), srand1 (generate random numbers), and abs (return absolute values). The specifications for the BDS C library functions are available in the BDS C documentation, which is available independent of the compiler itself.

(b) We must either modify the program to not use the BDS C functions or simply code them in our standard C dialect and include them into our program as additional functions. This would be the procedure followed with the qsort (in memory quicksort routine) function.

Step 6. program testing   At this point, the conversion process is completed and the program can be tested and implemented permanently in our collection of C software.

bdscio.h—Standard Header File for C Programs

```
/*                                                                         */
/* The BDS C Standard I/O header file — v1.41 October 14, 1980 */
/* This file contains global definitions for use in all C programs in */
/* place of common constants. Characteristics of your system, such as video */
/* screen size, interface port numbers and masks, and buffered I/O allocations, */
/* should all be configured just once within this file. Any program */
/* that needs them should contain the preprocessor directive: */
/*      #include "bdscio.h" */
/* near the beginning. If you go through and set all these as soon as you get */
/* the package, most terminal-dependent sample programs will run much */
/* better. */
/* ** Some console (video) terminal characteristics: *** */
#define     TWIDTH      64      /* # of columns */
#define     TLENGTH     16      /* # of lines */
#define     CSTAT       0x7E    /* console status port */
#define     CDATA       0x7F    /* console data port */
#define     CIMASK      0x80    /* console input data ready mask */
#define     COMASK      0x80    /* console output data ready mask */
```

```
#define    CAHI         1              /* console status active high */
#define    CRESET       0              /* status port needs to be reset */
#define    CRESETVAL    0              /* if CRESET true, value to send */
/* modify the following lines to the */
/* specific characters required by */
/* your computer system */
#define    CLEARS       ""             /* string to clear screen on console */
#define    INTOREV      ""             /* string to switch to reverse video */
#define    OUTAREV      ""             /* string to switch OUT rev video */
#define    CURSOROFF    ""             /* string to turn cursor off */
#define    CURSORON     ""             /* string to turn cursor on */
#define    ESC          '\033'         /* standard ASCII "escape" character */
/* *** Modem characteristics:        *** */
#define    MSTAT        2              /* modem status port */
#define    MDATA        3              /* modem data port */
#define    MIMASK       0x40           /* modem input data ready mask */
#define    MOMASK       0x80           /* modem ready to send mask */
#define    MAHI         1              /* modem status logic active high */
#define    MRESET       0              /* modem status port needs reset */
#define    MRESETVAL    0              /* if MRESET true, byte to send */
/* **** General purpose Symbolic constants: ******* */
#define    BASE         0              /* base of CP/M system RAM */
#define    NULL         0              /* used by some functions */
#define    EOF          -1             /* physical EOF for I/O functions */
#define    ERROR        -1             /* general "on error" return value */
#define    OK           0              /* general "no error" return value */
#define    CPMEOF       0x1a           /* CP/M end-of-text-file marker */
#define    SECSIZ       128            /* sector size for read/write calls */
#define    MAXLINE      135            /* longest line of input expected */
#define    TRUE         1              /* general purpose true truth value */
#define    FALSE        0              /* general purpose false truth value */
/* *** number of sectors to use for buffered I/O: ***** */
/* The NSECTS symbol controls the compilation of the buffered I/O routines in */
/* STDLIB2.C, allowing each user to set the buffer size most convenient */
/* for his or her system, while keeping the numbers totally invisible to the C */
/* programs using buffered I/O (via the BUFSIZ defined symbol.) For larger */
/* NSECTS, the disk I/O is faster, but more ram is taken up. Note that prior */
/* (pre 1.4) versions of the library were not set up to support this */
```

```
/* customizable buffer size and were always compiled as if NSECTS was 1 in this */
/* version. To change the buffer size allocation, follow these steps: */
/*     1. Alter NSECTS to the desired value here in bdscio.h. */
/*     2. Recompile STDLIB1.C and STDLIB2.C. */
/*     3. Use CLIB to combine STDLIB1.CRL and STDLIB2.CRL to make a new */
/*        DEFF.CRL. */
/* Make sure you declare all your I/O buffers with a statement such */
/* as: */
/*     char buf_name[BUFSIZ]; */
/*     instead of the older and now obsolete: */
/*     char buf_name[134]; */
/*     (and always #include "bdscio.h" in your programs!). */
/* ************************************************************ */
#define     NSECTS  8      /* number of sectors to buffer */
#define     BUFSIZ (NSECTS * SECSIZ + 6 ) /* Don't touch this. */
struct _buf {     /* Or this .... */
    int _fd;
    int _nleft;
    char *_nextp;
    char _buff[NSECTS * SECSIZ];
};
/* ************************************************************ */
/* If you plan to use the high-level storage allocation functions from the */
/* library ("alloc" and "free") then: */
/* 1. Uncomment (enable) the "ALLOC_ON" definition, and comment out the */
/* "ALLOC_OFF" definition from this file. */
/* 2. Recompile STDLIB1.C, and use CLIB to transfer "alloc" and "free" into */
/* the DEFF.CRL library file. */
/* 3. THIS IS IMPORTANT!!! Include the statement: */
/* _allocp = NULL; /* Initialize allocation pointer. */
/* somewhere in your "main" function PRIOR to the first use of the "alloc" */
/* function. DON'T FORGET THIS INITIALIZATION!! */
/* Remember to include bdscio.h in ALL files of your C program. */
/* The lack of static variables is the reason for this messiness. */
/* ************************************************************ */
/* Only ONE of these two lines should be uncommented: */
/* #define     ALLOC_OFF  1     disables storage allocation */
/* #define     ALLOC_ON   1     enables storage allocation */
```

```
#ifdef ALLOC_ON /* If allocation enabled, */
struct _header {
   struct _header *_ptr;
   unsigned _size;
   };
struct _header _base; /* declare external data */
struct _header *_allocp; /* used by alloc() and free (). */
#endif
```

Appendix D
General References

Chapter 1. Language Selection

The literature on language selection is quite extensive. I have listed below the more accessible guides for selecting a programming language that I have found useful in the preparation of this chapter:

ANDE82B Anderson, Gordon E., and Kenneth C. Shumate. "Selecting a Programming Language, Compiler, and Support Environment: Method and Example," *IEEE Computer* :29-36 (August 1982).

BLOO84 Bloom, H. J., and E. DeJong. "A Critical Comparison of Several Programming Language Implementations." In Feuer, Alan, and Narain Gehani (eds.). *Comparing and Assessing Programming Languages: Ada, C, and Pascal.* (Englewood Cliffs, NJ: Prentice-Hall, 1984), pp. 226-244.

DESS83A Dessey, Raymond (ed.). "Languages for the Laboratory, Part I," *Analytical Chemistry* 55(6):650A-662A (May 1983).

DESS83B Dessey, Raymond (ed.). "Languages for the Laboratory, Part II," *Analytical Chemistry* 55(7):754A-764A (June 1983).

FEUE82 Feuer, Alan R., and Narain H. Gehani. "A Comparison of the Programming Languages C and Pascal," *ACM Computing Surveys* 14(1):73-92 (March 1982).

FEUE84A Feuer, Alan, and Narain Gehani (eds.). *Comparing and Assessing Programming Languages: Ada, C, and Pascal.* (Englewood Cliffs, NJ: Prentice-Hall, 1984).

FEUE84B Feuer, Alan R., and Narain H. Gehani. "A Methodology for Comparing Programming Languages." In Feuer, Alan, and Narain Gehani (eds.). *Comparing and Assessing Programming Languages: Ada, C, and Pascal.* (Englewood Cliffs, NJ: Prentice-Hall, 1984), pp. 209-225.

GILB81 Gilbreath, Jim. "A High-Level Language Benchmark," *Byte* 6(9):180-198 (September 1981).

GILB83 Gilbreath, Jim, and Gary Gilbreath. "Erasthosthenes Revisited: Once More Through the Sieve," *Byte* 8(1):283-326 (January 1983).

KERN81 Kernighan, B. "Why Pascal Is not my Favorite Programming Language," *Computer Science Technical Report* #100 (Bell Laboratories, July 19, 1981).

MAGE82 Megenat-Thalmann, Nadia. "Choosing an Implementation Language for Automatic Translation," *Computer Languages* 7:161-170 (1982).

MATE79 Mateti, P. "Pascal Versus C: A Subjective Comparison." In *Proceedings of the Symposium on Language Design and Programming Methodology* (Sydney, September 10-11, 1979), pp. 37-69.

SHAW84 Shaw, Mary, Guy T. Almes, Joseph M. Newcomer, Brian K. Reid, and William A. Wulf. "A Comparison of Programming Languages for Software Engineering." In Feuer, Alan, and Narain Gehani (eds.). *Comparing and Assessing Programming Languages: Ada, C, and Pascal.* (Englewood Cliffs, NJ: Prentice-Hall, 1984).

SPRI79 Springer, Allen. "A Comparison of Language C and Pascal," *Technical Report* G320-2128 (IBM Cambridge Scientific Center, Cambridge, MA 1979).

WIRT84 Wirth, Niklaus. "Programming Languages: What to Demand and How to Assess Them." In Feuer, Alan, and Narain Gehani (eds.). *Comparing and Assessing Programming Languages: Ada, C, and Pascal.* (Englewood Cliffs, NJ: Prentice-Hall, 1984).

Chapter 2. C and BDS C

The books listed below are all valuable to the C programmer. The works by Plum concerning standards and the Bell Laboratory materials are perhaps the most specialized. The Traister work is oriented to the Supersoft C compiler and is therefore of interest to users of that C product. Those books marked by an asterisk (*) are perhaps most useful to someone just beginning to learn the language. Finally Kernighan and Ritchie's book is the definitive book on the language and its definition; it is essential for any C programmer. With the increasing popularity of C, the majority of these books are available in bookstores that carry computer-related books and magazines.

BELL83 Bell Laboratories. *Unix Programmer's Manual.* 2 volumes. (New York: Holt, Rinehart and Winston, 1983).

*CHIR84 Chirlian, Paul M. *Introduction to C.* (Beaverton, OR: Matrix Publishers, Inc., 1984).

FEUE82 Feuer, Alan R. *The C Puzzle Book.* (Englewood Cliffs, NJ: Prentice-Hall, 1982).

*HANC82 Hancock, Les, and Morris Krieger. *The C Primer.* (New York: Byte/McGraw-Hill, 1982).

HEND84 Hendrix, James E. *The Small-C Handbook.* (Reston, VA: Reston Publishing, 1984).

*HUNT84 Hunter, Bruce. *Understanding C.* (Berkeley, CA: Sybex, 1984).

KERN78 Kernighan, Brian W., and Dennis M. Ritchie. *The C Programming Language.* (Englewood Cliffs, NJ: Prentice-Hall, 1978).

*KOCH83 Kochan, Stephen G. *Programming in C.* (Rochelle Park, NJ: Hayden Book Company, 1983).

PLUM82A Plum, Thomas. *C Programming Standards and Guidelines: Version U (UNIX and Offspring).* (Cardiff, NJ: Plum Hall, 1982).

PLUM82B Plum, Thomas. *C Programming Standards and Guidelines: Version W (Whitesmith Version).* (Cardiff, NJ: Plum Hall, 1982).

*PLUM83 Plum, Thomas. *Learning to Program in C.* (Cardiff, NJ: Plum Hall, 1983).

*PURD83A Purdum, Jack. *C Programming Guide.* (Indianapolis, IN: Que Corporation, 1983).

PURD83B Purdum, J., T. Leslie, and A. Stegemoller. *C Programmer's Library.* (Indianapolis, IN: Que Corporation, 1983).

TRAI84 Traister, Robert J. *Programming in C For the Microcomputer User.* (Englewood Cliffs, NJ: Prentice-Hall, 1984).

*WAIT84 Waite, Mitchell, Stephen Prata, and Donald Martin. *C Primer Plus.* (Indianapolis, IN: Howard W. Sams, 1984).

ZAHN79 Zahn, C. T. *C Notes: A Guide to the C Programming Language.* (New York: Yourdon Press, 1979).

Chapter 3. File Tools

The article by Bolton (BOLT81) presents a set of C programs to provide date and time functions for an S-100 computer system. While the programs are hardware specific to the Mountain Hardware "100,000 day clock board," the ideas presented should be applicable and adaptable to any hardware-based time/calendar system.

The articles by Kater and Russell present programs to control an Epson printer's many print modes. This program is similar to the mxprint.h program of Chapter 3.

Finally, Parry and Roberts present more detailed word counting programs for analyzing writing samples.

BOLT81 Bolton, Bill. "Some Useful C Time Functions," *Dr. Dobb's Journal* 58:16-21 (August 1981).

KATE83 Kater, David. "Programming Epson's MX-80 Printer," *Popular Computing* (April, May 1983).

PARR81 Parry, Richard K. "Minding Your P's and Q's," *Microcomputing* :58-67 (June 1981).

ROBE82 Roberts, Steven K. "A Word Counting Utility for Writers," *Byte* 7:237-240 (June 1982).

RUSS83 Russell, Carlton P. "Mr. Epson Meet Mr. Pascal," *Creative Computing* (June 1983).

SOFT84 Softcraft Inc.

Finally, a commercial product (written in BDS C) provides incredible printer control with over 30 typefaces available, ranging from 8-point Roman to 40-point Old English. This product, Fancy Font, is available from:

SoftCraft Inc.
222 State Street, Suite 400
Madison, WI 53703

Chapter 4. Text Compression

The literature on text compression is quite extensive. The articles listed below provide a starting point for this interesting subfield of data structures and programming.

CORB82 Corbin, David. "An Introduction to Data Compression," *Byte* 6:218, (April 1981).

CORT82 Cortesi, David. "An Effective Text Compression Algorithm," *Byte* 7:397-403 (January 1982).

CORT83 Cortesi, David. *A Programmer's Notebook: Utilities for CP/M-80.* "Chapter 3: PACK and UNPACK" and "Chapter 4: TABBIT and UNTAB". (Reston, VA: Reston Publishing, 1983).

GUST82 Gustafson, David K. "Compress It!" *Microcomputing* :88-91 (May 1982).

PECK82 Peckura, M. "File Archival Techniques Using Data Compression," *Communications of the Association for Computing Machinery* 25:605-609 (September 1982).

PETE79 Peterson, James L. "Text Compression," *Byte* 4:106-113 (December 1979).

TANE81 Tanenbaum, A. M., and M. J. Augenstein. *Data Structures Using Pascal.* (Englewood Cliffs, NJ: Prentice-Hall, 1981).

TROP82 Tropper, Richard. "Binary-Coded Text: A Text Compression Method." *Byte* 7:398-413 (April 1982).

Chapter 5. General Editor References

Listed below are some of the major references available on the subject of editor design and construction. Also included are references to specific C-based editors.

CHRI82 Christensen, Ward. "Full Screen Program Editors for CP/M-80. Ed Ream's Editor in C." *Lifelines* 3(5):43-45 (October 1982).

EMBL81 Embley, David W., and George Nagy. "Behavioral Aspects of Text Editors," *ACM Computing Surveys* 13(1):33-70 (March 1981).

FINS82 Finseth, C. A. "Managing Words: What Capabilities Should You Have with a Text Editor?," *Byte* 7(4):242-282 (April 1982).

HOWA83 Howard, Alan. "Enhancing the C Screen Editor." *Dr. Dobb's Journal* 79:38-63 (May 1983).

JONG82 Jong, Steven. "Designing a Text Editor: The User Comes First," *Byte* 7:284-300 (April 1982).

KERN76 Kernighan, Brian W., and P. J. Plauger. *Software Tools*. (Reading, MA: Addison-Wesley, 1976).

LAND83 Landauer, T. K., K. M. Galotti, and S. Hartwell. 'Natural Command Names and Initial Learning: A Study of Text Editing Terms," *Communications of the ACM* 26(7):495-503 (July 1983).

MARK81 Mark of the Unicorn. *MINCE Internal Documentation*. "Chapter 5: Theory and Practices of Text Editing." (Mark of the Unicorn, 1981).

MARK83 Mark, Robert L., Clayton H. Lewis, and John M. Carroll. "Learning to Use Word Processors: Problems and Prospects," *ACM Transaction on Office Information Systems* 1(3):254-271 (July 1983).

MCWO83 McWorter, William A. "McWorder: A Tiny Text Editor," *Dr. Dobb's Journal* 82:36-42 (August 1983).

MEYE82A Meyerowitz, Norman, and Andries Van Dam. "Interactive Editing Systems: Part I." *ACM Computing Surveys* 14(3):321-352 (September 1982).

MEYE82B Meyerowitz, Norman, and Andries Van Dam. "Interactive Editing Systems: Part II." *ACM Computing Surveys* 14(3):353-415 (September 1982).

NICH82 Nicholson, Leonard K. "Background Information on Text Editors," *Dr. Dobb's Journal* 64:55-56 (February 1982).

REAM82A Ream, Edward K. "A Portable C Screen-Oriented Editor." *Dr. Dobb's Journal* 63:18-61 (January 1982).

REAM82B Ream, Edward K. "Screen Oriented Bugs," *Dr. Dobb's Journal* 67:4-7 (May, 1982).

REAM83A Ream, Edward K. "RED: A Better C Screen Editor, Part I," *Dr. Dobb's Journal* 81:34-65 (July 1983).

REAM83B Ream, Edward K. "RED: A Better C Screen Editor, Part II," *Dr. Dobb's Journal* 82:62-97 (August 1983).

Chapter 8. Text Formatters

The topic of text formatters has quite an extensive bibliography. The sources noted below will provide an introductory guide to the field. As noted above, the C Users Group has available a half dozen excellent formatters with source code that could solve any text processing need likely to be encountered. The article by Furuta, et al., provides an excellent overview of the concepts of text processing and gives examples of virtually all the major classes of such software. Kernighan and Plauger provide a batch text processor in their justly famous *Software Tools*. Finally, D. Knuth provides a discussion and analysis of a state of the art typesetter in *TEX and Metafont*.

FURU82 Furuta, Richard, Jeffrey Scofield, Alan Shaw. "Document Formatting Systems: Survey, Concepts and Issues," *ACM Computing Surveys* 14(3):417-472 (September 1982) (includes a bibliography of 93 items).

KERN76 Kernighan, B. W., and P. L. Plauger. *Software Tools*. (Reading, MA: Addison-Wesley, 1976) (chapter on "Formatting" includes RATFOR-based text formatter).

KERN81 Kernighan, B. W., and P. L. Plauger. *Software Tools in Pascal*. (Reading, MA: Addison-Wesley, 1981) (Pascal version of the above).

KNUT81 Knuth, Donald. *TEX and Metafont*. (Cambridge, MA: Digital Press, 1981).

Chapter 9. Sorting

If you are interested in sorts, the two major works on the subject are Knuth (KNUT73) and Lorin (LORI75). These advanced, technical treatises are complemented by the microcomputer-oriented articles noted below. Barron and Diehl provide an overview of sorting algorithms for microcomputers.

A two-directional bubble sort is described by W. A. Harrison and S. H. Sachs in "A Better Bubble Sort," *Microcomputing*, April, 1981. A bubble sort with "sinkers" is described by David Vergin in the October 1982 issue of *Microcomputing*. Albert Nijenhuis discusses the Shell sort in a series of articles on sorts and sorting techniques, "How Not to be Out of Sorts" *Creative Computing*, August/September, and October, 1980. The Shell-Metzner sort is discussed by John P. Grillo in "A Comparison of Sorts," *Creative Computing* November/December, 1976, pp. 76–80.

BARR83 Barron, Terry, and George Diehr. "Sorting Algorithms for Microcomputers," *Byte* 8:482-490 (May 1983).

KERN76 Kernighan, Brian W., and P. J. Plauger. *Software Tools* (Reading, MA: Addison-Wesley, 1976) (Chapter 4, "Sorting").

KNUT73 Knuth, Donald E. *The Art of Computer Programming: Searching and Sorting*, Vol. 3. (Reading, MA: Addison-Wesley, 1973).

LORI75 Lorin, Harold. *Sorting and Sort Systems.* (Reading, MA: Addison-Wesley, 1975).

Index to Programs

Subject Index

Note to Readers

As we all know, the microcomputer field is subject to rapid change. In the interest of continued accuracy, I would be interested in learning of program bugs, new and improved sources of C software and any other information readers might wish to relay. Please send all notices to the author at the following address:

Terry A. Ward
Academic Computing Services
University of Northern Iowa
Cedar Falls, IA 50614